To See Ourselves

To See Ourselves

Comparing Traditional Chinese and American Cultural Values

Zhongdang Pan,
Steven H. Chaffee,
Godwin C. Chu,
and Yanan Ju

Westview Press

BOULDER • SAN FRANCISCO • OXFORD

Copyright © 1994 by Westview Press, Inc.

Published in 1994 in the United States of America by Westview Press, Inc., 5500 Central Avenue, Boulder, Colorado 80301-2877, and in the United Kingdom by Westview Press, 36 Lonsdale Road, Summertown, Oxford OX2 7EW

A CIP catalog record for this book is available from the Library of Congress.
ISBN 0-8133-2075-5

Printed and bound in the United States of America

The paper used in this publication meets the requirements
of the American National Standard for Permanence of Paper
for Printed Library Materials Z39.48-1984.

10   9   8   7   6   5   4   3   2   1

Because of our tradition, everyone here
knows who he is, and what
God expects him to do.

And who has the right
as master of the house
to have the final word
at home?

The papa, the papa. Tradition.
The papa, the papa. Tradition.

Who must raise the family,
and run the home,
so papa's free to read
the Holy Book?

The mama, the mama. Tradition.
The mama, the mama. Tradition.

Sheldon Harnick, *Fiddler on the Roof*

Contents

Tables and Figures

Figures

Preface

Many starting points could be identified for this study. Reciprocal intellectual interest between China and the United States dates from the earliest contacts between these countries, in the nineteenth century. Reports to Western society on Chinese culture go back to Marco Polo. There have been anthropological studies of each culture by scholars from the other for most of this century. But the real stimulus for the present program of research has clearly been the Communist revolution in China and the consequent estrangement of these erstwhile allies of World War II.

China and America are not yet back to a friendly relationship at the macropolitical level, but already there are many contacts in the spheres of commerce, science, tourism, and education. In a way this book represents a form of contact in itself in that the three co-authors who were born in China now work at American universities. This is a bicultural study by a mostly bicultural group of social scientists. At times we will rely here upon our own personal experiences and knowledge of the two cultures that we are comparing rather than simply basing our conclusions on the empirical survey data that are the basis of our research project.

We could identify an entirely different kind of starting point for the project as well. Each of the co-authors of this book is a scholar in the field of communication, and we are thus indebted to the founder of that newest of the social sciences. This means that we stand in debt to Wilbur Schramm (1907–1987), the founder of our field. Schramm was a professor of two of us (Chu and Chaffee) at Stanford University in the early 1960s. Later he helped to found the Communication Institute at the East-West Center, where the research project represented in this volume has been based. Were it not for Schramm, a pioneer in the study of international communication and of the impact of mass media on culture, it is inconceivable that the research we describe herein would have been conducted. This book is dedicated to his memory.

China and the United States will be the major players in the coming Pacific era. Americans and Chinese need to understand each other—not only their different economic and political systems but, more fundamentally, their respective cultures. What common values do they share? On what values do they differ? This need is urgent because the little each knows of the other has probably been rendered invalid by what has happened in the two countries in the last half-century, particularly the Cultural Revolution in China and the soul-searching aftermath of the Vietnam War in the United States. This book is an effort to advance this process of mutual understanding between two former allies after their prolonged separation.

The research that produced this book would not have been possible without the generous support of many of our colleagues. We would particularly like to acknowledge the contributions of those who helped draft the instrument for the China survey: Francis Hsu, an anthropologist; Wang Gung-wu, a historian; Ambrose King, a sociologist; and Anthony Yu, a specialist in religious studies in China. Many Chinese scholars, especially Professor Xu Zhen of Fudan University, helped implement the field survey in China. Of the many American colleagues who participated in this research, we especially want to express our gratitude to Gary Heald, Jae-won Lee, Jack McLeod, John Mayo, Pamela Shoemaker, Leslie Snyder, and Diana Stover Tillinghast for implementing the data collection in the United States.

Other than Fudan University in China, six American universities provided support for the research reported here: Stanford University, San Jose State University, University of Texas at Austin, Cleveland State University, University of Wisconsin-Madison, University of Connecticut, and Florida State University.

Funding for the research in China and the United States came primarily from a generous grant by Mary and Laurance Rockefeller, with supplementary funding from the East-West Center, Honolulu, Hawaii, administered by Victor Li, then president of the East-West Center, and Mary Bitterman, then director of its Institute of Culture and Communication. The research in China and the United States was part of the Institute's project on cultural change in Asia and America. Michael E. Macmillan, senior editor of the Center's Program for Cultural Studies, provided editorial advice and prepared the camera-ready copy for this book. To all of them, we express our heartfelt appreciation.

The views and interpretations presented in this book are entirely those of the co-authors and are not necessarily shared by any of the cooperating scholars or institutions or the funding sources. We as co-authors, individually and collectively, bear full responsibility for any errors in facts or interpretation.

Zhongdang Pan
Steven H. Chaffee
Godwin C. Chu
Yanan Ju

tions—male-female, young-old, and super-subordinate—can tell us wherein and to what degree these two massive societies, the United States and China today, diverge. Cultures, in our view, differ most fundamentally in terms of these social relations, rather than in more superficial artifacts. It is in the degree of obedience wives owe their husbands, sons owe their fathers, or citizens owe their rulers that societies divide.

This book consists mainly of our report of two survey studies, designed to be as comparative as we can make them, of our own two cultures. As the title indicates, we are partly attempting "to see ourselves" in the process of conducting and reflecting upon the research reported here. While this is a social scientific study, and therefore intended to be objective, it is purposely written in the first person (plural). Each of us is either Chinese or American, or in some degree Chinese-American. We trust that our results will be of interest to members of each of these cultures and to others as well.

China and the United States are not simply our home countries, they are cultures of great moment in the world at large. China comprises the world's largest people and has traditionally represented (and deeply influenced) what is known collectively as "the East." The United States, in its turn, is the world's largest economy and is for many the prototype of "the West." Examining these massive and separated societies side by side should be of interest to anyone who hopes to understand the world we live in.

No one should imagine that such an undertaking can be straightforward and simple. We have in the project described here limited our inquiry to a few basic domains of human values and to field survey interview methods as a way of studying those values. Any single study must set for itself realizable goals. Our group of collaborating researchers—who number more than a dozen beyond the authors of this book—recognized from the outset that we could not reach all of our goals, certainly not immediately. We have not directly observed social behavior to see whether people act in accordance with the values they espouse. We have not examined cultural artifacts, such as stories and artistic creations, through which social relations are stored and transmitted. These kinds of research are of great value, of course, but they remain for other projects and other scholars.

We have also not literally examined change, although our long-range interest resides in how the cultural values of China and the United States are changing. This study is a baseline, cross-sectional comparison of these two cultures. Its value in the long run will lie in its use as a benchmark from which to compare subsequent, presumably more thorough, studies of this same type. We will be using variation between the two cultures, and between various subgroups within each, partly to locate clues about processes of cultural change. We do this not because our project is ideally designed for the study of change—it clearly is not—but because the question of change is uppermost in many minds when they consider these two countries, and especially China. Our inferences will be tentative, as inferences of social scientists always are, and our data will be even more inconclusive, regarding both comparison and change, than is usual in social science. But we will not shrink from venturing at least some inferences that go beyond our data. A sample survey is, after all, intended to project a larger picture. We will sketch in more of what we imagine than a literal reading of our survey questions and answers alone would yield.

Forces for Change in Cultural Values

Interpersonal relations in the domains of gender, age, and authority are often the focus of public policy and social change. In China, this has been particularly dramatic, especially in the past half-century. The same is true of the United States, if a bit more recently and less obviously. Debates over proper relations between men and women have in both countries led, for example, to laws prescribing more egalitarian treatment of women. Whether these macro-societal political changes have been mirrored by corresponding shifts in interpersonal behavior, or in the values people express—or more important, in their private feelings about what is right—is another question. Our study is designed to find out what values people express. There is ample reason in each country to believe that we are in an era of change regarding normative values in many domains of social relations. In the United States, for example, television has been charged with undermining children's deference to their elders (Meyrowitz 1985)—a hypothesis that would imply that traditional relations between generations had been the rule until TV's rather recent arrival.

There is considerable anecdotal and ethnographic evidence of different values concerning social relationships in the United States and traditional China (see Hsu 1981). The United States has much higher rates of divorce and premarital pregnancy while China is much more rigid in maintaining family stability and in prohibiting premarital or extramarital sex. We "know" too that Americans admire youth and energy whereas Chinese respect age and wisdom. Americans value individual personalities while Chinese appreciate family and group solidarity. Americans prize initiative and ambition whereas Chinese esteem personal sacrifice for family or state. These stereotypes of differences between the two peoples have accumulated for decades, suggesting a persistent static view of the two cultures.

A great deal of history has intervened in the century since this dualistic model was constructed, based upon early exchanges via Christian missionaries to China and Chinese students who ventured abroad to American universities. In that century China has changed from a semi-colonial feudal state to a republic, then shifted again, becoming a communist nation. In the course of several violent revolutions, Chinese intellectuals have launched a series of sweeping campaigns attacking Confucian doctrine. This occurred first in the May Fourth movement of 1919 (Chow 1960), more recently during the Cultural Revolution in the late 1960s and early 1970s, and again during the reform movement of the late 1980s. The land reform movement of the 1950s attempted to destroy the landlord class as part of a more general attack on traditional super-subordinate relations. Families were moved about and split up by a government policy of assigning people to jobs without regard to family location. Male-female role differentiation was obliterated wherever possible, such as in job assignment and promotion to supervisory positions. During the Cultural Revolution, filial piety in the form of ancestor worship was systematically prohibited. Even Confucius himself, that venerated secular philosopher of the sixth century B.C., came under attack. A scholarly tradition was created to examine the morality of his views regarding social relations (e.g., slavery) relative to the realities of his time. More often than not, Confucius was found wanting, as were the traditional patterns of social deference that were practiced in his name. It is not too much to say that the politics of China in its communist era has focused on cultural values of social relations more than on any other aspect of life.

The same might be said, albeit in less sweeping ways and with less dramatic formal policies, with regard to the United States. Work relations were overhauled at the turn of the last century through the labor movement and associated progressive reforms (Hofstadter 1955). Social relationships have obviously been at stake in this century's political struggle for women's suffrage and later for gender equality in the workplace, in the enduring controversy over abortion, and in the recent "family values" rhetoric of the Reagan-Bush-Quayle administrations. Youthful protesters against the Vietnam War encouraged one another with such slogans as, "Question authority," and, "Never trust anyone over 30." Ascriptive caste relations between the races, including many obligatory forms of deference by non-whites, lie at the core of American political struggles from the Civil War, to the Jim Crow laws enacted in the 1890s, on up to the Civil Rights movement, Affirmative Action programs, and urban unrest of recent decades.

Mass affluence, a rising standard of living, and universal public education have enabled Americans of whatever birth to aspire (with some reason) to the highest achievement levels. Cultural change has tended overall in the direction of decreasing role-prescribed deference in the United States. The Horatio Alger myth of the self-made man remains the American Dream in many people's minds. Age, as well as station, has lost much of its social cachet. Youth culture is fostered partly because young Americans enjoy a considerable amount of disposable income that can be converted into purchases of commercial products such as recorded music or clothing advertised on radio and television. Thus the economic means to break down traditional barriers that are analogous to those of the Confucian tradition have been expanding for a long time in the United States. In China the assault on Confucianism has been a more deliberate, conscious series of programs, but the long-term trend seems to have been roughly parallel to that in the United States.

Cultural change in the United States has not been without its detractors. Egalitarian movements with regard to gender, age, race, and authority are newsworthy precisely because they arouse a great deal of opposition in American society. Change is not inevitable, as the popularity of the reactionary Republican administrations of the 1980s demonstrated. The Equal Rights Amendment, which would have guaranteed women equality under the U.S. Constitution, failed to become law and died in the 1980s.[2] Power in business, the military, education, and other major institutions remains mostly in the hands of "old, white males"—a fact that would occasion no surprise in a traditional society. A true Confucian might in many respects feel more at home today in the United States than in contemporary China. At the least, one might argue that the cultural transformation of America in this century is as impressive as that of China, considering that the United States has passed from an agrarian society through an urban industrial society to a suburban post-industrial society (Bell 1973; Inglehart 1990).

Given these dramatic changes in each country and the very different paths of change that the two societies have experienced, one may well wonder to what extent the stereotypical contrast between the two cultures still holds. That is the central question we raise in this study. How much, for example, do traditional Confucian values remain in contemporary China after the indoctrination of communism and the "cultural invasion" from Western mass media? Where do most Americans stand today in terms of the fundamental human relationships in a society? Do the two cultures hold highly contrasting positions regarding these basic social relationships? If they do, how—and how much—do they differ? Do Americans and Chinese have a common basis for understanding one another? We seek, through this study, to see ourselves (both Americans and Chinese) more clearly, to identify what we share and where we differ.

The Present Study

The project we report here expands the comparative research tradition by adding survey interview evidence to the literature based on observational and artifactual research. Rather than rely on a few highly sensitized professional observers, of which Hsu is an exemplar, we are in effect turning over the task of observation to several thousand randomly sampled, non-professional members of each culture. By controlling the questions they are asked, and by directing the format within which they are invited to respond, we ask them to observe themselves and to tell us what values they hold regarding interpersonal relationships. Our interpretation of their many (and varied) answers to parallel questions that we have asked in each country is guided by the substantive literature that has preceded this project as much as by our own empirical findings. We do not claim to have dramatically new answers, or even improved questions, so much as evidence of a different kind that bears on issues raised in prior research.

This study is built around questions about gender, seniority, and authority hierarchies and about interpersonal relationships in general. We chose these values as representing the core of traditional Chinese culture (Liang 1987; Chu and Ju 1993). Studies on values in Western cultures (e.g., Williams 1970; Rokeach 1973, 1979; Inglehart 1990) are almost completely silent about these values. Individualism is such a basic assumption in the Western tradition that people are seldom asked in empirical surveys about their values in the sphere of relationships.

Still, it seems inconceivable that American culture should not incorporate some values regarding these basic social relationships, even if those values are not as obvious as in traditional Chinese culture. Individualistic concepts such as independence and privacy only make sense against a contrasting normative background of interpersonal obligation and mutual dependence. In approaching our topic from the Confucian perspective, we are making a conscious choice about which is to be "figure" and which "ground"—the individual or the social relationship. Hsu's (1981) contrast between the Chinese and American cultures notes that both contain important values concerning male-female, kinship, and family relationships, although these values may be differently configured in the two cultures. In other words, we do not consider that we are imposing an alien template on American culture in this study, although the values we are studying have been derived very consciously from explication of Confucian values.

This study examines three kinds of research questions. The first concerns the differences and similarities in prevailing cultural values concerning human relationships, across the two countries. This part of the analysis is primarily descriptive, intended to lay an empirical groundwork for cross-cultural comparisons. It is presented in Chapters 4 and 5, where we examine both the simple U.S.-China differences and then the differences between various subgroups in the two countries.

The second research question deals with a two-dimensional issue: empirical structuring of the value measures. Chapter 6 explores the empirical associations between values, across individual respondents—a kind of question that can only be addressed by survey research. If the same individuals support several values (even though those values are expressed differently), and if these correlations follow similar patterns in the two cultures, we will have evidence of a common structuring of parallel value orientations. That is, such results would indicate *empirical equivalence* of value measures across the two cultures, even if there are large U.S.-China differences in the levels of adherence to any particular value, and even if our studies in the two countries differ in their survey research procedures (e.g., language, sampling, interview administration). Parallel structuring of values needs to be established if comparative analysts are to attempt to locate the two value systems on global theoretical orders such as traditional-modern or materialism-postmaterialism. For our immediate purposes, evidence of empirical equivalence can enable us to compare the two cultures in terms of general value orientations (Kluckhohn and Strodtbeck 1961). That is, we need to know if the two cultures are *similar* in the overall structure of values before we can evaluate the extent to which they are *different* in adherence to a particular value cluster.

Our third research question focuses on the sources of influence on these cultural values, both factors that might maintain or account for stable values and those that might be producing change. This is a complex and intellectually challenging task, for which we must confess a lack of well-formulated theories. Given that ours is an early, exploratory investigation, we will break these factors into three general groupings that might account for differences within a culture. These we will group together as social relations, social structure, and social influence factors. The social relations and social structure measures in our study are usually lumped together thoughtlessly as mere "demographic variables" in survey research, but we see several of them as closely intertwined with specific value domains. The social influence factors we have added to standard demographics in this study involve the media of mass communication.[3]

Social relations factors are those demographic groupings that relate directly to the values in our study: gender, age, and marital status. These variables mean approximately the same thing in any society, and they define the person's place in relation to other persons in inescapable ways. That is, one's view of appropriate male-female relations—deferential or egalitarian—should be affected by whether one is a man or a woman. One's perspective on deference to elders (or the dominance of youth culture) is somewhat different depending upon the age of the person who is being asked the question. At the family level, norms regarding divorce might evoke different questions in the minds of married vs. single persons. Demographic measures of social relations are included conventionally in almost any survey questionnaire, simply because they are easy to ask and to code. But for our study, some of these descriptive variables have immediate implications for the very values upon which our study is centered.

Social structure factors, our second category, also involve conventional demographic measures; they include the person's education, income, and occupation. We see these variables not so much as absolute properties of an individual respondent as indicators of the relative position of the individual in an overall social hierarchy. The distinction between social *structural* demographics and social *relations* demographics is much clearer when one considers U.S.-China comparisons than it is in the usual single-nation survey. A high school graduate who is a factory foreman and who makes, say, $10,000 a year would stand relatively low in the American social structure—but quite high in China's. It is one's *relative* status, much more than the literal amount of education or earnings, that we expect to affect people's values regarding normative social relationships. Social structural factors are, then, essentially relational concepts, ordinal variables that indicate one's social stature much more than they reflect absolute qualities of one's personal circumstances. If values regarding personal relations vary across the social *structure* in predictable, relative ways, we should expect to see similar patterns of correlations in the U.S. and China data. If, on the other hand, individuals are truly atomized units in a non-traditional society, we might find similar expressed values in the two countries between, say, high school graduates—that is, people who possess equal, although not socially equivalent, educational backgrounds.

Social influences on cultural values, our third category, are virtually limitless, if interpersonal contacts are taken into account. In this study we are less ambitious than that, concentrating on mass communication influences only. Still, there are a host of separable influences to study here, and people differ in the degree to which they are exposed to each. We will distinguish particularly between media presentations of news and entertainment in both the United States and China. In China, we distinguish further between indigenous and Western entertainment media, and we also take into consideration exposure to propaganda from the communist government. Each of these sources, with its distinctive content, plays a specific role in shaping cultural values, and we shall examine those separable influences in Chapter 7. Insofar as Confucian values are concerned, though, the most usual view is that all mass media influences are likely to undermine traditional culture in some degree. Mass communication in the American sense, being almost by definition equally available to all, tends to have a homogenizing influence that is contrary to the patterns of deference that constitute the core of traditional culture (Meyrowitz 1985).

A final demographic variable that is basic to our analysis is urbanism. We will in fact analyze place of residence before the others, because one's geographic location is closely related to all the other factors we are examining. Urbanism is a social structural variable, and people in rural locations tend to be lower on the educational, income, and occupational ladders than those in cities and their suburbs. Moreover, urban areas abound with mass media, which may be scarce in rural locales. Change in cultural values, then, is normally expected to occur later and more slowly in rural locales.

Early studies of national development (e.g., Lerner 1958; Schramm and Ruggels 1965) suggested that a certain proportion of a less-developed country's population must be concentrated in cities before other processes of economic and social change will be set in motion. Mass media, for example, were not seen as contributing much to development in a predominantly rural country. We need not take a position for or against the modernization model (Lerner 1958; Schramm 1964; Inkeles and Smith 1974; Inkeles 1983) or on parallel images of political development (Almond and Verba 1963; Inglehart 1990). Our concern is with cultural values specifically, and it is enough that we begin here with the strong suspicion that people who live in urban centers are more likely to be touched by any wave of change in cultural values than are those living in rural areas.

Viewing One Another

Scholars of Chinese and Western civilizations have for years argued over differences between the two in terms such as individual versus group orientations, legalistic versus familial societal mechanisms, or horizontal equality versus vertical hierarchy structures (see Clark 1935; Forster 1936; Hsu 1981; Liang 1987). But there is little consensus over the dimensions of differences and similarities between the two cultures. Neither is there systematic accumulation of empirical evidence of such differences and similarities (Hsu 1981 being a notable exception).

A lack of consensus on this very large set of issues is not surprising. The problem facing every student of the two cultures is that each is highly complex, so that any classification based upon a selected set of dimensions falls short. Williams (1970:450–51) makes this point regarding American value systems: "Any attempt to delineate a national character or typical American values or a national basic personality type is extremely hazardous, not only because of serious gaps in the requisite data but also because of the enormous value-diversity of the nation." Further, "American society does not have a completely consistent and integrated value-structure. We do not find a neatly unified 'ethos' or an 'irresistible' strain toward consistency."

Although in any static comparison traditional Chinese culture seems more homogeneous than American culture, China's long history is also marked by many influences and great changes (Su and Wang 1988). We do not have, to date, much systematic knowledge on the extent and specific nature of the impact of the Cultural Revolution on traditional Chinese culture. One study (Zhao 1989) found considerable impact of communist media influences in terms of elevating state-oriented values above family-oriented values. But any attempt to reduce Chinese culture to a small set of abstract terms runs the risk of losing historical perspective and of covering up great diversity. It is fair to say that even though we often use singular nouns to refer to American or Chinese culture, each is more aptly characterized as a collection of diverse *cultures*.

Given the difficulty of summarizing either culture, it should be no surprise that the history of interchanges between the Chinese and Western civilizations has been marked by mutual misunderstanding. For much of her five-thousand-year history, China regarded herself as the imperial power centrally located under the sun (i.e., the Middle Kingdom). Until European colonial guns smashed the formerly closed door of China, most Chinese intellectuals presumed that their ancient civilization was far superior to that of the West. This sense of superiority persists in intellectual circles today (see Li 1979; Pang 1988; Su and Wang 1988; Tu 1987, 1991). A reciprocal arrogance can be found in the West, where many hope to see China adopt their values of liberal democracy, achievement orientation, efficiency, freedom of expression, and so forth. This missionary mentality echoes Forster's (1936) call for a "mentor-pupil" relationship between the United States and his conception of a modern China, and it continues to color Americans' views on national policy toward China (Nelan 1991).

Despite (or perhaps due to) their mutual misunderstandings, the two peoples seem to be chronically attracted to one another. American interest in China dates from the 1870s, when ex-President Ulysses S. Grant visited the Imperial Palace in Beijing. It is now two decades since President Richard Nixon and Premier Zhou Enlai shook hands at Beijing's old Capital Airport. In the past ten years, thousands of Americans have found their way to China as tourists or on business. But for most their interest centers around ancient archaeological discoveries, beautiful scenery, traditional customs, exotic cuisine, or business opportunities. Cultural values governing social relations, far from being a domain of understanding, are for American businessmen a major source of frustration in dealing with their Chinese counterparts. Chinese lodge their own complaints about American visitors, who operate from neither Communist nor Confucian principles in their dealings and interactions.

Since the turn of this century, though, many in China have admired the United States as the abstract model of a successful democracy. This enthusiasm among intellectuals dates from the May Fourth Movement of 1919 (see Chow 1960). This "Chinese Enlightenment" movement was spurred by such leaders as Hu Shih, a Columbia University Ph.D. who brought home an advocacy of vernacular language and a methodology of empiricism and pragmatism acquired from his American mentor, John Dewey. Seventy years later his call for "Wholesale Westernization" still haunts the memories of many Chinese intellectuals and policy makers, as both inspiration and humiliation. Meanwhile, during the Vietnam War era, many American students expanded their leftist sympathies into a new appreciation of Chinese culture, from Buddhism and Taoism to the best-selling "Little Red Book" of Chairman Mao Zedong. Forster's mentor-pupil model (how Confucian!) arose anew in China in the 1989 "Pro-Democracy Movement." Chinese students rallied around a "Goddess of Democracy" statue and recited catchphrases from American history: "We the people" and "of the people, by the people, and for the people." The present research project is partly inspired by an ongoing search for parallels between the two societies.

Interchanges between China and the United States are scarcely symmetrical. Americans today do not tend to look toward China for their guidelines.[4] But if they did, they could find much of value that would be familiar to them. One goal of this project is to foster mutual understanding, and with that in mind we do not apologize for beginning it with traditional Confucian values. To the contrary, we consider that a strength of this project, as so much research to date has instead proceeded from Western values and assumptions. The broad questions raised in our study, and the specific questions asked of the respondents in our surveys, concern basic human relationships that must be dealt with in some fashion in any society. If it takes a study based on the very hierarchical Confucian perspective to produce questions about where Americans stand on these eternal issues, the first central premise of our project is thereby validated.

Notes

1. We do not presume in this study to examine the enormous body of teachings that are ascribed to Confucius. Our concern here is merely with a few traditional prescriptions for human relations that are generally considered Confucian in character.

2. The women's movement behind the ERA campaign did, however, result in adoption of many egalitarian legal guarantees at the state and local levels.

3. Each of the authors of this book has been a professor in schools or departments of mass communication, and we consider ourselves students of the effects of mass media on society.

4. Many, especially in the business community, do look to Japan as a model for institutional organization.

2

Culture and Values

WE HAVE TO THIS POINT been using the terms "culture" and "values" in specific ways, but without much elaboration of their meaning. In this chapter we explicate the general domain of cultural values we are studying through an analysis of several intertwined concepts. This will include a review of both theoretical and empirical scholarship, including some prior studies of value differences between the American and Chinese cultures.

Defining Culture

To define "culture" with precision is a daunting task to say the least. In a review published forty years ago, Kroeber and Kluckhohn listed 164 different definitions—a clear indication of the evasive nature of culture as an analytical concept. As used in diverse scholarly and popular writings, the term "culture" means everything from fashion to ancient customs, from artifacts to traditional rituals, from enduring practices in the home and family to icons venerated in great national palaces.

Some core elements of "culture" can, though, be identified. Kroeber and Kluckhohn (1952:157) pointed out several key characteristics: "culture is a product; is historical; includes ideas, patterns, and values; is selective; is learned; is based upon symbols; and is an abstraction from behavior and the products of behavior." "All cultures are largely made up of overt, patterned ways of behaving, feeling, and reaction." In brief, Kroeber and Kluckhohn concluded, a culture is revealed by the commonalities in beliefs, value orientations, behavioral patterns, symbols of communication, and community relationships and rituals that are shared by most of the members (who both embody and experience them), despite variations among classes, areas, groups, and individuals.

Researchers have followed this tradition of defining culture by identifying its analytical components and describing the dynamics among them. Giddens (1989:31), for example, defines culture as consisting of "the **values** the members of a given group hold, the **norms** they follow, and the material goods they create. Values are abstract ideas, while norms are definite principles or rules which people are expected to observe." "Culture refers to the whole way of life of the members of a society."

This is also how Godwin Chu (1979, 1984, 1989) approaches culture as a concept in his long-standing research program, of which the present study is a part. Chu points out, in keeping with Giddens, that culture refers to "a way of life" shared by "the majority members of a cultural group." Culture also functions as a meaning system embodied in each individual's life experiences. Further, culture is identified explicitly with the individual's behavior and cognitions in a three-component conceptual scheme. In Chu's framework, "self," or individual, occupies the central position. The "self" perceives and participates in relationships with other "cultural elements." These "cultural elements" include (1) significant others, which form one's social environment; (2) materials and objects, which constitute one's physical environment; and (3) ideas (including ideology, values, and religious beliefs), which constitute a person's symbolic environment. The symbolic environment plays a significant role in determining how the self perceives the relationships with the social and physical environments, attributing meanings to these relationships, and setting priorities for decision making in dealing with these relationships. In this conception of culture, values play an important role in meaning construction, decision making, and behavior selection.

This tripartite conception of culture is represented schematically in Figure 2.1 (from Chu 1979, 1984). The bold lines represent directional relations: how the self interacts with significant others, how the self uses materials and objects in the physical environment and is in turn influenced by them, and how the self embraces ideas as relevant for social and material relations. The thin lines represent *perceived* relations, or linkages, that exist in the perceptual field of the self. That is, the thin lines represent the directional relations as each individual imagines, and interacts with, them. These connections may attribute individual-specific meanings to the relationships represented by the bold lines, and they influence how the self behaves in dealing with those direct relationships.

This conception of culture is consistent with a good deal of cultural anthropological literature. For example, White (1959/1976:61) described culture in a conceptual framework quite similar to Chu's tripartite model: "What is the locus of culture? The answer is: the things and events that comprise culture have their existence, in space and time, (1) within human organisms, i.e., concepts, beliefs, emotions, attitudes; (2) within processes of social interaction among human beings; and (3) within material objects...lying outside of human organisms but within the patterns of social interactions among them."

The interrelations among the elements of Chu's model constitute the

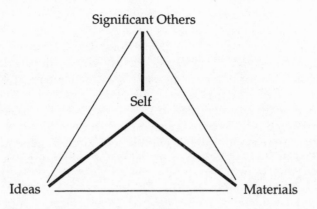

Figure 2.1 A Schematic Representation of Culture

potential forces for cultural evolution. There are both constraining and facilitating elements in the relationships among the three components of a culture. As the constraining elements generate forces to maintain cultural stability, the facilitating elements produce incentives for cultural change. These constraining and facilitating elements may be conceived as interactive forces that account in part for cultural evolution as a whole (Chu 1989). By incorporating social, physical, and symbolic environments, the Chu and White conceptions are compatible with the global notion of culture as "the whole way of life of the members of a society" (Giddens 1989). Chu also makes explicit linkages between culture, as a global macroscopic concept, and the cognition, affect, and behavior of individuals who share this culture. His model conceives of culture as embodied in and manifested through the relationships between a member of a society and his or her surroundings. These relationships are social in nature in that they involve others, as well as ideas, beliefs, and values that are shared with others. Through its linkages to individuals, this conception leads one to study culture through the behaviors, cognitions, and evaluative appraisals of individual members of a society.

Culture as a meaning system is materialized in patterns of human behavior and social interaction as well as in artifacts and observable rituals. Culture means more than physical materials or observed patterning of human interactions. It is also found in the evolution of distinct systems of ideas, beliefs, values, and their manifestations through symbols, forms of presentation, and patterns of social relationships. Culture is not static but dynamic, a constantly flowing current. Although occasionally major social interruptions or natural catastrophes might intervene to cause abrupt changes in a continuous cultural current (we think here of the 1949 communist revolution in China), cultural change is as a rule better described as a gradual evolutionary process. That is, all cultures are changing, and even the most abrupt changes do not imply wholesale discontinuity. For example, although the communist government in China enforced termination of ancestral-worship rituals during the Cultural Revolution, the idea of respecting one's ancestors remained. When political controls were loosened during the reform era in the 1980s, worship activities quickly resumed (Parish 1984; Link 1986). In this sense, culture is "social heredity—the total legacy of past human behavior effective in the present, representing the accumulation, through generations, of the artifacts, knowledges, beliefs, and values by which men deal with the world" (Williams 1970:25).

Values and Social Relationships

Each culture has its distinct value systems and orientations (Kluckhohn and Strodtbeck 1961). Values are often revealed in the behavioral patterns, community relationships, rituals, and cultural artifacts that make it possible for us to recognize and experience each culture. What are values then? One sociologist defines values "as those conceptions of desirable states of affairs that are utilized in selective conduct as criteria for preference or choice or as justifications for proposed or actual behavior" (Williams 1970:442). That is, values are learned and internalized by members of a society for their orientations and adaptations in a social world. Values are "a type of social cognition" (Kahle and Timmer 1983:44). This conception of values is shared to some degree by many others (Rokeach 1973, 1979; Kahle and Timmer 1983; Ball-Rokeach et al., 1984). It is values that provide cultural rituals, customs, and artifacts their meaning. Values also give each culture its distinct character. We focus in this study on values in order to study each culture as it is experienced and expressed by the people who carry and share a set of values.

A conceptual definition must differentiate values from other closely related concepts such as beliefs, attitudes, and norms. Values are a type of belief, but are not identical with beliefs, which are cognitive elements that have existential referents. In other words, one cannot empirically test the truthfulness of a value as one might a belief. Values are not the same as needs or desires, either. One can at least temporarily satisfy a need or desire, but fulfilling a value will not eliminate or reduce it in the slightest. A value resembles an attitude in that it involves an affective component, but values are more abstract and general than attitudes, and a value is not confined to any specific attitudinal object or behavior. Too, values differ from norms, although both concepts refer to one's sense of the way things "ought to be." A norm is a subjective perception of the attitudes of significant others, or of society in general (Fishbein and Ajzen 1975), and is thus related to specific behaviors or objects (Kahle and Timmer 1983; Rokeach 1973, 1979; Williams 1970). Norms usually carry sanctions that are enforced through group pressures, while values are internalized preferences held by the individual regardless of social context.

Each culture has its own hierarchically organized system of values (Kluckhohn and Strodtbeck 1961; Williams 1970; Rokeach 1973, 1979; Feather 1975). In Kluckhohn and Strodtbeck's terms, a value system is a set of principles that are "patterned" in a distinct configuration. This patterning of value elements distinguishes one value system from another. For example, both Chinese and Americans value family stability. But in traditional Chinese culture, family stability was built upon the supreme importance of one's obligations to ancestors, clan, and parents. The Chinese value of family stability is closely associated with many other values, such as prohibiting free male-female courtship and reliance on parental arrangement for marriages. This means that forces beyond the marriage itself, primarily those from clan and family elders, are involved in enforcing family stability. In American culture these broader social elements tend to be in the background, if they occur to marriage partners at all. Family stability in America is considered part of the "happiness" a couple seeks and is closely associated with other distinctly American values such as romantic love, individual happiness, and free courtship. Marriage constitutes the formal freeing of the man and the woman from their families of origin. Consequently, American marriage partners are their own primary enforcers of family stability.

These differences in patterning of the value of family stability with other values produce distinct patterns of social relationships in the two cultures. We can see these differences to some extent in divorce rates, in the manner of husband-wife interactions, and in male-female interactions in general. The effects of different patternings extend to the two cultures' distinctions between fraternal and maternal relatives, who is invited to the wedding, approaches to child rearing, and what the children are named.

One important area in which values differ across cultures is that of social relationships. Social relationships in this study are defined as those that are stabilized institutionally through culturally understood roles and responsibilities. For example, male and female relationships involve culturally accepted behavioral expectations in work situations, in families, and in social interactions. In each of these settings, there are socially accepted definitions of roles, through expected behavioral patterns and responsibilities associated with being a male or female. The same can be said about relationships involving authority hierarchies, seniority, or kinship.

Values concerning social relationships can be defined as the criteria or principles governing the choice of conduct in human interaction. That is, values are behavioral principles that function as standards of desirable ends and of the means to achieve those ends. They are manifested through comparisons of several equivalent behavioral options or individually expressed preferences (Williams 1970). When a value becomes a shared principle of the majority of a society, it may carry with it a moral or ethical power of sanction. It other words, a value can become a norm. It may develop further to become a legal regulation, so that legal sanctions come into play. Evidence of a society's core values is often found in its laws, but laws can be misleading. In 1982 it was written into law in China that love is the only basis for marriage. The very need to enact such a law tells us that this assertion was contrary to prevailing Chinese values. In the United States, where love is indeed the normative basis of marriage, such a law would strike most people as gratuitous.

Traditional Chinese Values and American Values

If each culture is distinct in its patterning of values, one might be tempted to identify a set of "core values" for each culture, based on their central importance in each value configuration. For example, many would agree that individualism, freedom, and equality of opportunity are core values in American culture (Williams 1970; Hsu 1981). Identifying and locating the core values in each culture is a particularly important task for a comparative study of cultures. If lists of core values could be compiled for the American and Chinese cultures, it would be possible to compare them, to "see" the different value configurations and to understand the differences at a more fundamental level of conceptualization.

Recognizing the core values of different cultures does not mean we should accept a static view of cultures or of value systems. In contemporary society, every value system is open to influences from, and spreads its own influences to, other value systems. Mutual influences are accomplished through communication, in its form as well as its manifest content. For example, international flows of communication technologies, or of messages from other cultures via those technologies, may change the value systems of developing nations (Lerner 1958; Schramm 1964; Salinas and Paldan 1979; Lee 1979; Hamelink 1983). This is welcomed by some proponents of modernization because, they argue, adopting such values as individualism, achievement orientation, or participatory democracy is both a necessary condition for and an indication of modernization (Lerner 1958; Inkeles and Smith 1974; Inkeles 1983; Almond and Verba 1963; Nathan and Shi 1993). Opponents of this view argue that the unidirectional flow of communication from a few dominant countries to developing countries destroys the "authentic national characteristics" for "an optimal synchronization of cultural values" (Hamelink 1983). The two sides share a common assumption, that no culture in today's world can remain segregated from the influences of others. Modern communication technologies and increasingly interconnected international economic systems make cultural isolation impossible in the long run. The political interpretation of international message flows is analogous to interpersonal communication, in that traditional patterns of deference are acted out daily according to rules about what children may say to their elders or wives to their husbands—and when and how they may say it.

Traditional Chinese culture is, as we have noted, widely considered to be built upon a value system crystallized in Confucianism. Confucianism itself has shown its "elasticity" through interpretations over the past two thousand years (Tu 1985). All schools of Confucianism agree, however, that this traditional value system is revealed through elaborate definitions, regulations, and moral and ethical principles regarding individuals' roles and relationships (Liu 1987; Hu and Cheng 1987; Liang 1987). These principles are not just ideas; they are materialized in social practices, including rituals, rites, ceremonies, and cultural artifacts.

At the heart of the Confucian system lies a linear hierarchy governing family structure, political structure, and the supernatural world (Liu 1987). This hierarchy was, as we have noted, characterized by various dominance-obedience relationships: men dominating women, old dominating young, and the emperor dominating everyone else. This hierarchy was delineated by clearly defined roles, responsibilities, rituals, and customs governing interactions among the occupants of designated positions at various levels.

This elaborated construction rests upon the foundation of the Confucian conception of kinship relationships. Filial piety, a principle that most literally governs the father-son relationship, constitutes a cardinal value of Confucianism. It entails unquestioned obedience of the son to the authority of his father (Tu 1985; Liang 1987) during—and after—his father's lifetime. Contrary to the popular conception of unidirectional control, this dyadic relationship implies active contributions by both parties. That is, the relationship is built on each party's internalizing his role, including his rights and obligations, and voluntarily fulfilling it (Tu 1985). This aspect of the father-son relationship is represented by the traditional phrase "benevolent father and filial son," a reciprocal system.

The basic dominance-obedience relationship characterized in filial piety is generalized to that of emperor-subjects *(jun-chen)*, treating the person's relationship with authorities as a natural extension of his relationship with his father in terms of dominance and obedience. A government official, by occupying his position and fulfilling his role, acquires obligations to obey his superior—and to obey, ultimately, the emperor—with complete devotion and self-sacrifice. In theory at least, this obedience extends to criticism of one's superior and even the emperor. Criticizing a superior through official channels, even in fear for one's life, is considered a supreme expression of loyalty to the emperor (Tu 1985). Therefore, both parties to this dyadic relationship must confine themselves in their own roles and obligations, which serve the ultimate goal of maintaining the emperor's "house and property" *(she-ji)*.

Where male-female relationships are concerned, there is an integrated set of traditional values to express male dominance: superiority of men over women, chastity for women, and lifelong submission of a woman to her husband and her husband's family. These values toward male-female relationships are manifested through clear definitions of female roles and the duties and obligations associated with those roles. Woman's role is to contribute through reproduction (in both physical and cultural senses) to her husband's family, so that the good family name is continued. She is also expected to share with her husband his filial duties to his parents and ancestors. Her commitment to her duties is expressed through her chastity throughout her life. Love between a woman and her husband (or fiancé) is irrelevant, even though she has the duty upon marriage to love her husband through fulfilling all her duties as a daughter-in-law of the family.

These three cardinal principles *(san-gang)* in the dominant interpretation of the Confucian value system are closely related and reinforce one another. For example, failing one's official duties may mean not only lack of loyalty to the emperor but also disgrace to the person's father and ancestors. A man with a wife whose chastity is questioned has failed to honor and obey his ancestors and has tarnished the grace of being an emperor's servant. Such dominance-obedience relationships continue in the supernatural world and are similarly defined. Social roles in the current world are personified in deities who occupy corresponding positions, and they continue indefinitely into the supernatural world after the annulation of human bodies. These concepts have no analogues in American culture.

We should not treat American culture as if it were all of one piece; the United States is too heterogeneous a country for that. But we can say that American culture, like others in Western civilization, contains no elaborated value systems based upon kinship clans (Liang 1987; Williams 1970). If anything, American culture would be characterized by individualism, equality, and freedom (Williams 1970; Spindler 1977; Hsu 1981), values that are as a set clearly incompatible with the Confucian tradition we have just described.

Regarding kinship relationships, American culture places much greater emphasis on the nuclear unit consisting of a couple and their immediate children. Close interactions with relatives beyond the two immediate generations are maintained and even considered socially desirable, but such interactions carry at most a weak obligation for continuing the family name, or for seeking not to dishonor it. Even between two immediate generations, adult children are expected to be independent both economically and socially, which includes setting up their separate households upon reaching adulthood. Rather few Americans know, or think it important, where their great-grandfathers are buried or how they conducted themselves in life.

Male-female relationships in the United States are also not governed by strong kinship obligations to either the fraternal or the maternal side. American women have, on the whole, a higher degree of legal and moral autonomy in marriage than was formerly the case in either the United States or China. In many respects there is literal equality between wife and husband; the political struggle for equal rights of American women has never needed to be fought in reference to a kinship system larger than the nuclear family. Although the typical American bride ritualistically promises to "honor and obey" her husband, she does so on an individual basis of love; it has nothing to do with his ancestors.

The lack of rigid definitions of women's roles in a kinship context may be partly responsible for the rather weak resistance to changes in family relationships and female status brought about by various social movements in the United States. As Williams (1970:90) points out, the "diminution of the extended family and the correlated loss of many previous functions of nuclear units" have led to emphasis on the family functions of "providing affection and security." These family relationships provide the "social basis for idealization of romantic love" in American society. Women are gradually occupying many roles that were traditionally reserved for males, such as holding public office, heading businesses, and practicing high-status professions.

It can be useful to contrast the two cultures as "ideal types," understanding that a certain degree of caricature is inherent in such an exercise. Williams (1970:501–502) outlined seven dimensions to characterize key features of American culture; six of these are useful to us here in creating a contrasting image of traditional culture. We will express these polar opposites in terms of traditional Chinese culture, which seems to us to fit in contradistinction point by point. But the reader might also consider that the traditional culture in question could in many respects be traditional American culture. Williams has set up his description of American culture partly to decry trends in modern U.S. life. There are many Americans who are concerned about traditional values, and virtually no politician runs for office without joining in the call for "a return" to an idealized past. With these caveats in mind, we may summarize six key differences between the two cultures in the following dualisms, drawing the characterization of American culture in each case from Williams's analysis:

1. American culture emphasizes "active mastery" in the person–nature relationship, whereas traditional Chinese culture emphasized "passive acceptance" of fate by seeking harmony with nature;
2. American culture tends to be concerned with external experiences and the world of things, whereas traditional Chinese culture emphasized inner experiences of meaning and feeling;
3. American culture is characterized by an open view of the world, emphasizing change and movement, whereas traditional Chinese culture was typified by a closed world view, prizing stability and harmony;
4. American culture places primary faith in rationalism and is oriented toward the future, whereas traditional Chinese culture rested upon kinship ties and tradition with a past orientation;
5. American culture emphasizes horizontal dimensions of interpersonal relationships, whereas traditional Chinese culture placed more weight on vertical interpersonal relationships;
6. American culture values the individual personality, whereas traditional Chinese culture weighed heavily a person's duties to family, clan, and state.

These dualistic contrasts summarize the distinct qualitative differences between the two cultures. However, such differences cannot be simplified into traditional versus developed societies, defined on a past versus present time continuum (Liang 1987; Pang 1988). These are two distinct types of differences. The East-West dichotomy recognizes different traditions and developmental patterns of the two civilizations while the past-present dimension implies a single continuous linear development model common to civilizations of both East and West. Confusion between these two conceptions underlies the repeated swings among Chinese intellectuals between "wholesale Westernization" and "preserving the national heritage" ever since the May Fourth movement of 1919 (Chow 1960; also see Tu 1987).

Value Changes and Sources of Influence

Cultural values can vary empirically in three general ways, two of which imply change (Chaffee and Chu 1992). First, values may differ cross-sectionally across the different members of the society. This is the kind of data we will present in this monograph, but it does not in itself indicate change—only differences. The other two kinds of variation constitute two different kinds of change: change within the individual members of the society and change in the composition of the society as old members die off and new members (with different values) enter. We will not be able to examine change empirically in either of these latter senses here. But we will consider both theoretically, as possible explanations for the cross-sectional differences we do find. That is, variation uncovered by this survey could indicate both cultural diversity and cultural change. We will be particularly interested in geographical differences within each culture, specifically the contrast between values in urban and rural settings. As a rule, social change occurs earlier and is more widespread in the cities and only gradually emanates from urban centers to the villages and farms of the countryside. We could, then, predict that the "American" values detailed in the six dualisms in the preceding section here would be more characteristic in urban than in rural samples. But in China matters will not be so simple. There are more than two diametrically opposing cultural forces at work, and each has been stronger at some historical periods than at others.

China specialists and scholars generally agree that three distinct and competing influences are operating in contemporary China: traditional Chinese cultural orthodoxy, Marxism and Maoism, and Western influences. Although these influences mostly conflict—as reflected in political clashes between the Party and intellectuals, between intellectuals and manual workers or peasants, and between the "liberals" and hardline Party conservatives—they may be allied regarding specific issues (Whyte 1989).

Male-female relationships serve to exemplify conflicts and alliances among the three different value orientations. China's Communist government advocates equal status of men and women and equal pay for equal work. It has adopted a marriage law stipulating that love be the sole basis for marriage (Platte 1988). The Communist value system in these areas of male-female relationships clearly aligns with Western influences. But the government just as clearly maintains an alliance with traditional Confucian male-female doctrine: both premarital and extra-marital sex are prohibited through strong moral sanctions, being denounced in the media as evidence of "Western influences."

Before 1949, China's traditional value system had commingled with Western liberalism; traditionalism was dominant, and communism was gradually emerging. With the success of the communist revolution and its repeated propaganda campaigns, communist ideology—with a Chinese accent—became the dominant cultural force (Tu 1987). Communism's dominance has declined since the economic and political reforms begun in 1979. This has included a movement to rehabilitate the reputation of Confucius, whose teachings had been severely denounced during the Cultural Revolution. Both traditional cultural elements and Western influences have since 1979 become increasingly powerful (Link 1986; Tu 1987), but communism remains the central fact of daily existence.

Evidence of the three forces in the contemporary scene can be found in Chinese media. Western entertainment such as imported TV series, movies, and rock music shares the stage with traditional Chinese entertainment (folk songs, vernacular dramas, and Peking operas) and with communist propaganda in the form of news, editorials, and officially sanctioned "entertainment" programs. The combination of these three forces has shaped a distinct culture. To date there has been little systematic documentation of the unique Chinese cultural discourse of the 1980s, but impressionistic observations indicate that the three types of influences are manifest not only in economic and political policy debates, but also in various cultural forms (Link 1986; Croizier 1989; Yang 1990).

Because the Communist Party controls the media system (Liu 1981; L. Chu 1986; Whyte 1989), media messages carry with them a seal of authority and, very often, policy implications. But the communist monopoly of media tends to detract from the credibility of official messages. Therefore, although messages from alternative sources lack the mass audience of official media, they do attract many young people by their freshness (and, often, sensationalism). With the loosening of communist control over alternative media in the late 1980s, local papers and magazines, underground publications, unofficial magazines, art performances, and exhibitions became important (Croizier 1989). Even many official and semi-official media outlets are forced to appeal to the market for their survival. The conflict between competing message systems and ideological orientations creates excitement in the Chinese media and attracts broad audiences.

The potential impact of these new media conditions on cultural values is difficult to estimate without good evidence of people's interpretations. On the one hand, China has been in transition for at least forty years, and instability and ambiguity are conditions that should intensify audience "dependency" on the media (Ball-Rokeach and DeFleur 1976; Ball-Rokeach et al. 1984). Mass media are thought to have their greatest influence when people are looking for guidance in an ambiguous situation. On the other hand, the media of China today are not as univocal as they were when the communist government maintained tighter control; they are more heterogeneous, if not so much so as the competitive, unfettered commercial media of the United States. The most common finding in studies of media effects when messages conflict is that people's predispositions—in any direction—get reinforced (Klapper 1960). The net effect is often near zero, although the total effect in strengthening various predispositions may be great. Two-sided political broadcasts, such as televised debates between competing candidates for president in the United States, tend to make Republicans more confident that their candidate is better—and Democrats equally confident instead that theirs is (Kraus 1979). Two-sided presentations, as contrasted with either one-sided messages or mere repetition of truisms, tend to strengthen the audience member's belief defenses so that the person is rendered more resistant to subsequent propaganda (Hovland, Lumsdaine, and Sheffield 1949; McGuire 1964). This theoretical analysis would not lead us to predict much net change from heavy exposure to a heterogeneous media message system. That is, in a survey such as the present study, heavy media users may not differ much from other people, because the effects on them tend to cancel out one another when aggregated across a heterogeneous audience.

China's economic reform begun in 1979 marked the collapse of the ten-year Cultural Revolution. It is impossible to review here all the social changes that have occurred in China since 1979, but it has been a period of declining communist dominance in ideology, revived traditional cultural elements, and opening of China to Western influences (Whyte 1989).

There have been no such comparable cultural dynamics and social changes in the United States. America's history with regard to traditional values has revolved around various dualisms and has been gradual and somewhat cyclical. That is, there are periods of seemingly rapid change in the direction of the "American" precepts outlined by Williams (1970), followed by reactionary eras when the dominant theme has been a call for a return to traditional values. The 1980s saw a resurgence of conservative power built upon the Reagan-Bush-Quayle "family values" slogan. Fundamentalist religious figures have become prominent (especially on television), and popular writers have flourished along with political leaders by harkening back to a past that is in many particulars similar to traditional Chinese values: family obligations, restrictions on abortion, traditional male-female role differentiation, and so forth.

But these traditional American values, whether they are in temporary ascendance (as in the 1980s) or widely ignored (as was the case in the

Vietnam War era of the 1960s), are in no serious sense Confucian. The ancestral linkages of Confucian culture, for example, are almost wholly lacking. Cultural conflict in America proceeds from an assumption that the individual, not the kinship system, is the unit of discourse. From this individualistic approach flow other concepts that are highly prized on all sides in the United States (and traditionally almost wholly unknown in China): freedom, independence, privacy, equality. The U.S. mass media happily propagate (and sell) whatever messages they can find on any side of the cultural divide, but these individualistic ideals remain central to any American construction of a political or social issue.

The infusion of Western media into China raises the question of whether these American values are being interwoven into the fabric of Chinese culture. The outward trappings of American society are easy to find in China today: free enterprise, self-reliance, technological innovation, conspicuous consumption. But many recent changes in China could easily be interpreted as a resurgence of traditional values (Chinese or American): family stability and prosperity, traditional male-female roles, and reduced governmental interference.

In the 1980s China and the United States took very distinct paths, but there are indications that the two cultures may share a degree of convergence. This is in effect one hypothesis we are examining in this project. Our suspicion, though, is that despite such surface similarities as China's movement toward a market economy, fundamental differences will persist. Chinese authorities have emphasized repeatedly that their goal is to establish a "socialist modern state with a Chinese character." There are, nonetheless, factors at work in both countries that might well produce additional similarities. Increasingly, the United States and China share a common pool of mass media messages—especially if the ubiquitous Western entertainment package is taken into account. The essential core of Western love stories, and of other staple themes such as crime and personal achievement sagas, is individualism. One survey of a group of Chinese women from three major cities in China reveals a strong correlation between these women's exposure to Western entertainment media and the priority they accorded to individual-level values (Zhao 1988). Education tends to encourage cultural change within the individual, as does urbanism (Lerner 1958; Inkeles and Smith 1974; Inglehart 1990). Both education and urbanization are on the rise in China, and both have already approached asymptotic, high levels in the United States—where suburbanization has succeeded the earlier trend toward urban concentration of people. China may be becoming more like the United States, at least where people are exposed to American models and opportunities to exercise individualistic values.

Mass media serve an educational and even a kind of "urbanizing" function as well, linking people in remote areas to the common culture. In this respect, too, China is moving down a modernization path that the United States has already traversed for the most part. We are not suggesting similar media content, similar media systems, or similar directions of media influences between the two cultures. But, despite differences in all these areas, mass media of any character play an important role in transmitting ideas that can be shared throughout a society. There is at least some evidence of significant media effects on values in both nations (e.g., Ball-Rokeach et al. 1984; Zhao 1988; Chu and Ju 1993). But the processes of mass media influence are complex and in many respects contradictory, and no simple unidirectional predictions can be made regarding their impact on cultural values. The best we can do at this point in our research is to examine variation in exposure to sources of media messages that differ in predictable ways and array this evidence alongside that relating to other factors such as location, education, age, and sex.

Summary

In this chapter, we have located values regarding social relationships in an important position in the symbolic universe of a culture. Values are conceived as principles and standards that guide human behavior in dealing with those relationships that form the basic fabric of a society. Values also contribute culturally distinct meanings to the social relationships that are present in all societies. Unique configurations of value elements constitute culturally distinct value systems, which characterize recognizable differences between American and Chinese cultures.

This study examines specific value elements in Chinese and American cultures related to several basic social relationships with the specific goal of cross-cultural comparisons. We are not proceeding from an assumption of a single dimension of traditionalism vs. modernism, nor do we assume that cultural change in either country proceeds in a unidirectional fashion. We assume that change may occur in some areas of social relationships, but that there will be cultural lags in other domains, and that underlying dimensions of a value system may not necessarily change.

We see cultural values as derived from, and leading to, social relationships that are represented in a rough fashion by demographic indicators: locale, gender, marital status, age, education, income, occupation. These in turn affect exposure to various channels of mass communication. At the heart of our conception lie value systems, not just discrete statements regarding a single value. We proceed in the chapters that follow to describe the project through which our data have been collected (Chapter

3), to examine U.S.-China differences and rural-urban differences in agreement with discrete value statements (Chapter 4), to evaluate demographic differences within and between the two cultures (Chapter 5), to explore patterns of association between sets of values (Chapter 6), and then to test the unique contributions to each of the value systems we identify, of both the demographic factors and exposure to various mass media channels (Chapter 7). In Chapter 8 we compare the marginal results of the U.S.-China surveys with parallel data from two Confucian countries, Taiwan and Korea. Finally, in Chapter 9 we review what we have learned from this study, and consider how it affects the way we might view Chinese and American culture today and what we should anticipate for the future.

3

Procedures

THE STUDY WE REPORT IN THIS book was conducted in various locations in the United States and the Shanghai region of China over a period
of several years in the late 1980s. It is part of a larger program of research
that began in the early 1960s under the direction of Godwin Chu and extends to a number of other countries as well. The culmination of this
project is not yet in sight. Hence this monograph is an interim report to
provide a baseline for comparison to other societies and for data that we
presume will be collected in future years. While China is changing in
many respects—as is, to a lesser extent, the United States—we presume
that the cultural values on which this project is centered are less amena-
ble to short-term change than are more superficial features of the culture
of each nation.

The story of this overall project began in 1964, when Chu returned to
his home in Taipei after completing his Ph.D. in communication at Stanford University. Interested in the impact of mass communication, he
secured a grant from the Asia Foundation in San Francisco to study
effects of media on cultural values. He conducted a survey of 317 people
in eight villages in northern Taiwan (Chu and Chi 1984). After a teaching
career at several universities, Chu came in 1973 to the East-West Center,
which has supported most of the rest of the research in this project.

In 1978 Chu returned to the same villages where he had first surveyed
traditional Chinese values fourteen years earlier, and with additional
support from the Pacific Cultural Foundation he was able to reinterview
185 of his original respondents. He also interviewed a new random cross-
section of 72 respondents in the same villages. Results comparing the
longitudinal panel data and the successive cross-sectional data (Chu and
Chi 1984; Chaffee and Chu 1992) indicated that the cumbersome panel
method is not necessary to the study of social change. More important, it
showed that despite the introduction of television and other modern
media in the intervening years, Confucian values remained strong in
rural Taiwan.

The Taiwan findings encouraged Chu, who had grown up in China
but left as a young man after the communist revolution, to wonder what
had become of traditional values in other Asian countries—including,
ultimately, his original homeland. He began to conceive of a larger

project to evaluate cultural change in several countries within the East-West Center's broad purview.

An East-West Center study of cultural values in Thailand was initiated in the spring of 1986. Among the scholars attending a workshop to evaluate the results later that year was Yanan Ju of Fudan University in Shanghai. Scholars in China, only recently in contact with their opposite numbers in the West, were caught up in a "Culture Fever," and the empirical data from Thailand particularly struck Ju as a productive way to approach the issue of traditional Chinese culture in the context of his country's newfound enthusiasm for modernization. He convinced his colleagues at Fudan University to undertake an empirical study of cultural change in China in cooperation with Chu and others at the East-West Center.

After several delays due to sporadic political turmoil in China, the project got underway in April 1987, concentrating on Shanghai and several towns and rural villages in its vicinity. The long-range plan was to conduct a baseline survey in 1987, assuming there would be a follow-up wave in the same sites some years later (following the model of Chu's Taiwan study).

The next task was to develop an appropriate survey instrument. The Taiwan questionnaire had been designed for village life on that island, and the Thailand study was built around Buddhism and Thai culture. In both cases, items were pretested locally in advance of field data collection. None of this quite fit the situation in China, where survey research was scarcely known before the Communists came to power—and then had been banned by the Party for more than thirty years. Some surveys were being conducted in China by the mid-1980s (e.g., Rosen and D. Chu 1987; Nathan and Shi 1993), but none of them dealt with cultural values in the area of social relationships. Chu and his colleagues had to start from scratch.

A planning workshop was convened at the East-West Center in Honolulu in May 1987. Participants were (with the exception of Steven Chaffee, whose role was to provide expertise in survey methods) leading scholars of Chinese culture within different disciplines. They included Francis L. K. Hsu, the last student of Bronislaw Malinowski and a past-president of the American Anthropological Association, whose work has been cited in earlier chapters of this book; Wang Gungwu, a historian who has written extensively on the role of merchants in a society that traditionally disrespected the mercantile class, and vice-chancellor (i.e., president) of the University of Hong Kong; Ambrose King, a senior sociologist at the Chinese University of Hong Kong, specializing in cultural values and modernization in China; and Anthony Yu, a professor of religion at the University of Chicago noted for his research on religions of China. The workshop went on for five days, conducted mostly in Chinese with occasional reviews in English for Chaffee's benefit. The result was a questionnaire designed for the Shanghai area study that is in this volume usually referred to as the "China" survey.

Several precepts governed development of the questionnaire. One was that the concepts represented in it would be those of traditional Confucian culture. Neither communist nor Western values would be included, due to space limitations; it was deemed more important to do a thorough job of one task than fragmentary work on several. No attitude scales were borrowed from instruments constructed in the United States or European countries. The governing concepts were instead those we have highlighted in the first two chapters here: the traditional Confucian concerns of interpersonal relations, male-female differentiation, authority relations, family values, and the like. In the workshop sessions, abstract cultural concepts were discussed extensively in Chinese, then presented in English to Chaffee, who attempted to convert them to usable survey interview questions. These questions were in turn translated back into Chinese by Chu and others. Many of the concepts were combined into multiple-item questions, for which the respondent would be given a list of terms from which to choose one or more answers.

Chu took the initial draft questionnaire to Shanghai in June 1987 for consultation with his colleagues at Fudan University. Upon review, some items were deleted and others were reworded in the Shanghai vernacular dialect. A number of items were added by the Fudan scholars to get at current social and political issues in China that had been overlooked in the Honolulu workshop. The resultant questionnaire was pretested in Shanghai and one village; in the process it became apparent that the personal interview method would not be feasible. The format was changed to a self-administered instrument in a small-group setting, which had the effect of excluding illiterates from the sample.

Final review of the pretest results led to creation of a novel list of eighteen traditional Confucian values, among which respondents were invited to indicate which ones they were "proud of" and which they felt "should be discarded." Emphasis in the questionnaire had shifted gradually from asking people about their behaviors to asking them about their values. Administration of the questionnaire was conducted by faculty and graduate students in Fudan University's Center of Communication and Cultural Studies, under Ju's direction. (Funding included a personal grant to the East-West Center from Mr. and Mrs. Laurance Rockefeller.) Final data collection for the China study took place near the end of 1987.

Meanwhile at the East-West Center a conference on communication and national development was held in the summer of 1987, co-sponsored with the East-West Center by the University of Hawaii. At this meeting, which was co-chaired by Chu and Joung-im Kim and featured Wilbur Schramm as keynote speaker, Chu reported to Chaffee on the pretesting in Shanghai. They began discussing the possibility of replicating the China study in other countries, including for the first time the United States. A year later Chu's proposal for a U.S. replication was funded by the East-West Center.

Chaffee invited two colleagues, Diana Stover Tillinghast of San Jose State University and Pamela Shoemaker of the University of Texas at Austin, to collaborate on data collection as class projects for their students. Working from the English translation of the Shanghai questionnaire, they began writing and pretesting items in a format suitable for telephone interviewing. During the 1988–89 academic year the first two surveys were completed, covering the adult populations of Santa Clara County, California, and Travis County, Texas. In this book, these are referred to as the California and Texas surveys, respectively.

The entire research group planned to present their data at the annual convention of the International Communication Association in May 1989. Events in China, now known collectively as Tiananmen Square, led to severe constraints on the Shanghai research group at this time, but Ju was able to present some limited results. Tillinghast and Shoemaker brought with them computer printouts and began comparing their results. The percentages agreeing with most of the value items were remarkably similar in the California and Texas surveys. This encouraged the collaborators in their assumption that they were indeed dealing with *national* cultural values in the United States, but it also pointed up the need to add some different locales, including at least one truly rural area.

The promising findings from the first two U.S. replications led to expansion of that side of the project, while the China side was placed on hold. In the summer of 1989 a workshop at the East-West Center brought together Chu, Ju, Chaffee, Tillinghast, and several new collaborators: Jack McLeod of the University of Wisconsin-Madison, Gary Heald of Florida State University, Leslie Snyder of the University of Connecticut, and Jaewon Lee of Cleveland State University. (Lee, a Korean-American, also brought in from Seoul Won-yong Kim, who had replicated the China survey there. It was clear from a glance at the Korean data that Confucian values were more widely held in Korea than in China.) During the 1989–90 academic year the new participants conducted surveys in their areas of the country: Dane County, Wisconsin; the rural counties surrounding Tallahassee, Florida; the metropolitan region of Hartford, Connecticut; and the metropolitan region of Cleveland, Ohio. These we shall call the Wisconsin, Florida, Connecticut, and Ohio surveys, although each of them is local rather than statewide in its sampling frame. The sample in Florida was deliberately designed by Heald to cover rural areas (i.e., to exclude the urban center, Tallahassee), so that the population surveyed consisted largely of poor white and black Southerners. The other five U.S. sites were essentially urban or suburban, centered on major cities that range in size from 200,000 to 700,000 population. In all cases, the U.S. interviews were conducted by telephone, and the sampling procedure was some variant of random digit dialing.

In 1990 Zhongdang Pan, then a graduate student from China who had worked on the Wisconsin survey as a Ph.D. student under McLeod, joined the research team. His primary responsibilities have involved data analysis and the writing of various reports, including drafting this book manuscript.

We have detailed this chronology of the project partly to explain why a "comparative" U.S.-China study should have so many noncomparable design features—timing, method of data collection, question format, and of course language—and partly to give some credit where a great deal of credit is due. Each of the collaborators in these surveys, in both countries, is truly a co-author of this monograph. They participated in questionnaire design, pretesting, data collection, data analysis, and other essential steps in the research process. Their subsidy from the East-West Center was just $2,000 apiece. In fact, this massive project, including more than four thousand interviews in the two countries, cost less than $50,000 if we include all the subsidies, travel, workshops, and incidentals. Most of this was paid by the Rockefeller grant to the East-West Center. Of course much of the remaining "subsidy" came from the collaborators, who devoted many hours of uncompensated intellectual effort to the project, and from the universities that pay their base salaries and encourage them to engage in research of their choosing. The entire data set from the project has been made available to all collaborators for secondary analysis, but the authors of this volume owe them an unpayable debt for their skilled and willing service to this project.

Methodological Issues

The sample survey method was deemed essential for this project for several reasons. First, we cannot expect that any value, or expression of it, will be literally universal in any culture. The empirical question to be answered is the *degree* of prevalence, of one value vs. another in one country vs. another. This requires asking many different kinds of people about many different kinds of values in a systematic fashion. That can only be accomplished by a structured questionnaire, so that every respondent is called upon to answer each of the questions in a format that will permit comparisons between different items and different kinds of people.

A second major reason for choosing the sample survey method is to represent a broad diversity of individuals. We cannot claim that our samples are literally representative of those two massive entities, China and the United States. No imaginable research program could hope to generate literally comparable data for both countries. But at the other extreme, interviewing just a few people in one or two locales would produce data that are subject to many idiosyncratic influences: the personalities of the interviewers and respondents, local and temporary concerns, oddities of geographical clustering, and so forth.

A third methodological advantage of our parallel-surveys design can best be seen in contrast with the other major method of scholarly inquiry on cultural values, which is insightful observation by a highly trained anthropologist who experiences life in both cultures (e.g., Hsu 1981). We have throughout this project drawn concepts from such fieldwork, and we have inevitably operated as amateur comparativists ourselves to the extent that we have lived in the two countries and informed our procedures and interpretations through our own reading and experiences. Even the most scientific of social scientists is also an individual with a personal history and a working knowledge of specific cultures, as well as an objective methodologist and theorist.

Our research has been sharpened too by other scholars' listings of contrasts between traditional Confucian culture and those of both communist China and the United States. But any single observer moving from one culture to another tends to be struck mainly by the contrasts, rather than the commonalities, and by the sense of change rather than of permanence. A relatively small shift in value emphasis can be experienced phenomenologically as a much larger difference than it might be when measured by a constant instrument, just as a person leaving a cold, dark room senses his new environment as warmer and brighter than it will seem once he is accustomed to it. Our survey interviews were conducted within each culture by indigenous personnel in each research site, so that there can be no analogous contrast effect. There was no reference in the U.S. study to China, nor vice-versa, for example. To the extent that we find differences between the two cultures, then, they cannot be ascribed to a perceptual contrast effect that exists only in the eye of the beholder. In this study, our comparisons are not inserted until an advanced stage of quantitative analysis of the data.

Survey interviews have been widely used in studies on values (e.g., Rokeach 1973, 1979; Kohn 1977; Kahle 1983; Inglehart 1990). Other methods are sometimes viewed as supplemental, and in other cases the survey is merely a supplement to the primary study (see Chu and Ju 1993 for a review). Survey methodology certainly has its weaknesses in the cross-cultural study of value change: (1) the validity of any standardized questionnaire item varies in different cultural contexts; (2) survey questions about generic categories of behavior or feelings may miss culturally meaningful but individually idiosyncratic revelations of underlying values; (3) survey interviews may arouse different cultural reactions to answering questions from strangers (Frey 1970; Verba 1969). We must throughout this report remain aware of these limitations, which go far beyond mere differences in language and in features of the interviewer-respondent interaction. All the sources of variation in human communication threaten to confound our interpretations of the data collected through the interviews on which this study resides.

No research method is by itself problem-free. While recognizing the weaknesses of survey methodology, we believe they can be remedied to a large extent through careful conceptualization, design, and statistical control. There exists a vast array of empirical studies on values, attitudes, and cultural changes based on survey methods in different cultures (e.g., Szalai and Petrella 1977; Frey 1970; Przeworski and Teune 1970; Verba 1969; Scheuch 1968; Almond and Verba 1963; Inglehart 1990; Inkeles and Smith 1974; Rokeach 1973, 1979; Ball-Rokeach et al. 1984; Schwartz 1992). These investigators have been successful because they approached their survey work gingerly, aware of its problematics as well as its promise.

Cross-national comparative research generates empirical data for us (1) to describe differences in human life across different societies; (2) to determine the cultural boundaries of a theoretical relationship, that is, to identify those conditions under which a proposition is validated; and (3) to reveal new empirical relationships not anticipated by other scholars (Przeworski and Teune 1970:ch. 1; Nowak 1977). Our project, while we should couch its goals in modest terms, has analogous purposes. We will describe values in the two nations—China and the United States—and we will explore their boundaries in relation to demographic subsets of people in each. These analyses are not simply ritualistic academic exercises; when we find the same question related to the same demographic variable in opposite ways in the two countries, we will automatically suspect that it means different things, at least in terms of the processes of social change, in the two societies. In our social influence (media effects) analyses, we will also be probing an area that has been largely neglected by prior students of cultural values.

Cross-national comparative research, properly executed, requires measurement of national-level variables (Przeworski and Teune 1970; Frey 1970). When basic *similarities* are observed between the nations under study, inferences can be made without referring to those attributes that differentiate the two cultures. But when cross-national *differences* are found, they need to be explained by functional variables, not just by naming the countries. That is, one will need explanatory factors, measures of the relevant cultural-level variables. Lacking such information—as is the case in many comparative studies—one can only refer to differences in a general sense, even though they may be due to identifiable differences between the two nations such as disparities in economic development, different political systems, or levels of income inequality (Nowak 1977). As Przeworski and Teune (1970:30) put it, "the role of comparative research in the process of theory-building and theory-testing consists of replacing names of social systems by the relevant *variables*" (emphasis ours). In the present case, where only two nations are involved and when they differ in so many respects, this warning may seem gratuitous. But it should remind us that the tendency to theorize grandly from such limited data deserves to be resisted.

A comparative study entails the unavoidable issue of measurement equivalence across cultures. Any meaningful comparison between nations requires cross-cultural concepts, that is, general variables common to all the cultures under examination, dimensions on which each culture can be located relative to the others (Frey 1970:187–190; Przeworski and Teune 1970:ch. 4). At the operational level, conceptual equivalence takes two forms: semantic equivalence and functional equivalence (Przeworski and Teune 1970; Frey 1970; Verba 1977).

Semantic equivalence in survey measurement would mean that questions for cross-cultural comparisons carry the same socially understood meaning in each culture. More exactly, semantically equivalent questions elicit responses that represent similar cognitive processes, as was assumed in the classical work on the measurement of meaning (Osgood, Suci, and Tannenbaum 1957). This criterion does not demand strict linguistic comparability, a standard that would preclude most cross-cultural research including U.S.-China comparisons. Later in this chapter, we will evaluate the semantic equivalence of the survey items used in our China and U.S. surveys.

Functional equivalence goes beyond semantic equivalence and questions whether two parallel questionnaire items compared between cultures represent events that play the same role in one's functioning in the two cultural systems (Nowak 1977:42). It is assumed in functional equivalence that each indicator is system-specific. Empirically, the criterion of functional equivalence implies that the items compared across cultures must bear similar relationships with other items that are known to represent common characteristics in these cultures (Przeworski and Teune 1970, 1969); this is a testable hypothesis. In terms of general research methodology, the issue here is one of construct validity (Cronbach and Meehl 1955), in the context of multiple cultures. As will be seen in our substantive chapters, some cultural values have a different *political* status in Communist China, due to the long-term governmental assault on the Confucian tradition, so that items that might seem semantically similar in the two countries have very different functional implications.

How much equivalence is necessary in the comparable items before we can compare two different cultures meaningfully? We attempt to answer this question by examining two intertwined factors that might produce nonequivalence. One is that an item in culture A cannot be compared with an item in culture B because they represent different phenomena in the two cultures. For example, engaging in rituals of worshiping ancestors in China may not be equivalent to attending church on Sunday morning in the United States. The other factor that might lead to nonequivalence is that two cultures are so different that the same act measured by semantically equivalent items in these cultures is differentially related to other characteristics. Verba (1977) gives an example to illustrate this dilemma. In both India and the United States, the act of voting involves the similar activities of going to a private booth to record one's vote and shares the similar legal meaning of selecting government officials. Whether or not one votes in the United States is related to a citizen's interest in politics, but it shows no such relationship in India. Two conclusions could be drawn. One is that voting as a measure is nonequivalent, so comparison of voting between India and the United States cannot be meaningfully made. The other is that the relationship between voting and interest, though not uniform across the Indian and American cultures, is still meaningful and reflects some characteristics inherent in the two cultures that function as different conditional variables. There is something to both conclusions (Verba 1977:190–192).

Equivalence of measures across cultures, as Verba's illustration suggests, can never be complete. This does not mean that no comparisons can be made. For example, ancestor worship in China and attending church in the United States might be considered semantically equivalent on one dimension: they are both religious and ritualistic acts, despite their fundamental differences. Relying upon this similarity, one might discuss the different meanings of the two acts in the two cultures as part of a meaningful comparison of levels of religiosity between Chinese and Americans.

In our analyses we will be alert to these problems of equivalence as we examine semantic similarities of items we wish to compare and the relational patterns among value measures within each culture. When differences are found, instead of simply concluding nonequivalence in measurement, we need to analyze carefully the similarities and differences of the items based upon other knowledge about each culture. We shall also examine the relationships within each culture between the value measures and other variables to infer similarities and differences in meanings of the value measures across the two cultures.

Various levels of analysis will be used in our study (consult Eulau 1986; Coleman 1986). Just as we noted above that national-level variables might constitute a part of explanations, so too might lower levels of aggregation, such as geographical areas or age groups, enter into our account of cultural values. We will be looking at these intermediate levels in our results chapters. Comparative research inevitably involves multi-level analysis (Przeworski and Teune 1970), at the least the level of the individual vs. the level of the social systems that are being compared. The basic analytical task is to estimate two portions of variance in values: within-culture (individual differences) and between-culture. In our study we anticipate, considering the differences in ideological, political, and economic systems, that between-nation variation will be larger than within-nation variation. At the first stage of our analysis, comparing aggregate level differences in values between China and the United States, we will in effect be treating the aggregate statistics within each culture as indicators of collective properties of that culture (see Lazarsfeld and Menzel 1961). The goal is to make inferences about two macroscopic units: the Chinese and American cultures.

Next, though, we should move on to examination of intermediate levels of analysis to evaluate whether the differences among these levels within each culture are as great as the differences between the two cultures. Again, our expectation is that the between-cultures variance will be greater, although we certainly do anticipate finding within-culture differences between demographic and other intermediate-level subgroups. These will not necessarily be the same patterns in each culture. When we find the same pattern of relationship, such as a positive correlation, between an intermediate-level (subgroup) variable and a value item, that will be some evidence on behalf of the functional equivalence of that item.

Our objectives in this study are narrower than those assumed by comparative social researchers who attempt to test theoretical hypotheses cross-culturally (e.g., Przeworski and Teune 1970; Frey 1970; Nowak 1977; Allerbeck 1977). We wish mainly to compare the differences in values between the American and Chinese cultures. Our basic units of analysis are, therefore, these two cultures. Even in the multilevel portion of the study, our focus is not on hypothesized relationships between individual-level characteristics. It is on patterns of differences between the two cultures and their robustness when other variables and other levels of analysis are taken into account.

Survey Procedures

In Shanghai a multistage stratified probability sample of two thousand respondents was drawn. At the first stage, two major areas were selected: the city of Shanghai and Qingpu county, which is one of the ten rural counties surrounding Shanghai. The second stage involved division of Shanghai sampling into that city's twelve urban districts and selection of two towns and twenty villages in Qingpu county. Finally, two thousand individual respondents were selected randomly, distributed among sites as detailed in Table 3.1. Sampling of individuals was relatively precise because in China there are complete records on all citizens. Residents below age eighteen or above age sixty-five in the selected areas at the second stage were excluded from the sample. We wanted to interview only adults, and only those who would not be too old to participate in follow-up interviews some years later. Self-administered questionnaires were filled out by the selected respondents in small group sessions held in local schools.[1]

The six sites in the United States were selected largely for convenience, in that each collaborating investigator replicated the survey in her or his home locale. (Each collaborator was given local option to add items to the basic questionnaire, but these came after the questions reported in this book so we will not detail those local variations here.) Collectively, the six sites were planned with an eye to diversity in terms of geographical region, socioeconomic status, and ethnic characteristics. Each collaborator selected telephone numbers through random digit dialing; interviews in most sites were conducted by students as part of a group project for a class taught by the collaborating professor. (In most cases these were research methods courses for advanced undergraduates and beginning graduate students.) The number of call-backs, instructions, and respondent cooperation varied somewhat from site to site.

Question wording on the values items was standardized for the six sites, with a few exceptions noted below due to changes that were deemed advisable after evaluating the results from the first two surveys, in Texas and California. Questions about mass media necessarily differed because local media conditions (e.g., number of newspapers, cable television channels) vary from site to site and because some of the investigators had stronger media research interests than others. The U.S. surveys were conducted between early 1989 and early 1990. Table 3.1 gives the sample size for each site.

Variations in operational procedures from country to country, and

TABLE 3.1   Sample Size by Location

Location	China	United States
Shanghai city	1,199	
Qingpu towns	304	
Villages	497	
Santa Clara County, California		559
Hartford area, Connecticut		197
Dane County, Wisconsin		509
Tallahassee region, Florida[a]		424
Cuyahoga County, Ohio		444
Travis County, Texas		349
Total sample size	2,000	2,482

[a]The Florida sample was drawn from counties bordering Tallahassee, but not from Tallahassee itself.

even from site to site in the United States, obviously add to our problems of interpretation. The U.S. and China studies do not represent those entire countries by any means. So despite the great effort to ask nearly identical questions of more than four thousand people in two vastly different cultures, we are faced with inherent problems in establishing comparability. Some of these are serious, but none is insuperable. We simply need to proceed more cautiously than would, say, an experimental psychologist "running subjects" in a laboratory.

Ours is not the only comparative study that falls short of an ideal design. In the context of a meta-analysis of such projects by Glaser (1977), the present study would be above average in coordination of data collection efforts and would rank high among those with a well-defined research objective. While different modes of interviewing (telephone, face-to-face, self-administered) sometimes affect survey responses (Groves and Kahn 1979), the differences due to these factors have not been shown to be profound (Schuman and Presser 1981). The lack of exact procedural equivalence needs to be kept in mind as we examine our results, but by no means would it invalidate the entire procedure.

Measures of Values

The core of all these surveys consists of an array of value measures. In this section, we will detail the wording, translations, and scales used in measuring values across the surveys.

For the initial survey in China, two general types of value items were developed. One was a forced-choice question, phrased in concrete terms with multiple options for the respondent to choose from. For example, one item in the China survey presented these alternatives: "Do you think old parents should be taken care of by their children, or should they take care of themselves?" ("Not sure" was considered a valid response also.)

The second kind of question is more like a Likert-type item, with a response scale tailored to the Chinese cultural context. This part of the questionnaire consisted of a set of eighteen fixed Chinese phrases that are widely known to virtually all adults in China. These phrases represent different aspects of traditional Chinese values, and many of them originated in the writings of Chinese scholars of the past[2] (Appendix 1 gives the Chinese and English versions). Respondents were asked whether they feel "proud of" each of these eighteen value items as a part of their cultural heritage, or if they think that the value in question should be "discarded." A third option, "not sure," was offered so that the respondents would not feel forced to make a choice between the two extremes.

Designing these two methods of questioning grew out of several considerations. First, the survey instrument was intended to cover both traditional Chinese cultural values and new elements developed in the past eighty years, that is, the republic system, followed by four decades of communist governance. As we noted, many traditional values contained in the popular Chinese language have been attacked in the years since the fall of the last emperor. But these traditional values remain in the people's everyday vocabulary in the form of fixed phrases and proverbs. Our questions and response formats used these available phrasings and gave respondents the opportunity to express their values by endorsing or rejecting the stock phrase.

In rural Taiwan, Chu (1964) had found it difficult to get the villagers to use the standard response scales employed in survey research in the United States. This stems partly from differences between the languages, but it is also a matter of acculturation. It is difficult to ask someone to "strongly agree" or "agree" or "disagree" or "strongly disagree" with a statement (a) if those phrases have no common equivalents in his language, (b) if the culture does not link agreement with strength, and (c) if the person has never heard of such questions. These are the reasons why the "proud of" and "discard" response format was used in surveying the values of Chinese respondents.

In planning the U.S. surveys, the collaborators encountered the flip sides of these problems. First, there are no English phrases that express the values represented by the eighteen Chinese phrases. We could only develop some general statements, each summarizing the main idea in the corresponding Chinese phrase. These transliterations could of course not be exact, because the phrases themselves represent concepts that had never existed in quite the same way in American culture. Second, in the United States we not only found we could use standard Likert-type scales, with their singular statements and agree-disagree response formats, it was virtually necessary to do so with American respondents. The agree-disagree item-by-item format is familiar to most Americans, who encounter it in school and in newspaper reports of public opinion polls. It has evolved because it is a very efficient and reliable way to collect opinion data in a telephone interview. Each item is a compact unit, and a long series of similarly worded statements can be administered quickly by this procedure. American respondents might have spent a lot of time pondering, forgotten the original question, or even terminated their interviews, if faced with the philosophical choices that the Chinese respondents encountered while poring over their paper-and-pencil questionnaires.

While we can readily justify these differences in question format, it is clear that responses from the China survey are not exactly comparable to those in the U.S. surveys. For example, being "proud of" the idea of "chastity for women" is not readily translatable into a value statement to which an American can respond on a five-point Likert scale.

It was not easy to concoct meaningful statements to represent the values expressed in the China instrument. While the researchers eventually wrote and successfully pretested items that covered most of the values in the China survey, certain value concepts simply do not exist in the American culture. Several items were abandoned from the U.S. phase of the project after pretesting indicated they aroused little other than incredulity in American respondents. For example, one item that was asked in Shanghai represented the Chinese tradition of ancestor worship:

How do you think you should treat your ancestors (select one)?
(1) burn incense, worship
(2) visit and sweep tombs
(3) memorial ceremony in family
(4) no ceremony is required

Almost any American respondent would be nonplussed if faced with such a question and would answer "4" only in self-defense against this entire foreign concept. Faced with such realities of cultural differences, the research team dropped from the U.S. survey several value items that seemed, like this one, to be meaningful only in the Chinese culture.

Table 3.2 lists the value items employed in the China survey (English translation) and the response scales for each. Listed on the same line is the comparable item used in the six U.S. surveys. A five-point Likert-type response scale ranging from "strongly disagree" to "strongly agree" was used in all cases. The midpoint of the response scale was suggested: "if you neither agree nor disagree with the statement" at most sites, or (in the Connecticut and Wisconsin surveys) "if you feel neutral."

Just as questionnaire construction proceeded with the goal of developing items that would be as comparable as possible, we continued this process in selecting the value items for the empirical analysis we are reporting in this monograph. Our first operational criterion for semantic equivalence between the U.S. and China surveys was comparability at the linguistic level. Where strict linguistic comparability was not feasible due to translation, some conceptual analysis was undertaken. That is, we attempted to make judgments as to whether statements employed in the two cultures would represent comparable psychological stimuli and therefore generate comparable responses (Frey 1970). The latter criterion might be called system-specific semantic comparability (see Przeworski and Teune 1969, 1970). This resulted in deletion of some items whose meaning seemed to be peculiar to only one of the two cultures.

In Table 3.2, the comparable items used in the China and U.S. instruments are listed in a parallel fashion, grouped into four major areas that represent the basic Confucian tenets with which this monograph begins: male-female relationships, kinship relationships, relationships in the authoritative hierarchy, and general interpersonal relationships. There are also a few items that do not fit clearly into any one of these four groupings, and we list them as a fifth category in Table 3.2. These include relationships between individuals and the state, and values regarding tradition. Because we have fewer items measuring these latter values, our analysis in those areas will be more limited. The main focus of our analysis will be on the values in the first four areas, which were long ago identified in the "three cardinal principles" of Confucian tradition, and the general interpersonal realm in which those principles are played out in daily life.

For male-female relationships, we have comparable items in both surveys regarding female sexual behavior and male-female social status. There are also comparable items for values toward kinship relationships: people's desire to have children and grandchildren and the responsibilities of parents and children. In the authority hierarchy, comparable items

TABLE 3.2   Comparable Item Wordings in the China and U.S. Surveys

China Survey Items	*U.S. Survey Items*
If a man and a woman are in love and they live together before they get registered for marriage, what do you think about this situation? 1. all right 2. depends 3. not all right	It is all right for a man and a woman who are in love to live together before they get married.
If a husand and wife have great difficulty getting along, and they have no children, do you think they should get a divorce? 1. no 2. other 3. yes	A husband and wife who don't get along and have NO children should get a divorce.
If a husband and wife have great difficulty getting along, and they have children, do you think they should get a divorce? 1. no 2. other 3. yes	A husband and wife who don't get along and HAVE children should get a divorce.
If an unmarried girl gets pregnant, do you think her family members will feel they have lost face? 1. yes 2. no	If an unmarried teenager gets pregnant, her family will feel ashamed.
If a man and a woman work in the same unit, do the same type of work, and have the same level of performance, do you think that 1. the man should get more pay? 2. the man should get a little more? 3. the pay should be the same?	If a man and a woman in the same company do the same kind of work, their pay should be the same.

(Continues)

TABLE 3.2   *(Continued)*

China Survey Items	*U.S. Survey Items*
Do you think old parents should be taken care of by their children, or should they take care of themselves? 　1. parents care for themselves 　2. depends 　3. children care for them	Aging parents should be taken care of by their children.
If parents face some financial difficulties, do you think they should ask their children for help or should they seek other means first? 　1. seek other means 　2. not sure 　3. ask children	If aging parents face some financial difficulties, they should ask their grown children for help.
Some people say that in Chinese society, network connections have their importance. What do you think? 　1. no important at all 　2. not very important 　3. somewhat important 　4. important 　5. very important	In American society, connections or who you know is very important.
Suppose you have a problem. If you follow the normal channel, it will take a long time, and the result may not be satisfactory., Do you think you should first try to go through some connections? 　1. first try some connections 　2. not sure 　3. should not try connections	When you have a problem that needs solving, you should go through normal channels before using your connections.
Do you think that human nature is benign or evil? 　1. evil 　2. neither 　3. benign	Human nature is basically good.

(Continues)

TABLE 3.2   (Continued)

China Survey Items	U.S. Survey Items
If you do not agree with the opinions of someone who is senior to you, will you express your different opinions? 1. no 2. sometimes 3. yes	If you do not agree with the opinions of someone who is senior to you, you should say so.
Do you think that younger people should show due respect to older people? 1. no need 2. some respect 3. yes 4. definitely yes	Younger people should show special respect to older people.[a]

Traditional phrases

Of the following elements of traditional Chinese culture, which do you feel proud of, and which should be discarded?

1. should be discarded
2. not sure
3. feel proud of

(a) Diligence and frugality	We should be frugal and not waste our money.
(b) Benevolent father, filial son	Fathers should be kind to sons and their sons should be devoted to their fathers.
(c) Loyalty to state	We should be loyal to our country.
(d) Differentiation between men and women	Men should have a higher satus in society than women.
(e) Three obediences and four virtues	A wife has an obligation to obey her husband.

(Continues)

TABLE 3.2 *(Continued)*

China Survey Items	U.S. Survey Items
(f) Tolerance, propriety, and deference	We should be tolerant toward people whose beliefs are different from our own.
(g) Chastity for women	Women should not have sexual relations until they get married.
(h) Pleasing superiors	We should try to please our superiors.
(i) A house full of children and grandchildren	It is good to have a house full of children and grandchildren.
(j) Harmony is precious	Out of respect for others, we should yield to their wishes.
(k) Generosity and virtues	We should be generous to others.
(l) Submission to authority	We should submit to authority.
(m) Respect tradition	We should show respect for tradition.

Notes: The questions are not shown here in the order in which they appeared in the original questionnaire. The response categories were finalized after data cleaning and collapsing some minor categories in the original questionnaire. The numbers in front of the answer options are the codes used in the analysis.

Not all six U.S. surveys contain every item listed here. In the subsequent analysis, the cases from the surveys that did not ask an item were excluded from the analysis involving that item.

[a]The California and Texas surveys used a slightly different wording: "Younger people should show proper respect to older people."

are available measuring beliefs about the way one should treat people with authority and people senior in age. In general interpersonal relationships, both surveys contain items measuring desirable conduct in dealing with other people, and in solving one's problems.

Despite these points of comparability, the two survey instruments differ in a number of ways. First, the China survey used two kinds of items to measure cultural values (see above). The U.S. surveys have only one type of questionnaire item: declarative statements followed by agree-disagree responses. Compared with the concrete terms in the China survey, the declarative statements in the U.S. surveys are more normative; that is, they often stress "oughtness" as shown by the frequent use of "should" in the wordings. But the declarative statements in the U.S. surveys may not stress the "normative" aspect strongly enough to match the Chinese phrases in the China instrument; these phrases drawn from traditional Chinese culture have been in the Chinese vocabulary for centuries, so much so that they are normative by nature. The many "should" wordings were inserted in the U.S. survey in an attempt to instill this prescriptive sense where it might otherwise not be understood. In our interpretations of the results we need to be attentive to possible influences of such vagaries of meaning.

The two instruments also differ in the response scales used, and there is no handy rule for equating the two metrics. For the China survey, except for a few items (e.g., importance of network connections in society, respect toward older people), most of the value items used one of two kinds of three-point scales. One consists of confirmation, "not sure or neither," or rejection. The other consists of three levels labeled "proud of, not sure, or discarded." We consider these two types of scales roughly equivalent within the China survey, as they are both ordinal scales indicating approval or disapproval. One item in the China survey used a simple "yes or no" dichotomous scale.

To convert responses on the Likert scales of the U.S. surveys into comparable three-point or dichotomous scales, we combined "strongly agree" and "agree" into one category of confirmation (equivalent to "proud of" and "yes" in China), and we combined "strongly disagree" and "disagree" into a single rejection category (equivalent to "discarded" or "no"). The "neutral" category in the Likert scale was retained as equivalent to the Chinese "not sure" or "neither" category. For the single China item that was answered on a dichotomous scale, we recoded the two "agree" categories of the Likert scale into "yes" and the other three responses into "no," assuming that only "agree" indicates "approval." In Chapter 4, we will discuss how differences in wordings and response scales might affect our inferences and the functional equivalence of measures that are not, on the surface, obviously comparable.

Social and Demographic Measures

Demographic data are routinely gathered in almost any general population survey, but in our study these variables also have clear theoretical relevance to the values that comprise our dependent variables. Demographics such as gender and age describe precisely the roles that are referred to in the three cardinal principles: male-female relationships, and youth-elder relationships. Whether a person is married or not just as obviously has something to do with one's perspective on husband-wife relationships. Other standard demographics, such as education, income, and occupational status, are all hierarchical in nature and therefore are related in some degree to Confucian principles of deference to authority. (The role of the teacher is especially venerated in the Confucian tradition.)

This is not to say that we expect each of these demographic variables to predict values about the corresponding relationships. Cultural values do not work that way. Both parties to a relationship, such as husband and wife, must accept the roles assigned them. Still, we would be remiss if we did not take advantage of the conventional battery of demographic measures as a central feature of our analysis. We should assume that these measures are determinants of the cultural values with which each demographic variable is intertwined. Here we will detail the measures and then compare the U.S. and China samples in terms of demographic profiles. Later, particularly in Chapter 5, we will examine the impact of these variables on values in the context of between-nations differences.

Gender (female) is a dichotomous variable with 1 representing males and 2 representing females. Simple as this measure is, its interpretation in the subsequent analysis may be complicated, challenging our best understanding of sex roles and socialization in the two societies. That is, while gender operationally takes on only two values, a host of latent variables lies behind this simple dichotomy.

Age of respondent is a continuous variable, which we would normally describe in discrete categories such as years or decades since birth (Chaffee 1991). In the China survey, age was coded into six categories: below 20, 20–29, 30–39, 40–49, 50–59, and 60–65. These were arrayed on an ordinal scale from 1 through 6. This same scale was used for the U.S. surveys, but an additional category existed in the U.S. samples: age above 65.[3] In the cross-national comparisons reported later, unless otherwise indicated, this above-65 category was excluded from the U.S. analysis. While age does not provide information about the life experiences and expectations associated with different age groups in each society, it is a comparable measure in two cultures in that it indicates biological maturation as well as the time periods during which people have moved through their various life stages.

To measure education, various response categories were used in the different sites. The China survey used seven categories: never went to school,[4] some elementary school, elementary school graduate, junior high school, senior high school, college, and postgraduate studies. One of the six U.S. surveys (Wisconsin) used the exact number of years of schooling in coding educational level. The others used ordinal scales ranging from

1=elementary school to 9=professional degree, with slight variations. These U.S. measures were converted into the ordinal scale used in the China survey.[5] We also constructed within-nation standardized scales of education to represent the relative (rather than absolute) meaning of education as a social structural variable.

Income, while it is a continuous variable, had to be measured in very different ways in the two societies, partly because they are wholly different economic systems (communist and capitalist). U.S. respondents were asked their annual household gross (before taxes) income. The Chinese survey asked for average annual income per member of the respondent's household, and this figure was multiplied by household size. But there are no taxes to enter into the calculations of income in China, and in any event the monetary units of the two nations cannot be placed on the same absolute scale. Adding to the complications, the six U.S. surveys used different income categories, ranging from five categories in Cleveland to nine categories in most of the other sites. Even when the number of categories was the same, different collaborators used different category boundaries to divide up the income distribution, partly because income ranges are much higher in some sites (e.g., Connecticut) than others (e.g., rural Florida). This nonstandardization of measurement reflects an implicit understanding among the collaborators that income functions as a relative, or social structural, variable. In that spirit, we moved straight to standardized scores within each survey before merging the data files. In China, all incomes were recalculated as deviations from the grand mean, and these scores were divided by the standard deviation for the entire array. This procedure was followed within each of the six U.S. sites, separately, as well. The standard units were then used as a common metric across the surveys. Clearly, though, it will not be meaningful here to translate the standardized scores back to either *yuan* or dollar figures.

The occupational structures of the United States and China are even more different than the income structures. Still, we consider that each occupational structure may be relevant to cultural values, particularly those relating to the authority hierarchy; we sought as much comparability as could be found in the data. The following categories were used to recode the occupations in all the surveys: agricultural workers, laborers (semi-skilled and skilled), service and clerical, managerial, professional, retired, and other. For the China survey, agriculture, husbandry, and fishing personnel were lumped as "agriculture." The U.S. surveys had no category that corresponds to this one, partly because (except for Florida) the U.S. surveys did not cover rural areas. Other recoding of occupations for the China survey: "service and clerical"=business service personnel, office worker; "managerial"=cadre in Party, government, and state-owned enterprises; "professional"=education, health and science, artist;

"retired"=retired. Self-employed and students were classified as "other"; there were few people in either category. Those in the military were treated as missing cases, since none of the U.S. samples included military personnel. For the U.S. surveys, the recoding is much simpler: sales and service as well as clerical were coded as "service and clerical"; both skilled and semi-skilled labor categories were combined into "laborer"; housewife (or housekeeper) and student were grouped into "other."

These rough groupings are based on the assumption that the central work activities within each occupational category are similar across the two nations. For example, college professors were considered professionals in both nations. Although the sociological and cultural meanings may differ somewhat, being a professor in both nations involves the activities of teaching and research. But not all the occupational categories can be so straightforwardly compared. For example, Party and government officials in China perform the activities of managing businesses, factories, and bureaucracies. On this dimension, they are comparable to managers and executives in the United States. But Chinese "managerial personnel" also perform ideological duties. Some differences between the two nations in these broad categorizations are inevitable. In our data analyses, we finally collapsed occupation into four categories that we treat as the comparable: (1) labor, (2) service, (3) professional, and (4) managerial. We also assume that these four categories are hierarchically ordered to some degree within each country.

Four marital-status categories for self-classification by the respondent were used in all the surveys: single, married, divorced, and widowed. Some U.S. surveys included a fifth category: other. Due to lack of detailed information, those in this category were defined as missing.

Comparing the Samples Demographically

Table 3.3 shows the differences in sample composition between the China and U.S. surveys on these demographic characteristics. Clearly, the samples differ greatly. For example, a little over 47 percent of the respondents in China are female, while the U.S. sample is more than 53 percent females. (The latter figure is what is usually reported as the percentage of females among American adults, based on U.S. census data.) All six U.S. samples included more female respondents than males, the proportion of females ranging from 50 to 55 percent across the six surveys.

The Chinese sample is necessarily younger, since those over age sixty-five were excluded; when we ignore those over sixty-five in the U.S. sample, however, the Chinese respondents are as a group somewhat older.

TABLE 3.3   Comparison of Chinese and American Samples (in percentages)

Demographics	China	United States
Gender		
Male	53	47
Female	47	53
Age		
Under 30	26	27
30–49 years	50	47
50–65 years	25	17
Over 65	(none)	9
Marital status		
Single	17	33
Married	79	51
Divorced	1	10
Widowed	3	6
Income[a]		
Low	21	18
Medium	61	60
High	18	22
Education (highest year)		
Elementary school	23	2
Some high school	39	6
High school graduate	28	56
At least some college	10	37
Occupation		
Agricultural	15	0
Labor	28	19
Service/Clerical	18	19
Managerial	6	9
Professional	12	25
Retired	15	14
Other	6	16

Note: Percentages are based on the number of valid cases. The sum of percentages within each group may not equal 100 percent due to rounding error.

[a]Income categories are relative to the distribution within each sample and are reported here only to show the approximate percentages used in later analyses. Most "low income" U.S. respondents had higher incomes in dollar exchange equivalents than did most "high income" Chinese respondents.

The two samples also differ with regard to marital status. A much higher percentage of American respondents are single, even though the two samples do not seem to differ much in age. We might attribute this difference to two factors: (1) Chinese tend to get married younger than Americans, and (2) it is uncommon to remain single in China after reaching a certain age.

Gender, age, and marital status, though, produce minor differences when compared with those that are dictated by the contrasting economic conditions of the two countries. The meanings of income, education, and even occupation are qualitatively different and quantitatively on vastly different levels. China is a "developing country" in which disposable income is very low[6] and a communist system in which many social goods (such as education) are not paid for out of one's family income. The United States is a market economy with an open educational structure and a competitive job market. Even allowing for these structural differences, though, comparability of demographic measures must be understood in relative terms.

The two countries cannot be directly compared on income levels, due to their totally different monetary systems. For the various U.S. sites, it is impossible for us to calculate ranges of dollar figures, given the different income categories used in the six surveys. For the China survey, however, we can represent the three categories in terms of *yuan*, the Chinese monetary units. The low category means annual household income ranging from 700 to a little more than 2,000 *yuan* ($147 to $421), the medium category approximately 2,500 to 5,400 *yuan* ($526 to $1137), and the high category from 5,500 to more than 12,000 *yuan* ($1158 to $2526).[7]

The Chinese respondents had much lower median education than the U.S. sample. This too is a well-established demographic fact about the two countries. More than one-half of the U.S. respondents had graduated from high school, while less than 30 percent of the Chinese respondents had a high school diploma. More than one-third of the U.S. sample had entered college, compared to only 10 percent of the Chinese. More than 60 percent of the Chinese respondents had a junior high school education or less, and more than 20 percent had terminated their education at the elementary school level. The corresponding figures for the United States, where compulsory education through secondary school has become the norm, are of course much lower.

In the occupational categories, we can see two significant differences between the two samples. First, the Chinese sample contains more people in the labor, or factory worker, category, reflecting the fact that Shanghai is a major industrial center. None of the U.S. survey sites (except for Cleveland) is noted for its manufacturing industry. Second, the U.S. sample includes at least twice as many professionals as does the China sample. These sample differences are consistent with general structural differences in the distribution of labor in the two nations, but they make comparison of correlations between occupation and other variables somewhat cloudier.

Any one of these factors distorting comparability of the measures may constitute an "extraneous factor" (Rosenberg 1968) that could spuriously produce misleading differences in cultural values between the two nations, or perhaps obscure actual differences that do exist. When we later compare the two cultures in terms of the salience of values, we take these differences in sample characteristics and national socioeconomic structures into consideration.

Analytical Approaches

Our data analysis is designed to make two types of comparisons between the two nations: comparisons of the distributions *for each value item* and comparisons *among the value items* and their demographic correlates. The per-item analyses might be called first-order comparisons, searching for salience differences between cultures; the across-items analyses might be called second-order comparisons, designed to find pattern differences between two cultures (Verba 1969; also see Leung and Bond 1989).

To make these two types of comparisons, we took three steps in data analysis. First, we cross-tabulated each value item by nation. This analysis produces estimates of aggregate salience differences in each value between the two cultures as a baseline. Cross-tabulation of each value item by each demographic variable in each culture then tests our working assumption that between-culture differences at the aggregate level are not due simply to compositional differences between the two samples. This first-stage analysis also provides information about relationships between each value item and the demographic variables.

The second step involves a series of factor analyses, which have two purposes. One goal is to examine the patterns of correlations among the value items to assess whether they indicate some smaller set of underlying value constructs. The other purpose is to assess the degree of similarity between the two cultures in these underlying value constructs. From this analysis, we seek a picture of the equivalence of value structures in the two cultures.[8]

The last step of our analysis involves a set of multiple regression models, with value indices as the dependent variables and the demographic variables as the main independent variables. Parallel regression models were fitted to the China and U.S. data separately. Through this analysis, we hope to detect patterns of relationships between values and demographic variables in a multivariate context that will illuminate similarities and differences between the two cultures.

Notes

1. Cooperation in China was virtually 100 percent, as it is not unusual there for residents to be brought together for such a group task.

2. The decision to use traditional wording for some items inadvertently led to an important dichotomy within the data set. Because traditional teachings had been under cultural assault in China for many years, there was a tendency to reject items so phrased, whereas items with seemingly similar content but worded in politically more neutral ways were more acceptable. This produced some complex interactions with various demographic comparisons between the two countries, which are noted in detail in later chapters.

3. As noted earlier, residents over age sixty-five were excluded in the Chinese sampling procedure, so that our respondents could potentially be recontacted some years from now in a panel survey.

4. The existence of this category does not mean the people in it were illiterate; truly illiterate people were excluded from the sample, as the China questionnaire was self-administered. Some people who have not attended school might have learned how to read and write through correspondence programs or through home instruction. The Chinese government has over the past forty years undertaken several campaigns to eliminate illiteracy, and the methods have not been limited to formal schooling.

5. For the Wisconsin survey, the following scheme was used to convert years of schooling to the common scale of the other surveys: 4–5 years=some elementary school, 6–8 years=elementary school graduate, 9–11 years=junior high school graduate, 12–15 years=high school graduate, 16–17 years=college graduate, 18 years and above=postgraduate degree.

6. Comments about the general character of the Chinese economic system should be understood as referring to China at the time of our survey, that is, circa 1987.

7. The dollar figures in parentheses are calculated according to the Chinese official exchange rates between the U.S. dollar and the Chinese *yuan* in 1989, approximately \$100=475 *yuan*.

8. This approach is called "relative equivalence" or "indirect equivalence" by Frey (1970:246). Limitations of this use of correlational data, in light of the classical measurement theory, is discussed by Hulin (1987; Hulin and Mayer 1986).

4

Differences in Value Prevalence Between China and the United States

HOW MUCH DO CHINA AND THE United States differ in cultural values? To answer this question, we will first look at the differences in percentages of people in each sample endorsing each of the value items. In making these comparisons, we are of course mindful of the methodological pitfalls such a procedure entails. The samples are not representative of the two countries, and the two surveys differed in mode of administration as well as in language and socio-political context. These are general caveats that need to be dealt with at each specific point in our analysis. That is, we choose not to admit defeat, in advance, due simply to the inherent difficulty of our research task. Rather, we will keep these and other issues in mind as we interpret the empirical results. Each finding will be considered in some detail before we decide whether to hazard a conclusion on the basis of the numbers before us.

This chapter also reports the within-culture differences in value prevalence between rural and urban areas.[1] This portion of our analysis represents a first-order check for possible artifacts of our research procedures. The China sample includes many more rural residents, for example, and could therefore appear to be more traditional if that is a general attribute (as one would expect) of rurality.

Comparisons Between China and the United States

Table 4.1 shows the proportions of respondents in the two samples endorsing each of the value measures. The presentation of results is organized into five areas: male-female relationships, family relationships, hierarchical relationships (including both seniority and authority hierarchies), general interpersonal relationships, and other. Percentage difference tests for two independent samples were conducted for each comparison (McNemar 1955:60–61).[2] Given the large sample size, we used an alpha level of .01 (or $z > 3$), two-tailed test, to evaluate statistical significance.

TABLE 4.1 Proportional Comparison of Values in China and the United States

Value items	Confucian values	China	United States	Test of difference	Communist values
Male-Female Relationships					
Differentiation between men and women (*Proud of*)	+	10%	13%	0	-
Three obediences and four virtues (*Proud of*)	+	8	30	-	---
Chastity for women (*Proud of*)	+	32	31	0	0
Family losing face for teen child's pregnancy (*Yes*)	+	85	41	+++++	+
A couple live together before marriage (*All right*)	-	11	59	+++++	-
Love is the most important in choosing a mate (*Yes*)	-	23	77	++++++	+
Equal pay for equal work for men and women (*same pay*)	-	84	93	+	+
Family Relationships					
Benevolent fathers and filial sons (*Proud of*)	+	63	74	--	0
A house full of children and grandchildren (*Proud of*)	+	21	54	----	-
Aging parents cared by their children (*Yes*)	+	79	74	+	+
Aging parents ask their children for financial help (*Yes*)	+	83	8	0	+

(Continues)

TABLE 4.1 (Continued)

Value items	Confucian values	China	United States	Test of difference	Communist values
A couple may divorce if they have no children (*Yes*)	-	77	50	+++	+
A couple may divorce if they have children (*Yes*)	-	36	37	0	+
Authority hierarchy					
Submission to authority (*Proud of*)	+	53	56	0	-
Pleasing superiors (*Proud of*)	+	7	59	------	-
Younger people respect older people (*Yes*)[a]	+	97	94	+	0
Express your opinions when you disagree with a senior (*Yes*)	-	23	78	++++++	0
Interpersonal Relationships					
Human nature is benign or evil? (*Benign*)	+	31	80	-----	0
Harmony is precious (*Proud of*)	+	49	24	+++	-
Generosity and virtues (*Proud of*)	+	59	92	----	-
Tolerance, propriety, and deference (*Proud of*)	+	47	94	-----	0
Importance of connections (*Important*)[b]	0	70	85	--	-
Using connections to solve problems (*Yes*)	0	72	11	+++++++	-

(Continues)

TABLE 4.1   *(Continued)*

Value items	Confucian values	China	United States	Test of difference	Communist values
Other					
Loyalty to state (*Proud of*)	+	77	92	--	+
Respect tradition (*Proud of*)	+	55	83	---	-
Diligence and frugality (*Proud of*)	+	90	81	+	+
Necessary to have religious faith (*Yes*)	0	28	68	----	-
Number of cases[c]					
Total *N*		2,000	2,482		
Minimum *N*		1,898	1,526		

Notes: Cell entries under China and United States are the percentages of respondents who gave the listed response to each item.

The first and last columns indicate expectations based upon China's two dominant value systems. The first column indicates the directions of the Confucian values with regard to the specific items, and the last column indicates the directions of the communist values. A zero in either of these columns indicates a lack of direct relevance of the value item to the corresponding value system.

The test of difference column indicates more (plus sign) or less (minus sign) prevalence of the *Confucian values* in China than in the United States. A zero indicates no significant cross-nation difference. When a value item is not directly derivable from the Confucian value system, a plus or minus sign simply indicates the result of subtracting the U.S. figure from the China figure. The magnitude of differences is indicated by number of plus or minus signs, with one indicating a single digit difference, two indicating a difference larger than 10 percent but smaller than 20 percent, three indicating a difference equal to or larger than 20 percent but smaller than 30 percent, and so on.

[a]The "yes" and "definite yes" categories are combined.

[b]The "very important" and "important" categories are combined.

[c]The number of cases varies from one comparison to another due to missing values. In the U.S. surveys, some of the value questions were not asked at all six sites.

The interpretive (i.e., nonquantitative data) columns of Table 4.1 are designed to follow the logic of our project. We began this study with Confucian values, and the first column indicates for each item whether we consider it to represent the Confucian tradition (+) or to be opposed to it (−). A zero (0) is entered in this column if the item seems neutral or ambiguous with respect to Confucian values.

The second column of the table reports percentages from our first data set, the China survey. This juxtaposition enables the reader to see at a glance, by comparing the plus and minus signs from column 1 with the agreement percentages in column 2, the extent to which Confucian values were endorsed by the Chinese respondents.

Column 3 of Table 4.1 shows the percentages agreeing with these same items in the U.S. survey, and column 4 indicates the net difference, in terms of both direction and magnitude, between the U.S. and China results. For items on which a Confucian value could be assigned (+ or −), a plus sign in column 4 indicates a direction consistent with the hypothesis that Confucian values would be endorsed more often in China than in the United States. A minus sign in column 4 means that the American respondents instead were more often favorable to that particular Confucian value item than were the Chinese. The larger the U.S.-China difference, the greater the number of plus or minus signs on the line in column 4. For those items for which we had no prediction on the basis of Confucian values (i.e., a 0 in column 1), the entry in column 4 is positive if agreement with the item is greater in China, or negative if it is greater in the United States, on the assumption that our items represent values that were at least at one time prevalent in China and therefore can be called "traditional Chinese values."

The final column of Table 4.1 indicates what we consider to be the Chinese communist values (+) or their antithesis (−). For example, the second line of the table shows entries for the traditional Chinese value of women's "three obediences and four virtues." This precept has been consistently attacked by the communist government in China. Hence there is a positive sign in column 1 to indicate that it is a Confucian value and a negative sign in column 5 to indicate communist rejection of it. The data show less prevalence of this value in China than in the United States, so there is a negative entry in column 4. This negative sign is easily compared with the corresponding negative sign in column 5. One notes at a glance that the communist program to eradicate this value has been successful—at least insofar as can be determined with these data.

Male-Female Relationships

One major characteristic of the traditional Chinese value system was male dominance. This was accompanied by rigidity in male-female sexual relationships, and this rigidity was asymmetrically imposed upon females more than on males. The results in Table 4.1 suggest that in terms of male-female sexual relationships, the Chinese sample is more rigid than the U.S. sample. Nearly 50 percent more American respondents would feel it "all right" for a couple in love to live together without a marriage certificate. More than 40 percent more Chinese respondents felt that families with pregnant teenage children would lose face. The two samples did not, however, differ in their emphasis on chastity for women; slightly less than one-third of respondents in each country endorsed the notion of chastity, which may be an artifact of the way the questions about this awkward subject were asked in each survey.[3] Chastity is probably of concern to most people in some measure, and may have been a loaded word in the survey interview context.

Male superiority in status did not receive much support in either culture. In both samples only a little more than 10 percent endorsed the traditional notion of "differentiation between men and women," that is, superior status of men over women in society. The popular concept that men and women should get equal pay for equal work received more support in the United States than in China. The American respondents, having experienced the civil rights movement, the women's liberation movement, and a steady increase in female participation in the labor force, expressed almost unanimous approval of the notion of equal pay for equal work. It is quite likely that the American and Chinese societies do not differ significantly in accepting gender equality as an abstract principle. But the contemporary Chinese value system remains more male-dominant than the contemporary American value system in terms of specific enactments of the abstract principle.

The main exception to this pattern is the difference between the two samples on the item asking about "three obediences and four virtues." The theme of this Confucian principle is that a married woman should be obedient to her husband. More than 20 percent more American respondents expressed acceptance of this notion.[4] The traditional Chinese phrase, "three obediences and four virtues," which was used in the Chinese questionnaire, has been severely attacked in propaganda campaigns throughout at least the last four decades. The male dominance represented by this principle was called a rope around Chinese women's necks (Mao 1927). One of the first steps taken by Chinese intellectuals seeking "emancipation from the past" was to take action opposing this principle. Even in the early years of the Republic of China, a small number of educated women from elite families, defying a hostile social climate, undertook to participate in business, in education, and even in politics (Hsu 1981). After the communist revolution, women's participation in all sectors of social life was promoted in keeping with the hegemonic communist ideology. Two-earner households have become the norm in contemporary Chinese society. Given the negative connotation resulting from propaganda campaigns, coupled with the changing social practices, it is not surprising that most of the Chinese respondents rejected this phrase. Most Chinese who grew up in the communist period do not even have a clear idea what the "three obediences" or the "four virtues" are other than the vague understanding of a woman's obedience to her husband.

This does not mean, however, that Chinese value equal status between husband and wife more than do Americans. Rather, it seems likely that the Chinese respondents rejected this ideologically negative phrase but that their fundamental values about male-female relationships show up more accurately in the more behavioral and descriptive items regarding living together and teen pregnancy (above). The Confucian tradition seems still prevalent in Chinese values when it is separated from its traditional symbolic expression.

The other way to look at the U.S.-China difference is to reconsider the caricature of the American value system, a system that may be more "traditional" in character than comparative observers have realized. That is, the relatively higher level of acceptance of the "obedient wife" idea by the U.S. respondents suggests that traditional American culture might be no less authoritarian in terms of husband-wife relationships than was traditional Chinese culture. One premise of fundamentalist Judaeo-Christian teaching is that the husband is head of the household; a husband should love his wife, whereas a wife should obey her husband. In seventeenth-century New England, proper conduct for a wife was to be submissive to her husband's commands. He was the head of the family, and she owed him an obedience founded on reverence, a mixture of love and fear (Kephart 1977). In addition, despite some conspicuous cases of women gaining prominent positions in traditionally male dominated occupations in the United States, participation in the labor force by married women remains lower today in the United States than it is in China. American working women tend to be in occupations marked by lower pay and lower prestige and to receive lower pay even within a prestigious occupational category. It is quite possible that in the traditional value system, the idea of a wife obeying her husband is no less important in American culture than in Chinese culture.

On the other hand, if we assume authoritarian values were dominant in both traditional Chinese and American cultures, and if we accept the validity of the measure employed here, the low levels of endorsement of the wifely obedience item are truly remarkable. After all, even in a culture influenced strongly by Judaeo-Christian beliefs, fewer than one-third of the respondents in our American sample seem to value an obedient wife. Hence, this may be a traditional value that is on its way out in both cultures.

We can also see how little the contemporary Chinese deviate from traditional Confucian values from their responses to the item on love as the basis of a decision to marry—a Western, and latterly something of a Chinese communist, precept. Fewer than one-fourth of the Chinese respondents accepted love as the most important factor in choosing a mate, while more than three-quarters of the American respondents agreed with that view. The low Chinese endorsement of this item may be more than a matter of values; it can be traced to harsh realities: marriage in China is a way of overcoming a lack of financial resources. Romantic love has never been regarded as directly relevant to marriage in Chinese culture, despite the fact that romance fills traditional Chinese operas, folk songs, and classic novels (Hsu 1981). There are a number of realistic factors that Chinese still take into consideration in deciding whom to marry: income, family prestige, location of one's job assignment, availability of housing, and the like. These were factors that families used to consider in deciding whom their children should marry, and today decisions are still based on these factors even though arranged marriages have become rare in China.

Family Relationships

Traditional Chinese culture greatly valued the extended family, including family relationships defined by specific roles and obligations of the family members. These characteristics marked significant distinctions between the traditional Chinese and American cultures (Hsu 1981). How are these cross-cultural differences surviving in contemporary Chinese and American societies? The second section of Table 4.1 provides an answer in three aspects of family life: the relationship between the members of a married couple, obligations to one's aging parents, and the desire to maintain traditional multigeneration families.

Times have changed, at least in China. Many more Chinese than American respondents are permissive regarding divorce, at least when the question asks about a childless couple having difficulty getting along. If children are involved in the marriage, though, the two samples are equally disapproving of divorce. In effect, then, the presence of children makes more difference to the Chinese than to the Americans when they consider the institution of divorce.

From the perspective of Confucian tradition, these findings can be interpreted several ways. Traditionally, marriage implied children, and even if no children had yet been born they would have been taken into account in considering divorce. Divorce would break up the entire family lineage and was therefore unthinkable. A strict Confucian view would not have led to the result in Table 4.1 where the absence of children markedly alters the Chinese respondents' opinion regarding divorce. On the other hand, this difference could be taken as an indication that many Chinese still hold strongly the traditional value of parental obligations to bring up children in intact families (see Hsu 1981). Or it could be simply a recognition of the reality that in China it is extremely difficult for a single parent to take care of small children and for children to grow up in broken families.[5] Even though divorce has been legalized by the communist government, and therefore might be easily approved if respondents took our question to be a simple public opinion item, divorce is in fact quite rare in China. In a society where courtship is still highly restricted, especially among those who have tied and then untied the matrimonial knot, a single woman has very limited opportunities to live a normal social life.

Surprisingly, the greater emphasis on extended families and family duties in traditional Chinese culture did not show up in other results in Table 4.1. Only slightly more Chinese than U.S. respondents thought that aging parents should be cared for by their adult children. The difference is minor in comparison with the overwhelming majority of people in both samples who thought that adult children should take care of their aging parents and that aging parents should ask their adult children for help if they face financial difficulties. In terms of obligations to offer such financial help, there was no difference at all between the two samples.

The lack of differences in endorsing the two values does not mean, however, that there are no cultural differences. The percentages reported here have quite different implications in the two societies. In the United States, the welfare of aging citizens has been a great concern not only among scholars but also in public policy circles. Social security and medicare have been enduring policy issues since Franklin D. Roosevelt's New Deal and Lyndon B. Johnson's Great Society programs. These two liberal policy thrusts were reversed in many respects in the 1970s and 1980s, but the specific programs devoted to care of the aged remain intact despite conservative assaults on social welfare in general. Compared with Chinese society, the United States has been taking more and more collective responsibility for the elderly. In China, older people still rely mostly on family members, especially their adult children. Only in the past decade did China start to produce the first generation of retirees supported primarily by their own pensions. Given this lack of substantial societal support for the elderly and safety net for the population in general, we might consider it alarming that fully one-fifth of our Chinese respondents do not value the traditional practice of adult children taking care of aging parents.

Extended family values may indeed be on the wane in China. Two items expressing family relationships, "benevolent fathers and filial sons" and "a house full of children and grandchildren," were endorsed much less often by Chinese than by American respondents. This is contrary to our understanding of traditional Chinese culture. The family as an institution was anchored in the Confucian concept of "benevolent fathers and filial sons," and fewer than two-thirds of Chinese respondents in this survey are proud of that traditional principle. The phrase, "a house full of children and grandchildren," describes an ideal state of happiness and the essence of the meaning of life in traditional Chinese culture. Only one Chinese respondent in five sees this value as a source of pride today—whereas more than one-half of the American respondents endorse it.

Hierarchical Relationships

At the core of the traditional Confucian value system is a set of behavioral principles enforcing vertical hierarchies of dominance, as expressed in the "three cardinal principles." In this system, seniority and authority were greatly respected. Such respect was unconditional and completely voluntary. Can we still find traces of the values supporting the seniority and authority hierarchies? There does not seem to be a clearcut answer in Table 4.1.

The one item that suggests a Confucian construction of authority is our question about expressing disagreement with a senior person. Fewer than one-fourth of the Chinese respondents said they would do this, whereas more than three-fourths of the Americans did. This suggests that traditional deference is still considered normative in China. On the other hand, there were virtually no U.S.-China differences in the percentages saying that younger people should respect older people, nor in the degree of endorsement of submission to authority. And fewer than one Chinese respondent in ten agreed with the statement about "pleasing superiors," while more than half of the Americans found this an acceptable value. The box score for Confucian values predominating in China might seem, from this brief accounting of these four items, to read: "one win, one loss, and two ties."

We do not consider the question to be so simply answered, even with our data, however. Two key items, both of which tilted toward the American side, were stock phrases from the Confucian tradition that in China had come under ideological fire in the Cultural Revolution. Knowing something about their respective histories can help us see why neither phrase is especially popular in China today and why one proved more acceptable there than the other.

Repeated propaganda campaigns over the past forty years have associated the phrase "pleasing one's superiors" with the unethical practice of manipulatively using closeness to a superior for personal gain. A person who is associated with this phrase is considered "slick" and "tricky," and the practice remains in great disrepute. The phrase "submission to authority," which Hsu (1981) felt was almost universally accepted in traditional China, likewise came under attack by the Red Guards during the Cultural Revolution. But it was a less conspicuous target of these attacks than were some other precepts, and its ideological connotation was rehabilitated somewhat during Deng's regime starting in 1979. When authority and law and order were revived, the value of submission to authority again came to be stressed in official discourse. The finding that only about half of the Chinese respondents endorsed this value is doubtless indicative of a major change from the past, but it may also represent a more recent upward swing from a low point in the 1970s.

As for contemporary American values, it is instructive that more than half of the American respondents accepted the notions of "pleasing one's superiors" and "submitting to authority." Both ideas, on their surface, would seem contradictory to values emphasized in the American stereotype: individualism, freedom, and equality (Williams 1970). Our evidence supports the view that a value system in a culture is a highly complex construction with rich historical deposits. Several scholars have noted the conflicting values that are simultaneously present in American culture (Williams 1970; Turner and Musick 1985). The figures presented here should remind us again not to derive a simplified and extreme image of Americans based on contrasts with the Chinese, traditional or otherwise. Conformity is also a prevalent value in the United States (Williams 1970), especially in relation to people in positions of power and authority.

Interpersonal Relationships

In the traditional Confucian value system, interpersonal harmony occupied an important role. Some argue that the goal of harmony underlies the other rules of deference; if each person in a relationship knows his or her place, interactions can proceed harmoniously. How do the contemporary Chinese and Americans differ in their values in this area? Table 4.1 includes six measures regarding interpersonal relationships. On the four for which there is a clear Confucian direction, there are large differences between the two samples—and in three of the four cases the Chinese less often give the Confucian response.

The one clear indicator of traditional Chinese values regarding interpersonal relationships is that approximately one-half of the China sample was "proud of" the Confucian principle that "harmony is precious," whereas scarcely one-fourth of the Americans held this view. This may say more about U.S. culture, though, than it does for the survival of traditional values in China. If social harmony had indeed once been as basic to other Confucian principles and as universal a value as many observers maintain, its rejection by the other one-half of the Chinese sample must represent a major cultural change.

The American tradition stresses competition, both economic and in the "marketplace of ideas." The need for dissent forms part of the rationale for widely shared values such as freedom of expression and independence from authoritarian control. Giving high priority to social harmony would obviously stand at odds with this American presupposition. It is likely that the statement used in the U.S. surveys is stronger than our China wording. The translation of "yield to others' wishes," while capturing the essence of the Chinese concept of harmony, conflicts with the American values of individualism and independence. In China the traditional phrase, "harmony is precious" has been undermined by propagation of the Maoist "struggle philosophy." This ideology of conflict was popularized during the Cultural Revolution, and only partially abandoned in the subsequent years of reform. Even after taking into consideration both these factors, though, it is safe to say that interpersonal harmony is valued less in the United States than in China. It seems to be valued less in China today than in earlier eras.

Americans in our survey are, on the other hand, much more likely than the Chinese to accept the more general (and Confucian) assumption that human nature is benign rather than evil. This item probably reveals a thoroughgoing impact of communist indoctrination. Belief in a benign human nature used to be a pivotal logical element of Chinese thought. This concept is found not only in the classic writings of Chinese philosophers but even in old schoolbooks. In fact, the traditional Chinese primer began with the lesson that human nature is benign. Marxist teachings based on a model of class struggle imply a different assumption about the basic nature of society. Today fewer than a third of our Chinese respondents subscribe to this pleasant assertion, compared with four of every five American respondents.

Two other sets of items from the list of Confucian phrases—"generosity and virtues" and "tolerance, propriety, and deference"—were accepted as virtual truisms by almost every American respondent, but only about half of the time by the Chinese. These traditional concepts were in Confucian teaching propounded as specific ways of carrying out social interactions that would help to preserve social harmony. Wording differences (our prime "usual suspect" to account for differences between the two samples) are unlikely to explain the large gaps on these two items in Table 4.1. A parallel survey in Taiwan, using exactly the same wording in the original Chinese, found these two traditional Confucian values being endorsed by 89 percent and 83 percent, respectively (Wang, Chung, and Chu 1991). It is far more plausible to infer that communism has brought about a significant erosion of traditional rituals, manners, and principles of social interaction in China (Chu and Ju 1993).

In practice, the principle of harmony led to an emphasis on using one's personal connections. This was not a Confucian teaching, and it is a practice subject to abuse, but it was a well-established fact of Chinese life in the traditional era. In an ascriptive social system, connections to well-placed persons become essential to getting ahead in life. The concept of *li* includes the basic values and principles of interpersonal conduct such as being generous, righteous, and respectful. Its pragmatic expression is known as *song li*, that is, sending a gift as a gesture of *li*, a show of respect in exchange for some favor.

In Table 4.1 we make no "Confucian" prediction for the two items that asked about use of personal connections, but we would expect such practices to have been much more readily endorsed in traditional China than in most cultures. Viewed from this perspective, the two items produce contrasting results in the U.S.-China comparison. Communist doctrine has been uniformly opposed to the practice of operating via personal connections, so that factor could not explain the difference between the two items in Table 4.1.

It is likely that questions about knowing people in power and being well connected to the bureaucratic hierarchy meant more to the Chinese respondents than to the American respondents, even though we would not argue that connections are any less important in the United States than in China. Our data, in fact, suggest as much; the American respondents are more likely than the Chinese to say connections are important, although more Chinese than Americans considered connections "very important." But the Chinese are far more likely than the Americans to endorse using their connections. Indeed, slightly more Chinese say they would use whatever connections they might have when normal channels are blocked than say connections are important. This pragmatic approach contrasts vividly with the United States, where only about one in ten would attempt to use connections rather than go through normal bureaucratic channels. Differences in wording might account for some of this disparity, but the contrast at the practical level is so great that we can have little doubt that a willingness to put one's connections to use is a Chinese cultural trait that has survived communist indoctrination to the contrary.

Other Comparisons

Several items reported in Table 4.1 do not fit neatly into any of our first four categories. Three of these clearly represented traditional Confucian teaching, and the fourth (the importance of having religious faith) is a hallmark of traditionalism almost anywhere.

Fewer Chinese than American respondents endorsed the value of "loyalty to the state." Americans are a notably patriotic people, and the figure for China (77 percent) is not low. Still, this is one value that both Confucianism and communism would promote. Perhaps some of the Chinese respondents are expressing their disapproval of the current communist government, or perhaps they were put off by the fact that the phrase as worded in the Chinese questionnaire is taken from Confucian teachings.

In the United States, loyalty is not only a widely trumpeted political slogan ("loyalty oaths" are still required for many teaching jobs, for example), it is also a virtually universal trait of Americans in fact. Despite the occasional eruption of right-wing charges of "fifth column" or "un-American" or "subversive" activities in the United States, there exists very little sentiment to the contrary in the general population. That is, our finding that more than nine of ten U.S. respondents endorse the value of loyalty to the state is quite plausible on its face. While China has undergone a number of revolutions and reform movements in this century, the U.S. political system has been remarkably stable, and the results for this item seem to reflect the differences one should expect between these two polities.

Another of the Confucian phrases, "respect for tradition," likewise receives less endorsement in China than in the United States. The lower Chinese figure (slightly more than half the sample) might indicate successful communist campaigns. The higher U.S. figure (more than four out of five) could represent a recent swing in American values in the traditionalistic Reagan-Bush-Quayle era. The item is, in the U.S. survey context, too vaguely worded to enable us to interpret the result with any confidence. Suffice to say that "tradition" seems to be a widely acceptable label in America.

Pride in the Confucian tradition of "diligence and frugality" remains widespread in China and is almost as broadly endorsed by the U.S.

respondents. These terms represent self-serving virtues and are encouraged by all governments, communist and Western alike. To American respondents, the wording resembles a truism more than a value to which one devotes oneself. In China, although the concepts are Confucian, they are not limited to that tradition, and they have not been attacked as have some of the other Confucian teachings we have examined above. These terms we might assign to the category of eternal verities, not values that would vanish with the passing of traditional culture.

Religious faith, while not Confucian, is characteristic of traditional societies and has been consistently opposed by communist regimes. In the United States, on the other hand, national leaders almost universally profess and champion formal practice of religion. Prayers are spoken at official functions, and some presidents have held regular prayer sessions at the White House. Reference to God has been incorporated into the Declaration of Independence and the pledge of allegiance to the flag and is stamped on every U.S. coin. Not surprisingly, then, the statement that it is necessary to have religious faith was endorsed more than twice as often by our American respondents as by the Chinese. Confucianism itself is not a religion in the usual sense, and we can safely conclude that formal religious faith is one traditional value that is more widespread in the United States than in China, by any accounting.

Of these last few findings, perhaps the most surprising is that only about half of the Chinese respondents endorsed the idea of "respecting tradition," a concept that once seemed to be accepted almost universally in China. During the Cultural Revolution, "destroying the old" was the motto for the young and the sentiment for the whole nation. Then in the ten years of economic reform after 1978, Chinese began questioning their own traditions in a search for reasons why China was lagging behind other countries. Heated debates over the traditional culture marked the period 1985–89. During this wave of "cultural fever" (Yang 1990), many young scholars subjected the traditional culture to critical reevaluation (Fudan University 1986). Some even called for complete abandoning of the traditional culture (Gan 1989). This idea trickled down to the general public through popular books and TV series, with considerable impact on public sentiment (Su and Wang 1988; Yang 1990; Tu 1991). Perhaps in view of this recent cultural history, we should wonder that even as many as 55 percent are proud of the value of respect for tradition in China today.

If we take the word tradition literally, then, we should conclude that China is the less traditional of the two societies we are examining here. But rejection of a label does not necessarily mean rejection of the values the label represents; surveys in the United States find that a small and decreasing percentage of citizens call themselves "liberal," for example, and yet most people hold liberal positions on many public issues. But overall we must admit with some surprise that our first series of comparisons of the two samples lends no support to the proposition that Chinese and American cultures differ in a consistent direction, Chinese values being the more traditional according to our Confucian indicators. Of the various items in Table 4.1, there are eleven on which the Chinese sample more often endorsed the traditional position, but eleven others on which the American sample was instead the more traditional. This first-stage comparison of our two samples results, then, in no clearcut conclusion. We shall have to dig deeper into the data to clarify the picture.

Urban Versus Rural Differences

Given the local nature of our samples, the results we have just reviewed can not be taken as representative of value prevalence in either the Chinese or American population as a whole. Our sampling was largely centered in cities, typically cities that house major universities. This is especially the case in the United States, where only one sample was drawn in a rural region (Florida). Are the U.S.-China differences we have found robust, or are they confounded with the greater incidence of rural respondents in the China survey? This is not just a methodological issue; we are also interested in urban-rural differences themselves. Traditional culture is normally associated with rural settings and cultural change with cities. In China, this can make urban-rural comparisons tricky, as many different waves of cultural change, pointing in different directions, have occurred in that country in recent decades.

By dividing our samples based upon urban vs. rural residency we can make two kinds of comparisons: between urban and rural areas within each nation and between the two nations within either urban or rural residency. Such comparisons would help us estimate the degree of development in value orientations from the so-called traditional values to modern values (Inkeles 1983). We have argued that different value orientations between Chinese and American cultures should not be confused with the differences between "traditional" and "modern" values defined on a time continuum. But we also have noted that the linear evolutionary model has been a dominant intellectual paradigm in cross-cultural studies. This is also the case in the studies examining urban and rural differences.

It is not difficult to find evidence of a linear evolution of cultures. In its quest for modernity, a traditional society will open itself and absorb resources from other cultures. In this cultural enrichment process, both

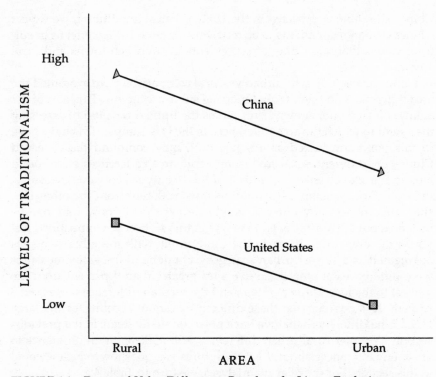

FIGURE 4.1 Expected Value Differences Based on the Linear Evolutionary Model

the "traditional" (or endogenous) cultural elements and the "modern" (or exogenous) cultural elements may be present simultaneously. Depending on one's point of view, increased presence of exogenous cultural elements may be interpreted in support of either "modernity" or "cultural hegemony" (Inkeles 1983; Hamelink 1983).

We cannot settle that ideologically charged debate in this study. What we can do is to examine our data to see the degree to which the prevailing cultural values in China depart from the Confucian tradition and, at the same time, resemble prevailing cultural values in the United States. Viewed broadly, we are attempting to judge whether we can validly compare the Chinese and American societies on the same dimensions, across different time periods of human development. If so, a linear evolutionary process would be a useful conceptual model to describe changes from "traditional" to "modern" values in China as transitional. The same paradigm could be employed to explain rural and urban area differences within each country. Our general expectation is that traditional Chinese values should prevail more strongly in rural areas than in urban areas in

China. The same is expected in the United States. In addition, we expect Chinese urban respondents to be relatively closer to the Americans in cultural values than are Chinese respondents in suburban towns and rural areas.[7]

Before proceeding with urban vs. rural comparisons, we examined the area differences among the six American survey locations. This part of the analysis (results not shown here) serves the limited purpose of assessing the extent to which the area differences in the U.S. sample, which we have to this point considered as a single unit, may confound the observed China-U.S. differences. Overall, some large area differences were found among the six U.S. sites. On fifteen of the twenty-seven value measures, the rural Florida sample stood out as most different from the other U.S. sites. (By chance, any one site would be extreme in only four or five instances out of twenty-seven.) We will in this section be contrasting Florida as the one rural setting in the U.S. sample with the other five sites aggregated as a single "urban" category. On none of the value measures were differences among these five sites greater than 9 percent from the highest to the lowest site per item, and the median difference was about 3 percent. It is obvious that these differences cannot account for the large U.S.-China differences that we have noted on many items in the previous section. Whether rural-urban differences will make enough difference to affect our inferences about the two cultures is a question to be answered in this section. For the relevant analyses, we turn to Table 4.2.

We followed the same conventions in Table 4.2 as in Table 4.1. The first four columns show the appropriate percentages, and the last two columns present the directions of the difference tests. The tests were analogous to those in a 2×2 factorial design, in which the test of, say, rural vs. urban difference was tested with the China vs. U.S. difference controlled for, and vice versa. For each value item, one interaction (between nation and area) was tested. Figure 4.1 shows the conceptual expectations of the China-U.S. and rural-urban differences in acceptance of the Confucian values, based on the linear evolutionary model. Clearly, the model would predict two main effects: China being more "traditional" than the United States and rural area being more "traditional" than urban area. Significant departure from such a pattern (e.g., Chinese rural residents are less "traditional" than they "should" be) will show up as an interaction. In the table, a plus or minus sign is used to indicate the significance of the corresponding comparisons. A 0 indicates no significant difference and × an sign indicates a significant interaction.

The area differences among the urban, suburban, and rural areas provide some clues about possible patterns of value changes in the two countries.[8] The linear evolutionary model fits reasonably well in the area of male-female relationships. Across four of the seven items, the cross-nation differences are consistent with the expectation of China being more "traditional." Rural areas were more "traditional" than urban areas on five of the seven measures. The two exceptions to the expected rural-urban differences involve a family's losing face for a pregnant teenage girl and chastity for women. They are due mainly to the China sample, in which rural residents more frequently value love in choosing a mate and less frequently say they are proud of "chastity for women." These views may be attributable to the fact that the rural Chinese respondents were much younger than their urban counterparts: more than 70 percent under thirty-nine years of age among the rural respondents vs. less than 50 percent among the urban respondents.

But the reversed rural-urban differences among the Chinese respondents are limited. With regard to divorce, a progressive openness was found, from rural to urban areas, in the China survey. There were larger differences between rural and township areas than between townships and the city, similar to the results for male-female relationships (data not shown). As Table 4.2 indicates, more urban residents would permit divorce, regardless of whether children are involved or not. Rural residents also more often endorsed aging parents' seeking help from their adult children, both in terms of care and of financial assistance. This pattern of differences is consistent with the expectations shown in Figure 4.1 and in two cases, aging parents being cared for by their adult children and permitting divorce when children are not a factor, this pattern also is revealed in China-U.S. differences.

This general pattern becomes more complex when we move to the next two value items in the family relationship category. Chinese urban residents are more likely to endorse "benevolent fathers and filial sons," a traditional concept, while the opposite holds for the U.S. sample. But many more Chinese rural residents would enjoy having a house full of children and grandchildren, while no urban-rural difference is found on this item in the U.S. sample. In general, greater urban and rural differences were found among the Chinese respondents than in the U.S. sample. By and large, Table 4.2 shows little difference between urban and rural areas in the United States in the value domain of family relationships.

For the seniority and authority hierarchies, the China sample showed very little resemblance to the pattern projected in the linear development model (Figure 4.1). More rural Chinese residents were willing to express their opinions when they disagreed with a senior, for example. But the respondents from the three geographical settings (urban vs. township vs. rural; township data not shown) did not differ in the respect accorded to older people; this is a high-consensus value everywhere. No significant differences among the three areas were found in submission to authority

TABLE 4.2   Cross-National Differences in Values in Rural and Urban Areas

Value Items	China Survey		U.S Survey		Rural-Urban[a]	China-U.S.[b]
	Rural	Urban	Rural	Urban		
Male-Female Relationships						
Differentiation between men and women (*Proud of*)	9%	13%	12%	14%	0	0
Three obediences and four virtues (*Proud of*)	11	7	41	27	+×	―――
Chastity for women (*Proud of*)	30	33	45	27	+××	0
Family losing face for teen child's pregnancy (*Yes*)	75	89	41	39	−×	+++++
A couple live together before marriage (*No*)	8	11	46	62	−×	―――――
Love is the most important in choosing a mate (*Yes*)	20	30	76	82	−	——————
Equal pay for equal work for men and women (*same pay*)	73	87	90	94	−×	——
Family Relationships						
Benevolent fathers and filial sons (*Proud of*)	57	65	84	72	0××	—
A house full of children and grandchildren (*Proud of*)	38	16	54	54	++××	―――
Aging parents cared for by their children (*Yes*)	90	76	78	74	+×	+
Aging parents ask their children for financial help (*Yes*)	88	81	83	81	0	0
A couple may divorce if they have no children (*Yes*)	60	83	53	49	−××	+++

(*Continues*)

TABLE 4.2   (Continued)

Value Items	China Survey		U.S Survey		Rural-Urban[a]	China-U.S.[b]
	Rural	Urban	Rural	Urban		
A couple may divorce if they have children (*Yes*)	23	40	39	37	–×	–
Authority hierarchy						
Submission to authority (*Proud of*)	50	54	70	53	–××	–
Pleasing superiors (*Proud of*)	13	5	73	56	++	-------
Younger people should respect older people (*Yes*)[c]	99	97	97	94	0	0
Express your opinions when you disagree with a senior (*Yes*)	32	20	82	77	+	-------
Interpersonal Relationships						
Human nature is benign or evil? (*Benign*)	36	29	80	80	0	-----
Harmony is precious (*Proud of*)	35	54	26	23	–××	+++
Generosity and virtues (*Proud of*)	49	62	96	91	0×	-----
Tolerance, propriety, and deference (*Proud of*)	37	51	93	94	–×	-----
Importance of connections (*Important*)[d]	73	68	88	84	0	--
Using connections to solve problems (*Yes*)	71	73	10	11	0	--------
Other						
Loyalty to state (*Proud of*)	76	77	95	91	0	--
Respect tradition (*Proud of*)	55	55	87	82	0	-·—

(*Continues*)

TABLE 4.2   *(Continued)*

Value Items	China Survey		U.S Survey		Rural-Urban[a]	China-U.S.[b]
	Rural	*Urban*	*Rural*	*Urban*		
Diligence and frugality (*Proud of*)	88	91	91	78	+×	+
Necessary to have religious faith (*Yes*)	22	31	77	65	0××	-----

Notes: Cell entries in the first four columns are the percentages of respondents who gave the listed response to each item. The number of cases varies from one comparison to another due to missing values. In the U.S. surveys, some of the value questions were not asked at all six sites.

[a]The plus and minus signs in this column show the directions of area differences after controlling for nations. The magnitude of differences is indicated by the number of plus or minus signs.

[b]The plus and minus signs in this column show the directions and magnitudes of the between-nation differences after controlling for area. They indicate the results of subtracting the percentages in the U.S. sample from the corresponding percentages in the China sample. They do not mean the same thing as in Table 4.1.

[c]The "yes" and "definite yes" categories are combined.

[d]The "very important" and "important" categories are combined.

either. But more rural residents endorsed the traditional notion of "pleasing superiors" than did residents in township and urban areas. Overall, the urban and rural residents differed less in their values related to seniority and authority hierarchies, compared with their differences concerning male-female relationships and family relationships (Table 4.2).

In comparison, the U.S. sample showed greater urban and rural differences in the authority-hierarchy value domain. Significantly more rural respondents endorsed "respecting older people," "pleasing superiors," and "submission to authority." If we assume that these are generally traditional values and thus characteristic of traditional American culture, the pattern is consistent with a linear evolutionary model. We should bear in mind, though, that the only rural area sampled in the United States was in Florida, and these might indicate regional (i.e., southern) values rather than the historical progression represented by the development model of value change.

In terms of interpersonal relationships, some significant differences were found between the Chinese respondents living in Shanghai, suburban towns, or rural areas (data not shown). Although a somewhat higher proportion of rural residents accorded importance to connections, it was the city dwellers who, as a group, were more willing to use their connections (Table 4.2). The opposite was true among the American respondents. A higher proportion of the rural Americans said they would use their connections to solve their problems.

The next three items express traditional Chinese values in handling interpersonal relationships. If there were the kinds of urban-rural differences predicted by the linear model, these three items would provide the critical tests because there is no dispute as to which response represents traditional values. We can see in Table 4.2 that in China, more urban residents endorsed these traditional values than did rural residents, a result directly contradicting the expectations in Figure 4.1. But consistent with expectations, significantly more rural residents believed that human nature is benign, compared with township and urban residents. No urban vs. rural difference was found in this domain among the American respondents. We have here no clear support for the linear model, in either culture.

Among the remaining value items, only two showed significant area differences. Among the Chinese respondents, rural residents and urban residents were quite similar in their support of the idea of "loyalty to the state." But more township residents appeared to endorse this value item than either rural or urban residents (data not shown). Also, more Shanghai city residents believed it necessary to have a religious faith. Among the American respondents, fewer urban residents endorsed either religious faith or frugality, a pattern opposite to that observed in the China sample. This finding is consistent with a linear development model for the United States, but we should note too that the degree of agreement with both the diligence/frugality and religious faith items was high even among urban Americans. Indeed, the percentage agreement that religious faith is necessary is more than twice as high in the urban U.S. sample than in any of the three Chinese locales (urban, suburban, rural). Far from a simple linear development away from traditional religious values, the China data may indicate that religion is recently experiencing at least a minor revival in urban Shanghai.

Urban-rural differences do not, taken as a whole, appear to be an important factor that would obscure or explain the overall cross-cultural differences shown in Table 4.1. Of the twenty-two cross-cultural differences we found earlier, nineteen of them remain significant when analyzed separately within the urban and rural subsamples. In other words, most of the cross-nation differences in cultural values could not be attributed to urban-rural differences within each nation, even though some of the within-nation differences were significant.

Some new patterns have also emerged here, and they suggest some contingent effects of urbanism. For example, although there is no general difference between the two cultures in the proportions endorsing "women's chastity," the unusually high proportion of the Florida rural respondents who agreed with this item created a significant cross-nation difference in the rural area. Similarly, the Florida respondents differed not only from their fellow Americans in urban areas, but also from the Chinese respondents in all locales in their orientations toward authorities.

There were also significant contingent effects of urbanism on the questions related to divorce. The Chinese sample appeared more permissive to divorce when children were not involved. The urban-rural comparison shows that the rural Chinese did not differ much from the U.S. (urban or rural) respondents on this divorce-without-children item. It was the Chinese urban (and township, not shown) residents who were unusually likely to endorse this rather hypothetical (in China) idea. But when children are involved in the situation, the Chinese rural respondents were much less likely to permit divorce, and the urban Chinese did not differ significantly from the two U.S. subsamples. In effect, the weight of children on people's tolerance for divorce was much greater among the rural than the urban Chinese respondents. The rural residents in China were also more likely to agree that aging parents should be cared for by their adult children. It was this unique characteristic of the rural residents in the China sample that was responsible for the overall cross-cultural difference on this value item. These findings suggest that the intergenerational features of Confucian thought remain more deeply ingrained in rural China than in the urbanized regions, regardless of how thoroughly Chinese respondents reject Confucian teachings when they are presented verbatim in a survey questionnaire.

Summary

Overall, the results reported in this chapter paint a picture of significant differences in value orientations between Chinese and Americans today. The Chinese respondents are more rigid about male-female relationships and seniority. They also attribute greater importance to personal connections and are more willing to use them for problem solving. However, the Chinese respondents also distanced themselves from some traditional Confucian values, such as, "benevolent fathers and filial sons" and "a house full of children and grandchildren." The English expressions of the ideas represented by these traditional Chinese phrases received far more support from the American respondents.

But this survey evidence does not convince us that the Chinese value families and family relationships less than their American counterparts. Rather, there are indications that the expressed support of the value items in this area is more a function of people's life experiences than a simple reproduction of either Confucian or communist ideology. The fact that rural Chinese respondents considered children more when asked questions about the maintenance of family stability indicates a pragmatic orientation. In a similar vein, rural Chinese seem to take for granted that adult children should care for their aging parents. This result too reflects pragmatism, given the almost total absence of societal care of senior citizens in rural China.

This chapter forewarns us to take a careful, not a simplistic, approach to our remaining analyses in this study. That is, one should not attempt to simplify the differences between China and the United States, nor between urban and rural areas. Values do not break down easily into patterns of "traditionalism" and "modernity." We have found some differences consistent with such a general model, but only a small number of the urban-rural patterns were consistent with linear evolution from "traditional values" to "modern values" in both countries. To be sure, when it comes to certain aspects of male-female relationships and family relationships, the rural residents in both nations appear to be more "traditional" than urban residents. But most of the cross-cultural differences reported in this chapter could not be accounted for by the simple notion of advancement toward "modernity." Rather, the differences reflect the divergent living conditions, life experiences, and cultural meanings of both the relationships addressed by the survey questions and the representations of these relationships in symbolic form as fixed phrases in a survey instrument. Given the complex cultural dynamics, especially those in contemporary China, we are unlikely to discern a single, overarching explanation of the complex patterns of value differences between China and the United States.

Notes

1. We are assuming that change proceeds unevenly across various sectors of a society, defined by characteristics associated with the speed of adopting new ideas, values, and behavioral patterns (Rogers 1983). If there is a linear pattern of development from traditional society to modern society (Lerner 1958), traditional

values would be more strongly held among rural residents than among their urban counterparts.

2. The proportion difference test assumes probability sampling from the target populations. In our case, each component sample was drawn randomly from the corresponding local population in a specific area.

3. The U.S. surveys used the statement, "Women should not have sexual relations until they get married," a straightforward principle of virginity. The Confucian phrase we are translating here as "chastity for women" is a much broader concept. Beyond prohibiting premarital sexual relations, it implies lifelong postmarital fidelity to the husband. The woman is not allowed to marry more than once. She is to submit to her husband and his family throughout her life—even if he were to die before consummation of the marriage.

4. In the traditional sense, the "three obediences" refer to a woman's obedience to her father before marriage, to her husband after marriage, and to her son if widowed; the "four virtues" refer to male-defined female ethics, language, manner, and work (*fude, fuyan, furong,* and *fugong.*) But in reality, the complex meanings of this phrase have been lost in China. What is left is the general notion of a wife's obligations to obey her husband, the statement used in the U.S. surveys.

5. This is not to say that these difficulties do not exist in U.S. society. But even without comparative studies on single-parent families or of children in broken families in the two nations, we believe the problems are much more severe in China.

6. In the U.S. surveys, only the Florida sample is clearly identified as a rural sample. Therefore, urban and rural differences in the U.S. data are operationalized as differences between the Florida sample and the rest of the U.S. samples. Such comparisons are potentially confounded by the differences between rural Florida and other rural parts of the nation.

7. Chinese society differs from American society in that there is no clearly formed middle class, nor people living in suburbs while working in big cities. City residents work and live in cities, while residents in outlying towns work and live in those towns. The same holds for rural residents. In general, there is a progressive "modernization" from rural areas, to small towns, to big cities.

8. To simplify interpretation, the urban and township residents in the China sample were combined into a single "urban" group for the urban-rural comparisons in Table 4.2.

5

Effects of Social and Demographic Characteristics

HAVING EXAMINED THE DIFFERENCES between the two cultures in the prevalence of the values at a macroscopic level, we are ready to address the next research question. Can social and demographic differences between the two nations help us account for the differences in value prevalence? Clearly, some of the traditional Confucian values are largely gone in China, while ideas similar to those values seem alive and well in the United States. This picture is quite different from the one depicted in Francis L. K. Hsu's (1981) analysis or in the outline of American culture proffered by Robin M. Williams, Jr. (1970). Further, many of the differences found in the previous chapter do not conform to the linear process from "traditionalism" to "modernity" (e.g., Lerner 1958). To further explicate these cross-national differences, we turn next to a more microscopic level of analysis.

For one thing, we need to show that our between-nation differences are not artifacts of the demographic makeup of the two samples (see Rosenberg 1968). We also need to examine the degree to which the two nations differ in their within-nation relationships between cultural values and relevant social and demographic variables (see Przeworski and Teune 1970:47–73). Cross-national comparisons of the relationships among variables may reveal clues to the processes of cultural change in each society.

In this chapter, we discuss the impact of six social and demographic variables on cultural values: gender, age, education, income, occupation, and marital status. We will examine how each of these variables affects the cross-national differences in value prevalence and how the two nations differ in the effects of each. These variables are closely implicated in at least some of the values in question in our survey. There are also general expectations regarding how each might affect traditional society.[1] For example, older people might be more traditional. Education, which is both an institutional method for enforcing the ruling ideology and a means for transmitting outside influences, might undermine many traditional values. Women might differ from men, or older people from younger, in their views on traditional patterns of deference. We will also

be looking for the possibility that demographic differences in the composition of our two samples might explain (or suppress) differences
between the two cultures.

Gender and Cultural Values

This study has from the beginning involved a central concern with
male-female relationships. This implies that there will be male-female differences in values that involve these fundamental relationships. Given
the recent campaigns in both countries to "give women equality" at long
last, one could well expect men to hold on to traditional values while
women would welcome change. This is one of many simplistic assumptions that our survey contradicts. As Table 5.1 shows, these expectations
were supported in only very minor ways.

The first four columns of Table 5.1 give the percentages of men and
women in each country who endorsed each value item. Column 5 shows
whether and in what degree the two sexes differed in their responses.
Column 6 reports the China-U.S. difference with gender controlled; these
results are very similar to what has been reported already in Chapter 4,
since the samples were quite alike in male-female composition. In China,
only four out of twenty-seven male-female comparisons were significant
($p < .01$); nine of the twenty-seven U.S. sample comparisons reached statistical significance. Overall, applying the more stringent $p < .001$ significance level for the larger total sample differences, only three of twenty-
seven items differ between the sexes in the pooled tests shown in Table
5.1. This is more than would be expected by chance alone, but scarcely
impressive considering the strong expectations one might have regarding
gender differences. As for our hypothesis that the males would be more
supportive of the traditional value structure in which they presumably
dominate females, only one, a wife obeying her husband (or three obediences and four virtues in the China survey), is in that direction to a statistically significant ($p < .001$) degree.

Indeed, of all the demographic variables we deal with in this chapter,
gender bears the fewest significant relationships with the value items.
The three instances where it makes a difference are of the type we
expected: all three have to do with marriage or the wifely role. There are
no differences in Table 5.1 that involve more general domains such as
family, authority, or interpersonal dealings. Even on divorce and the
equal-pay item, males and females agree to a surprising extent.

These few differences are obviously not sufficient to explain the basic
patterns of cross-cultural differences. Among the twenty-two significant

TABLE 5.1   Cross-National Differences in Values by Gender (in percentages)

Value Items	China Survey		U.S. Survey		Male-Female[a]	China-U.S.[b]
	Male	Female	Male	Female		
Male-Female Relationships						
Differentiation between men and women (*Proud of*)	12	8	14	12	0	0
Three obediences and four virtues (*Proud of*)	8	8	36	24	+	----
Chastity for women (*Proud of*)	31	34	28	33	−	0
Family losing face for teen child's pregnancy (*Yes*)	83	88	47	36	0	+++++
A couple live together before marriage (*All right*)	13	7	64	54	−	-------
Love is the most important in choosing a mate (*Yes*)	23	22	81	73	0	------
Equal pay for equal work for men and women (*same pay*)	82	85	93	93	0	−
Family Relationships						
Benevolent fathers and filial sons (*Proud of*)	64	62	75	74	0	--
A house full of children and grandchildren (*Proud of*)	20	23	52	56	0	-----
Aging parents cared by their children (*Yes*)	77	82	76	73	0×	+
Aging parents ask children for financial help (*Yes*)	83	83	85	80	0	0
A couple may divorce if they have no children (*Yes*)	74	80	49	51	0	+++
A couple may divorce if they have children (*Yes*)	39	31	33	41	0×	0

(Continues)

TABLE 5.1   *(Continued)*

Value Items	China Survey		U.S. Survey		Male-Female[a]	China-U.S.[b]
	Male	Female	Male	Female		
Authority hierarchy						
Submission to authority (*Proud of*)	51	55	56	56	0	0
Pleasing superiors (*Proud of*)	7	8	61	58	0	-------
Younger people respect older people (*Yes*)[c]	98	97	93	95	0×	0
Express your opinions when you disagree with a senior (*Yes*)	23	24	80	75	0	-------
Interpersonal Relationships						
Human nature is benign or evil? (*Benign*)	32	29	78	82	0	-----
Harmony is precious (*Proud of*)	49	50	25	22	0	+++
Generosity and virtues (*Proud of*)	58	59	93	91	0	----
Tolerance, propriety, and deference (*Proud of*)	50	44	93	95	0	-----
Importance of connections (*Important*)[d]	69	70	87	82	0	--
Using connections to solve problems (*Yes*)	74	71	12	10	0	+++++++
Other						
Loyalty to state (*Proud of*)	79	75	90	94	0	--
Respect tradition (*Proud of*)	55	56	81	84	0	---

(Continues)

TABLE 5.1 *(Continued)*

| | China Survey | | U.S. Survey | | Male-Female[a] | China-U.S.[b] |
Value Items	Male	Female	Male	Female		
Diligence and frugality *(Proud of)*	89	92	81	81	0	+
Necessary to have religious faith *(Yes)*	29	28	63	72	0	----

Note: Cell entries in the first four columns are the percentages of respondents who gave the listed response to each item. The number of cases varies from one comparison to another due to missing values. In the U.S. surveys, some of the value questions were not asked in all the six sites

[a]The plus and minus signs in this column show the directions of male/female differences after controlling for nation. The magnitude of differences is indicated by number of plus or minus signs. An × sign indicates a significant interaction.

[b]The plus and minus signs in this column show the directions and magnitudes of the between-nation differences after controlling for area. They indicate the results of subtracting the percentages in the U.S. sample from the corresponding percentages in the China sample. They do not mean the same thing as in Table 4.1.

[c]The "yes" and "definite yes" categories are combined.

[d]The "very important" and "important" categories are combined.

cross-national differences shown in Table 4.1, twenty remained significant in both gender groups. The other two significant cross-national differences were each maintained in one of the gender groups. There were only a few significant interactions between nation and gender. The difference between the China and U.S. samples as to aging parents being cared for by their adult children occurred mainly in the female group: significantly more Chinese than American women agreed with this item. Another significant cross-national difference, whether young people should respect older people, was mainly found among males: Chinese males endorsed this pattern of deference more than did American males. These interactions are so few, and relatively minor in magnitude, though, that we are hesitant to indulge in speculation as to why they are found in the data. Chance alone would not be a poor explanation, given the number of possible interactions that might have been found—and considering that we have no theoretical reason to predict any interactions of gender with nation.

Gender could be a suppresser variable (Rosenberg 1968:84-94) in that it concealed differences between the two nations with regard to divorce when a couple had children. More male Chinese respondents were permissive on divorce than male Americans (+6.1 percent, p<.01). The reverse was true in the female category (-9.6 percent, p<.01). This transverse interaction between nation and gender might suggest some interesting issues about sex roles and the marriage contract in the two nations, but it is an isolated finding that we simply note here without attempting an ad hoc explanation. In general, we found no more significant interactions between nation and gender than we found main effects of gender in Table 5.1. Given that we had seemingly good reason to expect gender effects, we deem it advisable to treat this particular analysis as exploratory rather than hypothesis-testing. Our exploration suggests that future research ought to focus on why the two genders do *not* differ on issues where one gender might seem to have more to gain than the other.[2] There are some particular findings that merit highlighting, though.

Chinese men and women showed no difference in their distaste for the old-fashioned notion of "three obediences and four virtues." It is the American men who are more likely to value a wife's obedience (p<.001). More than one-third of the American male respondents said a wife should obey her husband.

In both nations, higher proportions of females valued chastity in women. While this result on its face may seem to contradict the previous one (men value obedience, but women value chastity), it should be kept in mind that the Chinese question asked about being "proud of" the tradition of chastity. It is the woman who remains chaste in such a tradition, and therefore it is she who has something to be proud of. What has seemingly been abandoned is the more global Confucian view that chastity should be prized for its contribution to family stability and solidarity. The U.S. women too may have understood this as a statement about what they were proud of in themselves, rather than in the culture at large.

In both countries, men are more likely than women to endorse the practice of a couple living together before marriage. In China as recently as forty years ago, it was an indication of wealth and status for a man to have several concubines in addition to his wife (see Hsu 1981). But a woman was to be monogamous all her life, remaining dutiful to her parents-in-law and her children even if her husband had died early in the marriage. In the United States "living with a woman" has long been an acceptable (in some eyes, admirable) status for a man, but only recently has the reverse held true for a woman. If "living in sin" is no longer the universal pejorative it once was in the United States prior to the birth control pill (i.e., the early 1960s), the condition of being an "unwed mother" still occasions condemnation from the highest offices and media oracles of American society. This "double standard" still operates to some extent, and if there is a surprise in Table 5.1 it is that the male-female difference in the United States is not greater than the 10 percent we do find. Probably our wording has something to do with the result. The U.S. question asked whether living together without marriage is "all right," which is as close as we could come to translating the expression used in the China survey. Female respondents no less than males probably understood this item as an assertion of their personal freedom rather than as a normative statement about behavior they would approve of in others. The practice of living together before marriage seems to be an antitraditional trend that males welcome more than females, and that Americans accept more than do Chinese, at this time. The male-female difference does not, however, account in the slightest for the between-nation difference.

Over the remaining value measures no significant gender differences were found. Nor do gender differences in these areas in any way affect our earlier observations (Chapter 4) of the differences between the Chinese and American respondents. This pattern of null results seems remarkable considering that both these cultures have traditionally stressed male-female differentiation, and that a good deal of public policy in both nations has in recent decades been devoted to attempts to eradicate these traditional differences in treatment of the two genders. For whatever reason, men and women seem to think very much alike when it comes to cultural values of the kind asked about in our surveys. Perhaps different research methods would uncover more subtle or covert variations than we have been able to discern here.

Age Cohort Effects

Conceptually, age as a variable carries with it several possible theoretical processes of change at both the individual and societal levels. Age not only indicates an individual's maturation and progress through life's stages, but also reflects different socialization experiences, due to events in the surrounding social environment in one's formative years. Age variations thus can be decomposed conceptually into three components: aging, cohort, and period variations (Bengtson, Furlong, and Laufer 1974); operationally, though, this requires a richer data set than the present cross-sectional survey provides. The best we can do here is to examine the empirical correlates of our respondents' ages, bearing in mind that they might reflect either individual life-cycle changes or historical influences of a macroscopic nature.

While we cannot separate empirically all the possible implications of both age and aging, it is certainly meaningful to examine differences in value prevalence between age groups in each nation, as well as within each age group between nations. These comparisons are shown in Table 5.2. The three age groups in this table were created on the basis of both empirical and conceptual considerations. Empirically, we would like to maintain roughly equal numbers of respondents in each age category. Conceptually, we would like to maximize the homogeneity within each age group and the heterogeneity between categories in terms of people's life experiences.

For the China sample, some historical demarcations guided us in grouping respondents into the three age cohorts. The oldest cohort consists largely of individuals who went through their formative years before and during the communist revolution in the late 1940s and early 1950s; people in the middle cohort grew up during the 1950s and 1960s when revolutionary ideals and Maoist doctrines were at their strongest; the youngest cohort was largely socialized in post-Mao China.

These same cutting points were used to classify the American respondents, so we would have comparable age groups. These cohorts came of age, approximately, during similarly distinct eras of American history. The oldest (age 50–65 at the time of our U.S. survey) would remember World War II, and its carryover from the Great Depression, and would tend to be marked by their socialization during the postwar demobilization followed by the Cold War, the Korean War, and the staunch national policy of anticommunism. The 30–49 age group would have been born during the postwar "baby boom," a cohort that is often portrayed in popular writing as holding distinct values on social issues. The youngest cohort is composed of people born after the birth control pill ended that baby boom, sometimes jocularly termed "baby-busters." The socialization environment for "baby-boomers" as they came of age ranged from the optimism of the Kennedy era to the intense intergenerational and cultural conflicts of the late 1960s and early 1970s. Our youngest cohort learned their early lessons about life later, when a national wave of conservatism and a declining confidence in American dominance in the world was culminating in the reactionary "Reagan Revolution" of the 1980s. In all, there are significant historical shifts during the lives of our total sample that could produce marked age differences in values. In both countries, our rough reading of these recent histories is that they ought to produce curvilinear results if it is socialization, rather than aging per se, that generates differences in cultural values. That is, the historical period in which our middle (age 30–49) groups were presumably forming their values would have been distinct from both the earlier and the later eras. Just as "The Sixties" refers to the era in which young Americans were encouraged to question authority and in other ways cast aside traditional social values, the contemporaneous period in China was the most severe in terms of communist indoctrination under Mao Zedong.[3]

In any event, it appears from Table 5.2 that age cohort or aging differences within each nation are unlikely to account for our overall cross-cultural differences. Among the original twenty-two significant differences found between the China and U.S. samples, eighteen (more than 80 percent) remained significant within each of the three age groups, and the other four are replicated in at least one or two age groups. There are also indications across the domains that age cohort differences are much less linear (i.e., less traditional in younger than older cohorts) in China than in the United States. We find a much more thorough rejection of the traditional Confucian values among the Chinese who experienced their formative years during and immediately after the communist revolution.

Specifically, the significant cross-national difference on "equal pay for equal work for men and women" resulted mainly from the youngest and middle-aged cohorts (p<.01). Many fewer young and middle-aged Chinese respondents accepted the value of equal pay for men and women than did their American age mates; there was no significant difference between the two countries among respondents over the age of fifty, who are overwhelmingly supportive of this equality principle.

The significant cross-national difference on the item about caring for one's aging parents, for which we find a surprisingly negative effect of age, was due primarily to the oldest cohort. The older Chinese (for whom public support systems are almost completely lacking) were more likely than the older Americans to say that grown children carry this responsibility. There was much less between-nation difference at the younger age levels.

There was a slight interaction, one that is obscured by the overall cross-national difference, in the value accorded to the Confucian tradition of "benevolent fathers and filial sons." Agreement with this principle declined slightly with age in China, while it increased slightly with age in the United States. Still, the percentage agreeing at every age level in the United States was higher than at any age level in China. The net effect of age is zero, when results are aggregated across the two samples.

A clearer, transverse interaction was found concerning the value of chastity for women. The age effects were opposite in the two countries, while the central tendency was about the same in each country. Among respondents under the age of thirty, endorsement of chastity as a value was more than twice as prevalent in China as in the United States (p<.001). But among those aged fifty and older, American respondents were more than twice as likely as the Chinese to say they are proud of chastity for women as a cultural value. These countervailing patterns

TABLE 5.2 Cross-National Differences in Values by Age Cohort (in percentages)

Value Items	China Survey			U.S. Survey			Old-Young	China-U.S.
	<30	30–49	50–65	<30	30–49	50–65		
Male-Female Relationships								
Differentiation between men and women (*Proud of*)	9	12	9	11	12	14	0	0
Three obediences and four virtues (*Proud of*)	10	9	4	29	29	31	0	–––
Chastity for women (*Proud of*)	38	36	19	17	26	45	+×xx	0
Family losing face for teenager's pregnancy (*Yes*)	78	87	90	35	40	51	++	+++++
A couple live together before marriage (*All right*)	19	9	5	72	66	38	–––×	–––––
Love is most important in choosing a mate (*Yes*)	28	23	17	81	77	73	–	––––––
Equal pay for equal work for men and women (*Same pay*)	80	82	89	90	96	93	+	–
Family Relationships								
Benevolent fathers and filial sons (*Proud of*)	65	63	61	72	72	75	0	–

(Continues)

TABLE 5.2 (Continued)

Value Items	China Survey			U.S. Survey			Old-Young	China-U.S.
	<30	30-49	50-65	<30	30-49	50-65		
A house full of children and grandchildren (*Proud of*)	30	23	10	42	55	61	0	----
Aging parents cared for by their children (*Yes*)	81	83	71	78	80	64	--^	0
Aging parents ask their children for financial help (*Yes*)	86	86	74	86	86	73	--	0
A couple may divorce if they have no children (*Yes*)	77	79	72	43	49	58	+xx	+++
A couple may divorce if they have children (*Yes*)	40	36	31	34	38	41	0x	0
Authority Hierarchy								
Submission to authority (*Proud of*)	52	50	58	58	53	60	0	0
Pleasing superiors (*Proud of*)	9	7	6	53	58	66	+x	-----
Younger people respect older people (*Yes*)a	97	97	99	92	95	95	0	+
Express your opinions when you disagree with a senior (*Yes*)	25	22	23	76	79	77	0	-----

(Continues)

TABLE 5.2 (Continued)

Value Items	China Survey			U.S. Survey			Old-Young	China-U.S.
	<30	30–49	50–65	<30	30–49	50–65		
Interpersonal Relationships								
Human nature is benign or evil? (*Benign*)	26	27	45	77	80	81	++x	-----
Harmony is precious(*Proud of*)	46	49	54	24	21	24	0	+++
Generosity and virtues (*Proud of*)	57	58	62	92	92	91	0	----
Tolerance, propriety, and deference (*Proud of*)	45	48	47	92	96	94	0	-----
Importance of connections (*Important*)b	74	74	57	86	85	86	–x	--
Using connections to solve problems (*Yes*)	76	79	55	16	10	6	--x	++++++
Other								
Loyalty to state (*Proud of*)	79	77	76	89	91	95	0x	--
Respect tradition (*Proud of*)	55	58	51	80	82	87	0x	---
Diligence and frugality (*Proud of*)	83	90	97	69	83	89	++	++

(Continues)

TABLE 5.2 (Continued)

Value Items	China Survey			U.S. Survey			Old-Young	China-U.S.
	<30	30–49	50–65	<30	30–49	50–65		
Necessary to have religious faith (Yes)	28	27	31	60	66	74	+x	----

Notes: The American respondents aged sixty-six and older were excluded from the analysis. The number of cases in each column varies from one value item to another due to missing data and the fact that not all the items were used in all the U.S. surveys.

Cell entries in the last two columns indicate the proportional differences. The magnitude of a difference is indicated by the number of signs. The notations are:

+ = a significantly higher proportion in the oldest cohort or in the China sample.

− = a significantly lower proportion in the oldest cohort or in the China sample.

^ = a significant curvilinear function with the middle age cohort significantly higher than the other two.

x = a significant interaction.

0 = no significant difference.

[a]The "yes" and "definite yes" categories were combined.
[b]The "important" and "very important" categories were combined.

account for our not being able to find an overall significant difference between the two nations (Chapter 4).

Similarly, there is an age-by-nation interaction for the questions about divorce. This is particularly striking for the item where divorce would involve children. In China, the older respondents are less approving of this practice, while in the United States age is positively related to approval. The net result of these countervailing trends is that there is no overall age effect, just as there is no overall difference in approval of divorce-with-children between the two nations (Table 5.2).

Using connections to solve problems tends to be approved more readily by younger respondents in both countries, but the highest approval level is found in the middle Chinese subsample, thirty to forty-nine years of age; they are not much above the younger Chinese, though. One might speculate from this slightly curvilinear result that middle-aged Chinese have faced years of frustration in dealing with public officials for marriage certificates, housing assignments, promotions, and the like. Cultivating and using connections is clearly central to Chinese life, to judge from the huge between-nation differences we find on this item. Main characters in recent Chinese popular fiction are often middle-aged reformers who succeed or fail depending on their skills in use of connections. The older Chinese in our sample are less oriented toward using connections (Table 5.2) but still far above any age cohort in the U.S. sample.

With those interactions noted, let us return to the various value domains in order. First, in the area of male-female relationships, there was a progressive openness toward premarital cohabitation from the oldest to the youngest cohorts in both countries, despite the enormous between-nation difference we noted in Chapter 4. In the United States the age gaps are very large, the greater difference being that between the oldest and middle age groups (p<.001) as compared to that between the middle and youngest cohorts (p<.01). A similarly progressive openness with age, albeit at a much lower level, is also found among the Chinese respondents, although here the greater difference is found between the middle and youngest cohorts (p<.01). These age differences are understandable on a pragmatic basis; it is, after all, the young adults in any society who are most likely to wish to live together without yet committing to marriage. The age differences in Table 5.2 are notably larger than the gender differences on the same item, reported in Table 5.1.

Family shame over teenage pregnancy is another "generation gap" item in both cultures. The younger the person, the less common was this view. Among Chinese respondents, the significant difference is between the middle-age and youngest cohorts (p<.01), while the American sample produces a greater difference between the oldest and the middle-age groups (p<.01). Clearly, the younger adults identify more with teenagers and are reluctant to confer this social stigma on them. Still, the differences between China and the United States on this item are enormous in comparison with the age differences.

No age differences were found regarding differentiation between men and women, nor on the wifely "three obediences and four virtues" question. There were very minor cohort effects regarding equal pay for equal work between men and women: a progressive increase in support for this item with increasing age in China and a very weak trend in that direction in the U.S. sample as well. Ceiling effects may have prevented our detecting stronger age differences on this issue.

Love as the most important consideration in marriage is a value that appeals more to the young in both societies. But this age trend pales in significance alongside the huge cultural gap on the question. Fewer than one-third of the youngest Chinese, compared to more than two-thirds of the oldest Americans, give high priority to romantic love. Although romance and passion between sexes has been a continuous theme in both traditional and contemporary Chinese culture, it was not seen as important for a pragmatic decision such as marriage. Linking love to the institution of marriage is related to acceptance of other values such as individualism and choice. Clearly this Western norm has not penetrated far into Chinese culture, even among the young people who are more predisposed toward it, despite recent exposure of Chinese to Western romance and individualism in the mass media.

We have noted the opposite patterns of age effects on chastity for women in the Chinese and American samples. In China there was a progressive *increase* in being "proud of" the traditional value of chastity, from the oldest to the youngest, but in the United States there was a *decrease*. The upward slope in the United States was somewhat more marked than was the downward slope in China. We cannot pass this clear-cut difference by without speculating as to its origins, which are presumably different in the two cultures since the empirical relationships are in opposite directions.

Chastity, as a traditional value, would ordinarily be expected to appeal more to older people, as we find in the U.S. sample. For many in the over-fifty age bracket chastity may not be a pragmatic issue, nor a question with personal implications. As we said at the outset of this section, we expect older people to support traditional values more than young people do. Given that the simple hypothesis is supported in the U.S. data, our search for a more specific explanation for the interaction on this item should focus on China. Two possible factors occur to us. One is that the Chinese phrase for "chastity for women" has been under attack there since the May 4th movement seventy years ago. In contemporary China, the phrase we used in the China questionnaire carries strong negative connotations. We believe that chastity as a *global value* is prized (and still widely observed) in China, but this particular *phrase* is out of favor, and older people reject it as part of their greater general acceptance of the dominant culture to which they have been exposed. A second factor to consider is that, during the previous ten years of opening China to the world, premarital sex, extramarital sex, and sexual relationships among teenagers became increasingly frequent.[4] This trend of course involved the younger cohorts that are represented in our sample. Some of our young respondents are still in the marriage market, and others are parents of children who have reached the age of sexual (if not marital) readiness. In other words, younger respondents might be interpreting this question more pragmatically than ideologically and expressing their hope for a little more chastity in the system. In the United States, on the other hand, the term "chastity" is not politically dissociated from social practice, and young people are not as enthusiastic about it as their elders are for them.

Another plausible explanation in China might be that the same question wording evoked different referents in younger *vs.* older respondents. Chastity in the traditional Chinese phrase referred to the duties of a woman that are based on premarital virginity and marital fidelity, extending even to widowhood. But to young people not so oriented to the marriage context (nor to the traditional phrase used in our questionnaire), the term "chastity" might evoke what it means to most Americans: virginity. Premarital virginity is still heavily promoted and widely accepted in China, while postmarital fidelity has been stressed much less since divorce became permissible under law.[5] In any event, we doubt very much that the cultural value associated with the concept of chastity is held in the same degree in China and the United States, despite our failure to detect a difference (Table 4.1) between the two cultures. In survey research, equivalence of wording does not guarantee equivalence of meaning, nor of social or historical context. We consider that the strong interaction between age and nation in Table 5.2 is evidence that chastity is a cultural value that plays quite different roles in the two societies we are comparing.

The questions about acceptance of divorce produced interactions between country and age that are similar to those for the "chastity" item. In the United States, age was a positive predictor of approval of divorce, whereas in China the correlation was negative—with the slight exception that the middle-age group was highest in approval of divorce under the condition that no children are involved.[6] The effect of age in the United States was more marked than in China, the largest difference on either divorce question being the 15 percent increase from the youngest to the older American respondents (p<.001). When children are taken into account, the differences between the two countries were lessened within each age cohort. This is largely due to the fact that the older Americans were more affected by the children factor, whereas in China children made a huge difference in opinions about divorce, regardless of the respondent's age.

Age was correlated with opinions about the aged in both samples, but not in the direction one might predict from a simple self-interest theory. The oldest cohorts, consisting of people close to retiring from the labor force, expressed the *least* support for the propositions that aging parents should be taken care of by their adult children and that it is all right to ask one's adult children for financial assistance when needed. The significant age differences in both countries were found between the oldest and the middle-age cohorts. It could well be that these "older" respondents, a group centered on the late fifties in age, have even older, and highly dependent, parents to consider. Younger respondents, whose parents are also younger and presumably more able to care for themselves, may be too far removed from the time in question to be apprehensive about the vague obligations we asked them about. The results in China were slightly more supportive than in the U.S. sample at each age level in Table 5.2, which means that the between-nations difference we noted in Chapter 4 are in no way confounded with age differences between the two samples. The cultural value of responsibility for one's elders seems to remain slightly higher in China regardless of the person's age, and it is widespread across the age groups in both countries.

By contrast, the item asking about the traditional value of having "a house full of children and grandchildren" produced strong, but countervailing, age effects in the two countries. As a result there is no overall age effect; rather, there are two patterns, which are contrasting not only in a statistical sense, but also in our historical interpretation of the cultural changes they represent.

The "children and grandchildren" item must be interpreted against the background of China's national policy limiting a family to one child. The older Chinese respondents seem to have more thoroughly accepted this abandonment of traditional values. Only one in ten in the oldest cohort in China remains "proud of" the tradition of having large families, whereas in the youngest cohort three times as many respondents endorsed it (p<.01). The reverse pattern was found in the United States, where overall support for this value was on the average twice as widespread as in China. That is, about four in ten among the youngest U.S. respondents (i.e., those most likely to be thinking about having children) favored the "house full" notion, compared to six in ten in the oldest cohort (i.e., those more likely to be thinking about having *grand*children) (p<.01).

Americans are increasingly delaying or eschewing marriage and having fewer children per couple (Sweet and Bumpass 1987). The positive age trend we find in Table 5.2 is probably an accurate reflection of a general shift in American values away from the traditional emphasis on progeny. We might imagine, though, that in decades to come, when our younger respondents have moved into the older cohort, they will look more fondly on children, especially their children's children—a cohort that lies far in the future of their lives. What about the Chinese respondents? Perhaps the older Chinese experienced harsh times bringing up their youngsters during the 1950s and 1960s and had been left to see their children dependent upon them for taking care of grandchildren again. The younger Chinese, on the other hand, might simply resent the strict one-child policy. This is quite a different meaning of our question compared to the view of the senior Chinese, who may feel that they have been prevented from enjoying the promise associated with having children and grandchildren.

A hint of this same interaction is also found in Table 5.2 for the item regarding pleasing one's superiors. This traditional value was rejected overwhelmingly by the Chinese, and its acceptance was negatively correlated with age. In the United States, by contrast, this item was positively correlated with age, a finding that accords with a common-sense prediction. That is, in the United States, where the longer people work the more likely they are to hold senior positions, the older respondents (all of whom were still of working age) were most supportive of this traditional practice. In China, that value has virtually disappeared and is not one to which senior people display any attachment. Age may, in this respect too, reflect in China a combination of different histories of people of different ages, plus unedifying personal experience under a regime that has overturned traditional values as thoroughly as possible. The other items in the authority hierarchy group showed no relationship to age.

Age was positively related to the first item in the interpersonal relationships area, the belief that human nature is benign. While this item was more widely endorsed in the United States, there was a big jump in China from the middle to the oldest age group. There were no linear or strong age differences for the other interpersonal abstractions in Table 5.2: harmony; generosity and virtues; or tolerance, propriety, and deference.

Age seems to have some negative effect on the importance accorded to using "connections." In China, the oldest group saw connections as markedly less important, and in both countries the older respondents were less inclined to say they would use connections for problem solving ($p < .01$). There was a progressive decrease in the acceptance of using connections from the youngest to the oldest cohorts in the United States, while the two younger groups in China did not differ significantly.

Of the remaining items at the bottom of Table 5.2, all show positive correlations with age in the United States. That is, older Americans were more traditional than were younger respondents, in each respect: they expressed greater loyalty to the state, respect for tradition, pride in diligence and frugality, and a greater need for religious faith. These findings all accord with our global expectation that traditional values will be endorsed more widely as people age and among people who were socialized to their cultural values at an earlier time in history.

The picture is much more complex in the Chinese sample. While the traditional view of diligence and frugality (values one need not be Confucian to accept) did get near-unanimous support in the oldest Chinese subsample, the other values did not seem to increase with age. It is as if traditional culture, under siege throughout most or all of these respondents' lifetimes, has been submerged so that the expectable effects of aging are not to be found in China today—at least not via the survey research methods we have employed.

Education and Traditional Cultural Values

Education is one of the least comparable (between nations) of the independent variables in our study. Because of very different structural conditions, the educational standards have reached very different levels in the two countries. Most Chinese complete their education with high school, whereas sizable numbers of Americans today go to college at least for a while (see Table 3.2). If we literally compared high school graduates, say, in the two countries we would be matching students of relatively high attainment in China with those of only modest attainment in the United States. Whether such a comparison makes sense depends upon whether one conceives of education in absolute or in relative terms. As we shall see, for most of our purposes here the evidence supports a relative rather than an absolute interpretation of the implications of education for cultural values. But as often as not, the relational effects of education are different in the two countries.

The education ladder is related to two variables that are otherwise unmeasured here, in ways that are probably similar in the two countries: First, education is an indicator of social status, and second it is dependent upon cognitive abilities and thus a rough locator of individual intelligence within each society. (That is, a very good student in China is likely to finish high school, whereas a very good student in the United States is likely to finish college; the opportunities open to the bright student are radically different.) We have no strong reason to predict that either social status or intelligence will be systematically related to the traditional cultural values in our study, but there is at the same time no justification for assuming that they are not. Intelligence is presumed to be a predictor of susceptibility to "modern" ideas (Lerner 1958), and socio-economic status is a traditional correlate of many of the behaviors—such as use of "serious" mass media—that we vaguely associate with cultural innovation. If we would venture any global expectation, it should be that education would as a rule be negatively associated with traditional perspectives on social relationships. Certainly we would be remiss if we did not examine the question of the relationship between education and traditional values as defined here.

Testing separately for the relationship between education and cultural values in each country enables us to check for possible artifacts. Because the normal educational attainment levels in the two samples are so different, it is possible that the differences in values that we have ascribed to between-nation differentiation is instead due simply to the fact that the U.S. sample includes many more college graduates, and the China sample includes many more people whose education was terminated short of a high school degree.

Our strategy for comparing the influence of education on values in the two nations was first to standardize the education measure within each survey and then to group each sample into three equal-sized subsamples. Cross-country comparisons of these three *relative* educational categories are shown in Table 5.3.

Controlling for educational levels in each nation did not alter our first-order estimates of cultural differences. Among the twenty-two significant cross-national differences, eighteen (i.e., more than 80 percent) remained significant in each of the three educational categories. Each of the other four remained significant in one or two educational categories. Four additional significant between-nation differences were found that are specific to some educational level(s).

A cursory inspection of Table 5.3 suggests that education is not a general variable with similar value functions in the two societies. Of the twenty-seven value items, only eight show similar correlations with education in both countries. Less-educated people are consistently more traditional with respect to: male-female role and pay differences; wifely obedience; disapproval of living together before marriage; prizing children and grandchildren; submitting to, and pleasing, people in authority; and the belief that human nature is benign. There is some evidence of a general effect of education eroding traditional values, but there are more exceptions in our data than there are values that follow this simple rule.

In few instances do these trends for education represent especially strong correlations, although the relationship in each instance is monotonic. For no single item that we noted in the previous paragraph are there differences in both countries of as much as 10 percent between the lowest and the highest educational categories. Thus the expected influence of education as a force that undermines traditional values may be overstated in popular lore. It is not a general effect that cuts across countries and value domains, and it is not an especially powerful effect when one considers the wide educational variation represented in our total sample here. Given that many factors are correlated with education as a measured survey variable, one may rest assured that schools themselves are not responsible for a wholesale undermining of traditional society, as has at times been charged in both countries. Since our study here is not primarily about educational effects, but rather about cross-national comparisons, we will not dwell on the reasons that might lie behind these eight items for which we find parallel correlations in the United States and China.

More interesting to us are the nine items for which the patterns are *opposite* in the two countries. On six of these nine, the direction of education's effect in the United States is away from the traditional value while in China education seems to impel toward the traditional view: filial father-son relationships; expressing disagreement with a senior; prizing harmony and generosity; loyalty to the state; and the need to have religious faith. Three other items produce the reverse interaction, that is, education is negatively correlated with the traditional view in China, but positively correlated in the United States. This is the case for both of the items regarding divorce, and also for the question about grown children taking care of their aging parents. These latter items may represent pragmatic responses in the United States, in that families of lower socio-economic status (a strong correlate of education) are more likely to experience divorce and the strain of intergenerational dependency.

These interaction effects between education and nation are mostly not very strong correlations, certainly no stronger as a set than those we noted in the previous section regarding items for which education did account for antitraditional trends in values. But the fact that the patterns are opposed in the two countries makes the interactions in many of these cases rather strong. And the fact that in Table 5.3 we find at least as many countervailing between-nation patterns as we find consonant trends suggests that education does not have a univocal effect on values. It operates differently within each culture, in different spheres of values.

One general conclusion we could offer, though, is that the large differences in absolute educational attainment between the two countries will not explain much of the overall between-nation variation that we have noted to this point. If we consider that the "high" education group in China is roughly as educated, in terms of number of years, as is the

TABLE 5.3 Cross-National Differences in Values by Educational Level (in percentages)

Value Items	China Survey			U.S. Survey			Low-High	China-U.S.
	Low	Med.	High	Low	Med.	High		
Male-Female Relationships								
Differentiation between men and women (*Proud of*)	14	10	9	22	9	9	+	0
Three obediences and four virtues (*Proud of*)	11	10	5	40	28	22	++x	---
Chastity for women (*Proud of*)	26	35	33	37	31	24	0x	0
Family losing face for teenager's pregnancy (*Yes*)	83	85	87	42	41	43	0	+++++
A couple live together before marriage (*All right*)	7	9	14	52	60	65	--	-----
Love is most important in choosing a mate (*Yes*)	25	20	24	80	79	73	0	------
Equal pay for equal work for men and women (*Same pay*)	77	82	89	89	94	96	-	-
Family Relationships								
Benevolent fathers and filial sons (*Proud of*)	53	65	68	78	75	69	0xx	--

(Continues)

TABLE 5.3 (Continued)

Value Items	China Survey			U.S. Survey			Low-High	China-U.S.
	Low	Med.	High	Low	Med.	High		
A house full of children and grandchildren (*Proud of*)	29	24	14	59	52	52	++	-----
Aging parents cared for by their children (Yes)	85	82	73	72	75	77	0x	+
Aging parents ask their children for financial help (Yes)	83	85	81	77	84	87	0x	0
A couple may divorce if they have no children (Yes)	60	77	87	52	49	48	--xx	+++
A couple may divorce if they have children (Yes)	23	34	45	39	38	34	-xx	0
Authority Hierarchy								
Submission to authority (*Proud of*)	56	55	49	63	59	46	++x	0
Pleasing superiors (*Proud of*)	12	8	3	64	60	53	++	-----
Younger people respect older people (Yes)a	98	98	96	95	95	93	0	0
Express your opinions when you disagree with a senior (Yes)	26	25	20	72	78	82	0x	-----

(*Continues*)

TABLE 5.3 (Continued)

Value Items	China Survey			U.S. Survey			Low-High	China-U.S.
	Low	Med.	High	Low	Med.	High		
Interpersonal Relationships								
Human nature is benign or evil? (Benign)	42	31	25	84	79	76	++	-----
Harmony is precious(Proud of)	39	49	56	32	23	16	0xx	+++
Generosity and virtues (Proud of)	54	58	62	93	92	91	0x	----
Tolerance, propriety, and deference (Proud of)	38	45	55	90	96	95	--x	-----
Importance of connections (Important)b	71	68	71	81	86	87	0	--
Using connections to solve problems (Yes)	67	71	77	12	10	11	0x	++++++
Other								
Loyalty to state (Proud of)	72	77	80	93	92	89	0x	--
Respect tradition (Proud of)	56	60	51	87	83	78	+	---
Diligence and frugality (Proud of)	91	93	87	84	80	79	0	+

(Continues)

TABLE 5.3 (Continued)

Value Items	China Survey			U.S. Survey			Low-High	China-U.S.
	Low	Med.	High	Low	Med.	High		
Necessary to have religious faith (Yes)	25	28	31	77	68	59	+xx	----

Notes: The three educational categories are based on the within-nation distributions of the respondents in each of the nations. The number of cases in each column varies from one value item to another due to missing data and the fact that not all the items were used in all the U.S. surveys.

Cell entries in the last two columns indicate the proportional differences. The magnitude of a difference is indicated by the number of signs. The notations are:

+ = a significantly higher proportion among the oldest cohort or in the China sample.
– = a significantly lower proportion among the oldest cohort or in the China sample.
^ = a significant curvilinear function with the middle age cohort significantly higher than the other two.
x = a significant interaction.
0 = no significant difference.

[a]The "yes" and "definite yes" categories were combined.
[b]The "important" and "very important" categories were combined.

"medium" group in the United States, this disparity cannot account for any of the between-nation differences. The easiest way to see that is to note that there were no significant curvilinear effects of education in the United States, which there would be if the "medium education" group stood out in any fashion in Table 5.3. By contrast, the "high education" group in China was either the lowest or the highest on twenty of the twenty-two value items in that survey. These are the two groups that are most similar in absolute years of formal schooling in the two samples.

Most important to our purpose here, what are we to make of the six traditional value items that in the United States do seem to be eroded somewhat by education, but that in China produce the opposite pattern? We suspect the answer lies in a kind of transaction between one's individual judgment and the indoctrination programs of the communist state. Each of these items represented a traditional Confucian teaching: filial piety, deference, harmony, generosity, loyalty, and faith. It may take a strong sense of self-efficacy—which we would expect of better-educated people—to hold to such values in the face of an extensive campaign to undermine them. (Only loyalty to the state is an exception to this characterization, in that the communist government has stressed loyalty to it at least as much as any government does. But, nationalism and patriotism have always been among the motives as well as important components of Chinese intellectuals' discourse, both the official and the oppositional.) In its broad assault on Confucian doctrine, the Chinese government may have failed to dent the belief structures of its better-educated citizens on these questions of global values. Or, these people were quick to recover these traditional values from their memory after the change of political climate in the reform era. To be sure, on almost all of these values the absolute level of agreement was lower in China than in the United States. (The one exception is the item regarding harmony, which seems not to be much of an American value even among the least educated.) Our conclusion, then, is not that the anti-Confucian counter-structuring program of recent decades in China has by any means failed—we strongly believe that it has succeeded in eradicating traditional values—but that it may have been restrained to some extent by resistance in the minds of the most self-assured and competent members of the society.

Effects of Income on Cultural Values

Income is another variable that is far from directly comparable. Not only are the absolute levels and indeed the monetary systems vastly different, but so are the variances and the social meanings of low income.

Few Americans in our sample have incomes nearly as low in absolute monetary equivalents as the highest-paid Chinese, but the "floor" standard of living for poor people in the United States may be considerably worse. Money buys different things, at different prices, in the two countries, and there are commodities that one need not buy in one country that are quite dear in the other. We cannot interpret our results with respect to these massive structural differences between the two economies. All we can do here is to examine the *relative* impact of income on values. There does not seem to be very much, especially in China.

Given the lesser variance in income, we expected to find much smaller income effects on values among the Chinese respondents than among the American respondents.[7] For this analysis, the incompatibility of the monetary systems in the two nations was handled by classifying respondents in each sample into low, medium, and high income categories. The comparisons across the two nations were thus made on the basis of common locations of the respondents in the income *distribution* within their own nation. A global "modernization" prediction would, as with education, presumably be that increasing income implies declining support for traditional values. The results of our analysis are shown in Table 5.4.

Overall, controlling for income made very little difference in our between-nation findings. Of the twenty-two cross-national differences in cultural values, eighteen remained significant after income was controlled for. Three of the twenty-two cross-national differences were replicated within certain income levels, and two additional income-category-specific cross-national differences were found. These latter differences had to do with adult children's responsibilities for their aging parents, a concern that seems logically related to income. More low-income Chinese than American respondents (p<.01) thought that aging parents should be cared for by their adult children, and fewer Chinese than American high-income respondents saw a responsibility to give financial assistance to aging parents (p<.01). As we have noted earlier, the two countries differ in the provision of support systems for the aged, so these differences are probably not merely due to income. In any event, we are discussing two items on which agreement was very high in both nations, and only slightly higher in China than in the United States.

Overall the "effects" of income were not only small, but also inconsistent. Only two traditional value items showed successive monotonic decreases with higher income in both samples: wifely obedience and chastity as a virtue were more widely endorsed by the lowest-income groups. Indeed, across the twenty-seven value items, we find in Table 5.4 monotonic effects of income on only twelve in the U.S. sample and for just six of the twenty-seven items in the China sample. (None of the monotonic effects in China involved a difference greater than eight per-

TABLE 5.4 Cross-National Differences in Values by Income Level (in percentages)

Value Items	China Survey			U.S. Survey			Low-High	China-U.S.
	Low	Med.	High	Low	Med.	High		
Male-Female Relationships								
Differentiation between men and women (*Proud of*)	14	9	10	18	11	12	+	0
Three obediences and four virtues (*Proud of*)	10	9	5	40	29	22	--×	---
Chastity for women (*Proud of*)	37	31	30	41	28	25	++	0
Family losing face for teenager's pregnancy (*Yes*)	84	86	85	39	43	40	0	++++
A couple live together before marriage (*All right*)	9	11	10	51	62	62	-×	----
Love is most important in choosing a mate (*Yes*)	25	22	21	77	77	75	0	------
Equal pay for equal work for men and women (*Same pay*)	80	85	82	89	94	96	0	--
Family Relationships								
Benevolent fathers and filial sons (*Proud of*)	59	65	62	76	74	70	0	--

(Continues)

TABLE 5.4 (Continued)

Value Items	China Survey			U.S. Survey			Low-High	China-U.S.
	Low	Med.	High	Low	Med.	High		
A house full of children and grandchildren (*Proud of*)	29	19	20	56	54	54	+	----
Aging parents cared for by their children (*Yes*)	84	78	79	73	75	77	0×	+
Aging parents ask their children for financial help (*Yes*)	85	84	77	79	83	86	0	0
A couple may divorce if they have no children (*Yes*)	71	78	79	51	49	52	0	+++
A couple may divorce if they have children (*Yes*)	32	38	33	39	36	39	0	0
Authority Hierarchy								
Submission to authority (*Proud of*)	54	52	54	65	56	50	+×	0
Pleasing superiors (*Proud of*)	10	6	8	63	60	55	+	------
Younger people respect older people (*Yes*)[a]	98	97	97	95	94	94	0	0
Express your opinions when you disagree with a senior (*Yes*)	23	24	22	75	81	80	0	------

(*Continues*)

TABLE 5.4 (Continued)

Value Items	China Survey			U.S. Survey			Low-High	China-U.S.
	Low	Med.	High	Low	Med.	High		
Interpersonal Relationships								
Human nature is benign or evil? (Benign)	28	31	36	80	80	82	–	––––––
Harmony is precious (Proud of)	45	51	50	33	21	20	0×	+++
Generosity and virtues (Proud of)	56	59	59	94	92	91	0	––––
Tolerance, propriety, and deference (Proud of)	47	47	50	89	95	95	–	–––––
Importance of connections (Important)b	71	71	64	83	84	90	0×	–
Using connections to solve problems (Yes)	73	73	70	13	10	12	0	++++++
Other								
Loyalty to state (Proud of)	77	77	73	93	91	91	0	– –
Respect tradition (Proud of)	59	54	57	86	82	83	0	–––
Diligence and frugality (Proud of)	91	90	91	82	82	76	0	++

(Continues)

TABLE 5.4 *(Continued)*

| Value Items | China Survey | | | U.S. Survey | | | | |
	Low	Med.	High	Low	Med.	High	Low-High	China-U.S.
Necessary to have religious faith (*Yes*)	25	29	29	74	67	61	0×	----

Notes: The income categories are based on within-nation standardized distributions. The number of cases in each column varies from one value item to another due to missing cases and the fact that not all the items were used in all the U.S. surveys.

Cell entries in the last two columns indicate the proportional differences. The magnitude of a difference is indicated by the number of signs. The notations are:

+ = a significantly higher proportion among the low income category or in the China sample.
− = a significantly lower proportion among the low income category or in the China sample.
× = a significant interaction.
0 = no significant difference.

[a]The "yes" and "definite yes" categories were combined.
[b]The "important" and "very important" categories were combined.

centage points from the lowest to the highest income group.) For one item (financial help for aging parents) the results were monotonic in both surveys, but in opposite directions and in only slight degree at that.

The implications of income for values are, upon close inspection of Table 5.4, often linear, and more often than not these are similarly linear for the two countries. In the area of male-female relationships, for example, not only were there the two parallel monotonic relationships we noted above, but there were also subtler (admittedly slight in magnitude) parallels as well. The high-income group was in both samples lowest, for example, on the male-female differentiation items and highest on the teen-pregnancy item. In both samples the lowest income group was also lowest in endorsing men and women living together and receiving equal pay, and the highest income group was the least likely to say that love is the most important factor in choosing a mate. Apart from this last, ambiguous, item all these findings are in accord with a general hypothesis that traditional male relationships will be more widely endorsed in the lower-income strata of society.

The most conspicuous overall impression of Table 5.4 is that income does not have much effect on the cultural values of the Chinese respondents. (Perhaps this conclusion testifies to the success of communistic practices, which putatively aim at producing a "classless society.") Of the eighty-one comparisons between proportions within each line of the table, only nine (11 percent) reached significance in the Chinese sample, and the largest difference was just 10 percent. This was the distance between the low and middle-income categories ($p < .01$) regarding the value of "a house full of children and grandchildren." The middle- and high-income groups did not differ significantly on this item.

Even in the American sample, where we had substantial income variation, income did not correlate strongly with the values we asked about in our survey. Again looking at the eighty-one comparisons between row entries in Table 5.4, for the U.S. respondents only fifteen (19 percent) produced significant differences. Of the twelve monotonic relationships, only five involved a difference as large as 10 percent between the low- and high-income subsamples. While income did appear to have more effects on the American respondents than the Chinese, and while the differences were greater than one would expect by chance, they are not impressive as a set.

As with education, we found some instances where the effects of income seemed to be opposite in the two countries. This kind of interaction occurred in some degree for the traditional Confucian values of harmony, generosity, and religious faith, which were endorsed in China least often by the low-income group; in the United States, the low-income respondents were the ones most likely to agree with these items, although not all the differences in this pattern were significant. These results are mindful of our similar findings for education (Table 5.3) and may be attributable to the education-income correlation, or to a more general effect of one's social status, which is an unmeasured correlate of both these variables in our survey.

Effects of Occupational Categories

The economic systems of China and the United States are so very different that literal comparisons of occupations might seem meaningless. We have already examined here two related features, education and income, that are also quite different in the two countries and that are also related to occupation. For example, occupations are often ranked in order of prestige, and this ordering invariably turns out to be correlated with the education required to enter a field and the income one receives from working in it. We will not in this chapter attempt to replow that ground. We can, however, make some comparisons of certain generic categories of work that are defined in common ways in both countries. Some of our value questions refer specifically to the workplace (e.g., "pleasing superiors") and thus might produce different results depending upon the occupational composition of the samples from the two countries. So our first purpose here is to check on the possibility that differences reported in Chapter 4 are due to the differing distributions of respondents in the two samples across types of work situation. Our second purpose here is to inquire into possible correspondences between occupation and cultural values.

For our first-order tests, of the robustness of our overall findings, we grouped occupations into four categories that we consider to represent reasonable commonalities between the two nations in the nature of activities involved in each occupational category: labor, service workers, professionals, and managerials. People who did not fit into one of these categories were excluded from this analysis.

Our most general finding was that controlling for occupation does not diminish the overall cross-national differences in cultural values. Overall, seventeen of the twenty-two significant cross-national differences remained significant across all four occupational categories, and three retained their significance in some specific occupational categories. Only two of the twenty-two were no longer significant in any of the four occupational categories. There were also three additional occupation-specific cross-national differences.

The two significant cross-national differences that disappear when we control for occupation were on "aging parents cared for by their adult children" and "respecting older people." Neither of these had been noted as a major difference between the two samples in Chapter 4.

The three additional significant cross-national differences had to do with "differentiation between men and women," "chastity for women," and "submission to authority." American laborers endorsed the idea of "differentiation between men and women" more by a margin of 8 percent when compared with their Chinese counterparts (p<.01). In the service industry, more Chinese than American respondents (by 14 percent) accepted the notion of "chastity for women" (p<.01), and 13 percent more American than Chinese respondents in this industry endorsed "submission to authority" (p<.01).

The partial replications of the overall cross-national differences came primarily from the labor and service categories. Chinese respondents in these industries were less likely (p<.01) than their American counterparts to accept the idea of equal pay for equal work for men and women by margins of 7 percent and 12 percent, respectively. The same was true with regard to "benevolent fathers and filial sons," by 15 percent in the labor category and 12 percent in the service category. Also in the service industry, more Chinese respondents endorsed the idea of "diligence and frugality" than did their American counterparts.

Within each nation, the occupational categories did not produce many differences in values. In the China sample, only 7 of the 108 (or 6.5 percent) comparisons between occupations on each value produced a significant (p<.05) difference. In the U.S. sample, just 9 of the 108 (or 8.3 percent) percentage comparisons were significant. These findings are not much better than chance, and only a few of the differences we did find seemed to be conceptually meaningful.

One general finding in both nations was that a much higher proportion of people in the labor and service sectors endorsed the notion of obedient wives, compared with those in professional and managerial occupations. More respondents in service industry accepted the notion of "pleasing superiors" than in the other occupational categories. These results are roughly consistent with the sociological evidence showing greater authoritarian and conformist tendencies among the working class, compared with the middle class (e.g., Kohn 1979; Alwin 1988). But overall our findings on occupation are rather meager.

In Table 5.5 we have summarized the results for just two of the occupational categories, labor and professional. These two kinds of work clearly contrast, in any society, and they serve to illustrate how little difference occupation makes to our results. To show all four categories that we compared would take twice as much space but would not add appreciably to the picture. There are eight items for which the labor-professional differ-

TABLE 5.5   Cross-National Differences in Values by Occupation (in percentages)

Value Items	China Survey		U.S. Survey		Labor-Prof.	China-U.S.
	Labor	Prof.	Labor	Prof.		
Male-Female Relationships						
Differentiation between men and women (*Proud of*)	12	12	19	8	+×	0
Three obediences and four virtues (*Proud of*)	10	4	45	25	++×	---
Chastity for women (*Proud of*)	36	25	33	23	++	0
Family losing face for teenager's pregnancy (*Yes*)	88	89	43	41	0	------
A couple live together before marriage (*All right*)	12	15	62	65	0	------
Love is the most important in choosing a mate (*Yes*)	24	27	82	78	0	------
Equal pay for equal work for men and women (*same pay*)	80	92	91	97	−	−
Family Relationships						
Benevolent fathers and filial sons (*Proud of*)	61	66	79	71	0×	--
A house full of children and grandchildren (*Proud of*)	27	11	58	50	++	----
Aging parents cared for by their children (*Yes*)	83	75	78	78	0	0
Aging parents ask their children for financial help (*Yes*)	85	80	83	86	0	0

(Continues)

TABLE 5.5   *(Continued)*

| Value Items | China Survey | | U.S. Survey | | Labor-Prof. | China-U.S. |
	Labor	Prof.	Labor	Prof.		
A couple may divorce if they have no children (*Yes*)	72	87	48	48	0×	++++
A couple may divorce if they have children (*Yes*)	31	44	32	38	–	0
Authority hierarchy						
Submission to authority (*Proud of*)	54	51	62	51	+	0
Pleasing superiors (*Proud of*)	8	3	67	57	+	------
Younger people respect older people (*Yes*)a	98	97	95	93	0	0
Express your opinions when you disagree with a senior(*Yes*)	25	17	77	82	0×	------
Interpersonal Relationships						
Human nature is benign or evil? (*Benign*)	31	26	81	76	0	------
Harmony is precious (*Proud of*)	47	52	32	17	0××	+++
Generosity and virtues (*Proud of*)	58	62	93	92	0	---
Tolerance, propriety, and deference (*Proud of*)	45	51	92	96	0	-----
Importance of connections (*Important*)b	75	70	84	90	0×	--
Using connections to solve problems (*Yes*)	77	71	12	11	0	+++++++

(Continues)

TABLE 5.5 *(Continued)*

Value Items	China Survey		U.S. Survey		Labor- Prof.	China- U.S.
	Labor	Prof.	Labor	Prof.		
Other						
Loyalty to state (*Proud of*)	75	77	91	90	0	--
Respect tradition (*Proud of*)	56	49	84	80	+	----
Diligence and frugality (*Proud of*)	87	90	88	83	0	0
Necessary to have religious faith (*Yes*)	28	33	67	61	0×	-----

Notes: Only those respondents who were classified into labor/agriculture and professional categories are represented in this table. The number of cases varies from one comparison to another due to missing data. In the U.S. survey, some of the value questions were not asked at all six sites. The first four columns show the raw proportions in each occupation within each nation. The fifth column indicates the direction of differences between occupational categories after controlling for nation. The sixth column indicates the between-nations differences after controlling for occupational categories. Similar to Table 4.1, the magnitude of differences is indicated by number of plus or minus signs. Unlike Table 4.1, the last column simply indicates the result of subtracting the U.S. figures from the China figures.

[a]The "yes" and "definite yes" categories are combined.
[b]The "very important" and "important" categories are combined

ence is significant and consistent across nations: Professionals were less supportive of the survey statements on behalf of wifely obedience, chastity for women, a house full of children and grandchildren, submission to authority, pleasing superiors, and respect for tradition. Professionals were also, in both countries, more supportive of equal pay for equal work and divorce (given children). In all these respects we could say that the professionals are less traditional in their viewpoint.

These occupational differences in Table 5.5 were small, however, and the majority of items showed no significant differences between labor and professional workers. There were eight items, though, on which the labor-professional differences were in opposite directions in the two countries. For each of these, the direction in the United States was the expected one, that is, that professionals were the less traditional group; in China, professionals gave more traditional answers than laborers. The strongest interaction of this form is on the "harmony" item, where most of the difference was found in the U.S. sample. This could be due to different meanings of the value statement in the two cultures. While to many in China, interpersonal harmony is interpreted as a return to "normality" after decades of practicing Mao's "struggle philosophy," reaching such harmony by "yielding to other's wishes" is contradictory to the independence cherished by American professionals. There were also fairly sizable interactions for the questions on filial sons, on expressing differences to a senior, and on religious faith. These results are similar to, but not as strong as, the parallel findings for education (above). The interactions mostly occur for questions where there is a very large U.S.-China difference, and in no case did the lower occupational group in the United States approach that of the upper group in the Chinese sample. What we see in these interactions is mainly a tendency for the professional Chinese to express traditional views that have been opposed by the regime in power in China for some decades. This may be evidence that those traditional values remain in the culture, but are suppressed. There is no way to test such a premise with the kinds of data available to us. But the pattern observed in Table 5.5 is largely consistent with those observed with age and education. For those younger, better educated, and holding professional jobs in China, there seems to be a modest revival of traditional Confucian values.

Effects of Marital Status

We expected marital status to affect some of the values concerning male-female and family relationships, if only due to situational perceptions. That is, we do not expect the fact of getting married to affect one's cultural values at any deep level, but there is good reason to imagine that married people might hold somewhat different operational norms for interpersonal behavior in the context of marriage and the family. Table 5.6 examines the differences we found, which turned out to be few and small.

Marital status as a variable for empirical analysis presented us with several problems: Most people in each sample are married, and married people tend to be older than single people. In China we had so few widowed ($N=49$) and divorced ($N=27$) respondents that we did not include these categories in the analysis. The confounding effects of age remain in Table 5.6, but will be removed from the effects of marital status in our multivariate analyses (Chapter 7).

Overall, marital status had little effect on the observed cross-national

TABLE 5.6 Cross-National Differences in Values by Marital Status (percentages)

Value Items	China Survey		U.S. Survey		Single-Married[a]	China-U.S.[b]
	Single	Married	Single	Married		
Male-Female Relationships						
Differentiation between men and women (*Proud of*)	8	11	12	12	0	0
Three obediences and four virtues (*Proud of*)	9	8	27	30	0	--
Chastity for women (*Proud of*)	33	33	23	33	−x	+
Family losing face for teenager's pregnancy (*Yes*)	80	86	42	41	0	+++++
A couple live together before marriage (*All right*)	20	9	66	55	++	-----
Love is the most important in choosing a mate (*Yes*)	28	22	77	80	0	------
Equal pay for equal work for men and women (*same pay*)	80	84	91	94	0	--
Family Relationships						
Benevolent fathers and filial sons (*Proud of*)	65	62	72	75	0	--
A house full of children and grandchildren (*Proud of*)	24	21	48	57	0x	---
Aging parents cared by their children (*Yes*)	79	80	77	76	0	0
Aging parents ask their children for financial help (*Yes*)	84	83	83	84	0	0
A couple may divorce if they have no children (*Yes*)	82	76	50	48	0	+++
A couple may divorce if they have children (*Yes*)	46	33	36	36	+x	0

(Continues)

TABLE 5.6   *(Continued)*

Value Items	China Survey		U.S. Survey		Single-Married[a]	China-U.S.[b]
	Single	Married	Single	Married		
Authority hierarchy						
Submission to authority (*Proud of*)	48	53	54	58	0	−
Pleasing superiors (*Proud of*)	6	8	53	61	−	−−−−−−
Younger people respect older people (*Yes*)[c]	97	98	93	95	0	0
Express your opinions when you disagree with a senior(*Yes*)	24	23	81	77	0	−−−−−−
Interpersonal Relationships						
Human nature is benign or evil? (*Benign*)	26	32	81	78	0	−−−−−−
Harmony is precious (*Proud of*)	48	50	24	23	0	+++
Generosity and virtues (*Proud of*)	60	58	93	92	0	−−−−
Tolerance, propriety, and deference (*Proud of*)	47	47	94	95	0	−−−−−
Importance of connections (*Important*)[d]	75	69	86	84	0	−−
Using connections to solve problems (*Yes*)	77	72	12	9	0	++++++
Other						
Loyalty to state (*Proud of*)	82	76	87	93	0×	−−
Respect tradition (*Proud of*)	51	56	80	84	0	−−−
Diligence and frugality (*Proud of*)	80	92	78	81	−	+

(Continues)

TABLE 5.6 *(Continued)*

Value Items	China Survey		U.S. Survey		Single-Married[a]	China-U.S.[b]
	Single	*Married*	*Single*	*Married*		
Necessary to have religious faith *(Yes)*	28	29	65	67	0	-----

Note: Cell entries in the first four columns are the percentages in each marital category who gave the listed response to each item. The number of cases varies from one comparison to another due to missing values. In the U.S. surveys, some of the value questions were not asked at all six sites.

[a] The plus and minus signs in this column show the direction of differences between marital status categories after controlling for nation. The magnitude of differences is indicated by number of plus or minus signs.

[b] The plus and minus signs in this column show the direction and magnitudes of the between-nation differences after controlling for marital status. We subtracted the percentages in the U.S. sample from the corresponding percentages in the China sample. They do not mean the same thing as in Table 4.1.

[c] The "yes" and "definite yes" categories are combined.

[d] The "very important" and "important" categories are combined.

differences: for eighteen out of the twenty-two differences noted in Chapter 4, the result remains the same when marital status is controlled. Three of the remaining four differences were replicated within one of the marital status categories, which means that only one of the twenty-two was no longer significant with this control. Meanwhile, two additional U.S.-China differences emerged within one marital status category.

The three partial replications of the significant cross-national differences resulted from a lack of significance when we compared the single people, that is, the smaller subsample group of respondents. The significant (all $p < .01$) differences that were found only between the two sets of married respondents were on whether aging parents should be cared for by their children, "loyalty to the state," and "diligence and frugality." The married Chinese were significantly more supportive of the first and third of these items; the married Americans were higher on loyalty to the state.

Diligence and frugality was one of the few items that married respondents in both countries more often endorsed, so there is both an effect of marriage and an interaction. For the married Chinese, this item may not be so much a value as a pragmatic choice forced upon them by conditions of low wages, high inflation, and crowded housing.[8]

Marital status did not have much net impact on the value items. In both nations, singles are much more likely than married respondents to accept premarital cohabitation (both at p<.01). This probably indicates a bit of self-interest, not an enduring value difference. Married people are more likely in both countries to be proud of the tradition of pleasing superiors, which may bespeak a slight conservatism that accompanies marital responsibilities.

There were a few weak interactions, where the effects of marital status were opposite in the two countries: Both "loyalty to the state" and "a house full of children and grandchildren" were endorsed more often by the married in the United States but by singles in China. The latter finding is probably additional evidence of the problems that beset a married couple with children in contemporary China. One-sided interactions are found on two other items: In the United States, singles are less likely than the married to prize chastity for women, and in China singles are more likely to approve of divorce when there are children involved; in each case there is no difference according to marital status in the other country.

These are almost all slight differences that do not disturb the overall picture we have developed in our earlier analyses. Indeed, almost all of the findings with regard to marital status could be explained by the larger, parallel differences noted above (Table 5.2) with regard to age cohorts. Single people are, almost by definition, younger as a group than are the married, and it is likely that even the few small marital status effects we have noted here will be eliminated when we control simultaneously for these correlated factors in multiple regression (Chapter 7).

A Brief Summary

One of our objectives in this chapter has been to test the robustness of the cross-national differences we reported in Table 4.1. The overwhelming conclusion is that we have found very little evidence for an alternative explanation apart from our original conclusion that there are some large differences in cultural values between China and the United States. In each test against a demographic variable here, some 80 percent of the twenty-two significant differences between the two nations held up at each level of the partitioning variable. There is no case where a between-nation difference could be explained away as an artifact of different sample compositions, despite the enormous differences between the two samples on structurally determined factors such as education, income, and occupation. The two samples are simply located in very different value planes.

The analyses in this chapter have a second purpose too. We have been asking along the way how each of these demographic variables affects the values in our survey and whether they have the same effect in each country. We hoped that such analyses would shed some light on the processes of cultural change. For example, we have kept track of a general hypothesis that there is a linear progression toward greater "modernity" in cultural values from the old to the young and from low to high levels of education, income, and occupation. We have also kept in mind that one's particular social status (e.g., occupation, gender, age) might affect one's answers to questions that directly concern that status. Do men and women hold different values about husband-wife norms? Do young and old, or professional and labor workers, hold different views on superior-subordinate relations? In some cases we have found such differences, although the results were not especially in accord with a simple-minded "self-interest" prediction.

The three most important variables in explaining variations in cultural values within each sample have been age, gender, and education. For each, we found some surprising differences in the patterns of the within-nation relationships between these variables and the value items. For example, we found opposing age-related patterns between the two nations concerning chastity and divorce. In general, the evidence reveals much more than a linear progression, from the old to the young age groups, toward less "traditionalism" in values. This is inconsistent with the modernization theory. For many traditional values, we found education predictably (according to the modernization theory) eroding support for the statements of the traditional ideas in the U.S. sample; but in China the reverse was true. More-educated respondents were more traditional, perhaps in defiance of heavy-handed governmental attempts to eradicate traditions that many people still feel are valuable guides to daily living. Similar patterns were found with regard to age cohort differences. These interactions between nation on the one hand and education and age on the other were echoed, more weakly, in the analyses on income and occupation, which along with marital status proved not to be important demographic predictors of values in this study.

There are generalizations to be made. In both countries, males more often endorsed "differentiation between men and women" and valued romantic love as the most important consideration in selecting a mate, for example. Education consistently worked as a force for greater openness in male-female relationships and family relationships. So for the most part did age; fewer younger respondents accepted most of the traditional male-female and family values. There probably is a general process under way, in both countries, from "traditionalism" to "modernity" in some cultural values concerning male-female and family relationships. But this theoretical pattern certainly does not capture all the findings revealed here. Value endorsement often turns out to be an indication of pragmatic concerns, closely related to social and historical conditions that influence people's lives directly.

Our analysis is complicated by a number of factors, chief among which is the problematic of cross-country equivalence. It has been obvious from the beginning that we could assume no more than a rough equivalence in the meanings of the value items in the two cultures. We have noted several instances where a finding was probably due to differences in the context in which people responded to questions that we had intended to be identical. Beyond the non-equivalence of value measures, even our demographic measures may mean somewhat different things in the two countries. Even a variable as fixed and unarguable as age or gender has different implications where much of the culture has traditionally been built around it, especially when there have been major pressures toward change in the relationships it defines. And of course the enormous structural differences between China and the United States in their educational, monetary, and economic arrangements have forced us to interpret the standard demographics of education, income, and occupation in only relative, not absolute, fashion. What should be surprising is how *few* differences we found on some of these factors, considering that they carry such very distinct sociological and psychological meanings in the two countries. While the similarities in the patterns of relationships between these demographic variables and many of the value items strengthen our confidence in the comparability of the variables involved, the absolute proportional differences in values across categories of a demographic variable pose difficulties in interpretation. Our interpretations are only valid within the limitations of our knowledge of the two societies and our assumptions about the measures.

Notes

1. In this study, the term "traditional" is used to refer to the codified Confucian ideas and values. This narrow working definition is necessary to avoid other ideologically laden connotations of the term.

2. The assumption that only men benefit from the prescribed male-female relationship may be questionable. Traditional role prescriptions insure many benefits for a wife in return for her submission. This issue is far from being thoroughly resolved in modern feminist theory.

3. Our characterization of these eras can only be approximate and is also offset by several years. That is, if we assume that everyone in each country is socialized at about the same age, that age would have come historically earlier in China since our U.S. interviews were conducted two or three years after the

China survey that we are reporting here. This difference could be exacerbated, too, if the end of one's schooling marks the critical phase of socialization to adult values; most of our Chinese respondents completed their education with high school, which is to say they were several years younger than the more typically college-educated Americans in our sample.

4. We are not aware of any statistical study showing increases in sexual promiscuity in China. But social concern has been rising in the past few years, to judge by the frequent news articles, columns, and editorials appearing in Chinese newspapers and magazines. Some evidence of an increase in extramarital and premarital sex is also offered in Zhang Xin-xin's work (1989). Of course, it is possible that the generally more open atmosphere of recent years has made reports of sexual activity more available without any real change in what people are doing.

5. Opposing the rigid notion of postmarital fidelity had been an important part of the antitraditional and anti-Confucian discourse in the May 4th tradition. Dr. Haiou Yang pointed out to us that her research shows that many older women had suffered under the traditional "chastity" rule. In that value system, a widow in effect had to sacrifice her entire life to her dead husband's family. Our Chinese respondents over age fifty may well remember such cases, and it is they who account for the negative age trend in Table 5.2. The women's rights movement in China has been intertwined with major political upheavals in the past fifty years. The cry for women's liberation from the male-centered value system and social relationships has been an important part of the overall revolutionary discourse in China. In the United States, the women's movement gained some impetus from the general pressure toward social change during the Vietnam War, but women's rights legislation has, from suffrage to state equal rights amendments, not been closely associated with other kinds of reforms.

6. Notably, all Zhang's (1989) instances of extramarital affairs, divorce, and marriage crisis involve people from this age cohort.

7. Almost all general population surveys show that income is positively related to educational level in the United States. But the comparable relationship is much weaker in China. Part of the larger income effects that we expect in the United States could be a result of education and will disappear in later regression analyses when we control for these two variables simultaneously. See Chapter 7.

8. In China, single people mainly use their own salaries to support themselves, and some even get a supplement from their parents. Married couples, though, have to support themselves, their children, and sometimes their parents as well. And, while many singles live in dormitories or in their parents' houses, married couples often have trouble finding any place to settle their families

6

Configurations of Cultural Values

BECAUSE THIS IS AN EXPLORATORY STUDY in an area where little has been done before, we have proceeded quite methodically to this point. We have examined cultural value items in relation to demographic variables. We have, in the analyses so far, grouped items on the basis of assumed commonalities, which are based on our explication of the value concepts these items represent. But we did not want to force our assumptions upon our data before providing a detailed descriptive account of value prevalence in the two nations. Items were kept separate in statistical tests, so that we could see whether those we thought to be similar in their value implications performed similarly in relation to other variables. Many times they did, although we have also noted a number of instances in which they did not. With that set of detailed analyses behind us, we turn now to tests of our conceptual assumptions.

The idea of cultural values goes beyond endorsement of specific value items in each culture. As we argued in Chapter 2, each culture is characterized by a unique recognizable value *system*, revealed as a unique *configuration* of various values. Different value systems may differ from one another in at least three separate aspects: levels of prevalence of the values that are meaningful to all cultures, different configurations of these commonly meaningful values, and values that are unique to each system. The previous analyses were based on the presumption that the Confucian value items could be interpreted meaningfully in both Chinese and U.S. cultures. Operating under this assumption, we showed some expected (and some surprising) differences between China and the United States in these values. Now we must examine the extent to which these value items indeed were interpreted similarly by the Chinese and U.S. respondents.

Addressing the question of cross-cultural comparability in meanings of the value measures overlaps considerably with another more substantive task. That is to examine how the twenty-seven value items are interrelated in each culture, that is, the configuration of the commonly meaningful value items in each culture. Two cultures could be compared in this respect. In the previous chapters, while analyzing the twenty-seven value items separately, we were not assuming that they represent twenty-seven distinct value dimensions in each culture. Rather, we presume that there are structural relationships among these items. In other words, there are considerably fewer dimensions of values than there are items in our survey. For example, permitting male-female cohabitation before marriage should be related negatively to the value accorded to chastity. It is quite possible that there is such a correspondence in the *covariances* among the value items between the two nations, even though the central tendencies for each item in each country may differ.

These tasks involve comparing intercorrelations among the value items that we presume to be commonly meaningful in the two nations. Identifying the underlying value structure *within each* culture—our substantive task—makes it possible to compare the within-culture value configuration between the two cultures. Such comparisons can shed light on the comparability of the value items that belong together conceptually in both cultures, our measurement task. We know that different languages and cultural contexts furnish meanings to our measures and may lead respondents toward different interpretations and responses to our questions. And yet we have assumed all along that the underlying relationships and the values associated with them are at least analogous, or we would not have undertaken to compare the United States with China at all. We need not only to distill our long roster of items down to a more reliable and cross-culturally comparable set of dimensions, but also to present evidence of the empirical comparability of these value dimensions.

Establishing measurement comparability in a cross-cultural study is a daunting task. We have made a serious effort from the onset of this project to achieve *semantic equivalence* by (1) constructing survey items with similar wordings, (2) adjusting question wording and format to suit the custom and context of each culture, and (3) selecting items that we deemed semantically comparable in each conceptual domain. But that conceptual work only tested our items on ourselves. We now need to examine empirical evidence that sets of items in our questionnaires function as *psychologically equivalent* stimuli in the two cultures (Frey 1970; Przeworski and Teune 1969, 1970). That is, we are testing here the extent to which, in both cultures, an item that was intended to tap a general value orientation is associated with a second item that had approximately the same purpose.

The first kind of evidence needed for establishing cross-cultural equivalence in measurement is similarity in the relationships between items that are designed to measure the same underlying construct (Przeworski and Teune 1970; Nowak 1962). To the extent that a set of items in the two cultures forms cross-culturally parallel factors, these items are considered to be cross-culturally equivalent, that is, they are related to one another similarly in both cultures.

What if these cultural value items do not conform to the same underlying factor structure in the two cultures? In that case, we should consider two possibilities: Either the measures are not equivalent (i.e., they have different meanings) across the two cultures, or else the two cultures contain very different configurations of the values in question. These two possibilities have different theoretical implications, the first implying an operational weakness in the measurement instrument and the second implying genuine cultural differences. But the distinction is really a specious one. Because a value item gains its meaning from its placement in a semantic network of related value items, if a similarly worded value item relates to established cross-culturally common value items differently in two different cultures, then the item is given different meanings in the two cultures. Different value configurations involving one value item imply different meanings of the item in different cultures. Therefore, we rely on the same data to draw inferences of empirical equivalence of value items between two cultures and of cross-cultural comparability in value configurations.

We do not have sufficient data to accomplish all our research goals. For one thing, we do not have measures of all the important values in each culture. (The study was conceived, as noted earlier, in Confucian terms, and gives little consideration to value domains that are considered distinctly Western.) Any attempt to examine value configurations will be incomplete. Second, we do not have well-formulated theories to help us specify precise measurement models that would link indicators of values in each culture to more universal constructs. Our analysis is truly exploratory in nature. But, we do bring some broad common-sense categories to the analysis. We think it is quite appropriate at this stage to maintain this level of balance between conceptual imposition and data exploration in our analysis.

We have already differentiated four conceptual domains, into which many of our survey questions have been grouped: male-female relationships, family relationships, hierarchical relationships, and general interpersonal relationships. Each of these is rather clearly specified in the Confucian tradition, so that we can identify a presumably "traditional" end of each continuum of survey responses in both countries. We assumed that these four domains are universally present in any society and that they deal with four of the most fundamental social relationships. These are our conceptual impositions upon the data. We do not consider it too strong an imposition by identifying *a priori* the four domains of social relationships. We did have some theoretical guidance from sociological research on values and social institutions, as well as from cultural anthropological studies (Williams 1970; Hsu 1981), but this guidance was rather general in nature. Ours is the first survey we know of that has dealt with these specific value domains at a detailed empirical level of inquiry. Some subjective imposition drawing on our personal knowledge of the two cultures is necessary.

Our standard procedure here is to conduct a factor analysis of the cultural value items in each of these domains separately for the Chinese and American samples. To the extent that the items in each domain produce similar *structural patterns* in the two cultures, we should be more confident of their cross-cultural equivalence and of the validity of that conceptual domain.

For the factor analyses, all value measures were restored to their original scales. In the China survey, responses were measured on either three-point or two-point scales (except for the two items concerning personal connections, which used five-point response scales). In the U.S. surveys, all responses were recorded on five-point Likert scales. These vagaries of measurement produced differences in reliability and skewness of the empirical distributions in the two countries, meaning that the inter-item correlations in China tended to be lower than those in the U.S. survey. Given all these differences, it is quite clear that the data impose severe difficulties upon any attempt at identifying structural similarities between the two cultures. Operating under such constraints, if cross-cultural similarities in value configurations are observed, we would be able to place greater confidence in the results.

The analyses we report here represent one step in an exploratory process. We are searching for clues, rather than testing hypotheses, about the configurations of cultural values in China and the United States. Given this exploratory approach, we did not confine our factor analysis to a single, predetermined model, such as to assume either orthogonal or correlated factors. There is no theoretical rationale to support either kind of model to the exclusion of the other. Instead, both orthogonal and correlated structures were fitted to the data, on the assumption that we would learn most from finding which solution provides the better fit to the data. As it turned out, none of the correlated structures produced a significantly improved solution over the simpler orthogonal structure (due largely to the modest raw correlations between items). Accordingly, only the solution with orthogonal structure is reported here, in each domain.

Male-Female Relationships

We expected at least two underlying factors to emerge from the seven value items in the male-female domain: traditional views on sexual relationships and on equal status of women. One item in this group, "Love is

TABLE 6.1   Factor Analysis of Value Items Related to Male-Female Relationships
(Principal Components with Varimax Rotation)

Value Items	China Survey		U.S. Survey	
	I	II	I	II
A couple live together before marriage (*All right*)		−.73	−.85	
Family losing face for teenager's pregnancy (*Yes*)		.69	.42	
Chastity for women (*Proud of*)	.70		.85	
Three obediences and four virtues (*Proud of*)	.72		.39	.68
Differentiation between men and women (*Proud of*)	.60			.77
Equal pay for equal work for men and women (*same pay*)		.47		−.77
Percentage of variance	24.2	20.6	38.7	19.6
Eigenvalue	1.5	1.2	2.3	1.2

Note: The questions in the U.S. surveys used a five-point Likert scale. Cases with missing values were excluded from the analysis. The resulting sample size for the U.S. is *n*=1145. For simplicity, factor loadings below .30 are not shown.

most important in choosing a mate," proved to be anomalous in both cultures, in that it did not relate to the other items or factors consistently. In the China survey, including this item in the factor analysis resulted in a three-factor solution that did not invite meaningful interpretation; in the U.S. data, the "love" question became a single-item factor by itself. Dropping this question, on the other hand, left us with clear and overlapping patterns in both cultures. The resulting factor analysis is presented in Table 6.1.

Each sample produced a two-factor solution regarding male-female relations. In the American survey, the two factors in Table 6.1 seem clear in meaning: the first has mainly to do with sexual relationships (chastity, living together, and teen pregnancy), while the second is related to social and family issues regarding the status of women. Both scales happen to face in the traditional direction, and we interpret them as, respectively, *traditionalism in sexual relationships* and *traditionalism in status of women*.[1]

The China data produced more complexity in terms of literal content, although the factor structure itself was a bit cleaner. Factor I for the Chinese sample contained two items related to women's status, male-female differentiation and obedient wife. The other item that loaded on this factor, chastity for women, would normally be interpreted as related to sexual relations. Similarly, the second factor consisted mainly of two items related to sexual relations, living together before marriage and family losing face for a pregnant teen. But it also included one status question, equal pay for equal work.

This factor analysis thus shows both similarities and differences in the interrelationships among the value items on male-female relationships. Upon closer examination, one explanation emerges. It takes us back to the issue of sign-referent separation. The first factor for the Chinese sample consists of three traditional Confucian *phrases*—"chastity for women," "three obediences and four virtues," and "differentiation between men and women." Although they might designate different value referents in Confucianism, they were forced to a closer proximity by all being targets of repeated propaganda campaigns.[2] But this unique meaning of these items in the China survey does not seem to overshadow the similarities between the two samples. We note that the conceptually anomalous item on each factor—the one that does not conform to our expectations, nor to the factor structure in the U.S. survey—has the weakest loading on the Chinese factor in Table 6.1. Therefore, we conclude that, while colored somewhat by the anti-Confucian propaganda effect that attaches to certain traditional phrases, the overall pattern in China is similar to that in the U.S. That is, there is a sexual relations issue, and there is a status of women issue. The two are conceptually distinct, and in both cultures these factors would seem reasonably coherent if we imagine what the Chinese results would be if the specific phrases were not associated with a particular political program.

Overall, a two-factor solution worked reasonably well in both samples. The two factors accounted for nearly 45 percent of the total variance in the China survey, 54 percent in the U.S. sample. The eigenvalues are, for both factors in both samples, well above 1.0—which is the level represented when a factor explains no more of the common variance than would a single item. The more dominant of the two factors in the United States is the one involving sexual relationships, which may mean that traditionalism in male-female relations is mainly sexual in its definition. In China, there is more of a balance between sexual traditionalism and traditional male-female status relationships. While these hints of a difference would accord with our general sense of differences between the two cultures, we consider the similarities to be more striking.

The underlying structure of cultural values concerning male-female relationships, then, seems to us reasonably consistent cross-culturally, if we allow for the Chinese respondents' sensitivity to politically controversial phraseology, despite the overwhelming differences in the prevalence of these values in the two cultures. Recall that in our first-order comparisons (Table 4.1), male-female relationships produced some of the largest differences between the two samples; it is encouraging for our comparative approach that the commonalities between items are *similarly structured* in these two contrasting cultures. Still, we need to be responsive to our data. We did not find the same factor structure in this domain of values, and it behooves us to withhold judgment on the conclusion we are entertaining, that the patterns are similar in the two countries even when absolute differences in acceptance of certain traditional values may be rather large.

Family Relationships

The expected similarity in the patterns of relationships among value items in the family relationship domain is shown clearly in Table 6.2. In each survey, the same three factors emerged from the analysis, although the China data are weak in that the eigenvalue for the third factor barely reaches unity. We have preserved all three factors so that the similarity between the two samples is clear. Not only is the structure quite clean in each case—every factor consists of two items, with no secondary loadings to report—but the relative strengths of the factors are so similar that they appear in the same order in the two samples.

This pattern suggests that the two cultures share three underlying family relationships value dimensions, even though the levels of prevalence were in some respects quite different (see Chapters 4 and 5). The first factor is clearly *permissiveness toward divorce;* the second is *obligation for parent care;* and the third consists of *vertical kinship ties.* Together, these three factors accounted for 60 and 68 percent of variance in the China and U.S. surveys, respectively. Each item's factor loading is high, as might be expected on the basis of commonality of wording for the first

TABLE 6.2   Factor Analysis of Value Items Related to Family Relationships (Principal Components with Varimax Rotation)

Value Items	China Survey			U.S. Survey		
	I	II	III	I	II	III
A couple should divorce if they have no kids (*Yes*)	.76			.90		
A couple should divorce if they have kids (*Yes*)	.77			.90		
Aging parents cared for by their kids (*Yes*)		.76			.84	
Aging parents ask their kids for financial help (*Yes*)		.80			.85	
Benevolent fathers and filial sons (*Proud of*)			.78			.75
A house full of children and grandchildren (*Proud of*)			.64			.76
Percentage of variance	23.1	20.3	16.5	28.2	24.6	17.5
Eigenvalue	1.4	1.2	1.0	1.7	1.5	1.1

Note: The questions in the U.S. surveys used a five-point Likert scale. Cases with missing values were excluded from the analysis. The resulting sample size for the U.S. sample is $n=1619$. For simplicity, factor loadings below .30 are not shown.

two factors and the commonality of traditional phraseology for the third.

It is instructive to compare these parallel between-item structures for the two samples with the considerable differences we found for the levels of prevalence on these items. In Table 4.1 we reported that the Chinese gave the more traditional responses on the items loaded on Factors I and II here; the U.S. respondents gave the more traditional responses on the Factor III items. But since the latter were phrases from the attacked tradition in China, we might infer that in the values of family relationships overall the Chinese are more traditional—although not by much.

We also noted quite a few interactions for these items, between country and such demographics as age and education (Chapter 5). So the picture from the previous two chapters is not one of cross-cultural similarity in prevalence. But the meaning of the three dimensions in question seems to be comparable in the two cultures.

The similarities of factor structure, in other words, encourage us to interpret the differences in the locations of the two cultures on these common underlying dimensions; they are not apples and oranges. The only difference we found in this factor analysis was the relatively weaker covariations among the items in the China sample. This difference was expected on the basis of the less fine-grained (and hence less reliable) measurement scales used in the China survey. In our later analyses we can be confident that, as we sum items to create indices that represent each of these dimensions, we are not sacrificing measurement validity just to improve reliability. We will be merging variances that share a good deal of commonality.

Hierarchical Relationships

Again, although the two samples produced enormous differences in the levels of agreement on several of the items dealing with the authority hierarchy (see Table 4.1), they are quite similar in the structuring of these cultural values. Table 6.3 presents the factor analysis, which yields the same two factors in each sample: *acceptance of authority hierarchy* and *acceptance of seniority hierarchy*. These two factors accounted for 56 percent and 58 percent of the total variance among the items in the two samples respectively.

There are a couple of differences between the two samples in this value domain. First, the second factor barely reached unity in its eigenvalue, indicating it is a very weak factor. Second, the item on younger people respecting older people is located closer to the first factor, authority hierarchy, than to the second one, where it would seem to belong conceptually. However, in general, the similarities, both in terms of the underlying dimensions and the relative weights of the individual items on each dimension, are more striking than the differences.

The first factor in both samples is the one involving superiors, or those in authority. In China, this commonality could be ascribed to phraseology, as these two items used traditional Confucian wording; but the fact that we find the same first factor in the United States, where traditional Chinese phrasing and government campaigns directed against it are

TABLE 6.3   Factor Analysis of Value Items Related to Seniority and Authority
Hierarchy (Principal Components with Varimax Rotation)

Value Items	China Survey		U.S. Survey	
	I	II	I	II
Express your opinions when you disagree with a senior (*Yes*)		.78		.95
Younger people should respect older people (*Yes*)	.35	.69	.36	.30
Pleasing superiors (*Proud of*)	.64		.77	
Submission to authority (*Proud of*)	.73		.80	
Percentage of variance	28.7	27.3	34.1	24.9
Eigenvalue	1.2	1.1	1.4	1.0

Note: The measures in the U.S. surveys used a five-point Likert scale. Cases with
missing values were excluded from the analysis. The resulting sample size for the
U.S. sample is $n=1577$. For simplicity, factor loadings below .30 are not shown.

completely unknown, suggests that this is a coherent underlying dimension.

In addition, Table 6.3 shows that in both samples, seniority and authority overlap somewhat through the item of "respecting older people." This result could be accounted for by the fact that in the day-to-day world seniority and authority tend to be correlated; because the typical career trajectory is upward over time, for most people the boss is more often than not older as well. Furthermore, in the China sample, "respecting older people" overlaps verbally with the two items on authority, all being traditional phrases.

At the least, it seems justified to conclude that authority and seniority hierarchies exist and that deference within those structures is a common facet of social relationships in both countries. This means that we can treat each of these as a general domain of values and interpret them comparatively, even though endorsement of particular statements may vary a great deal between China and the United States.

General Interpersonal Relationships

Earlier we found large differences between China and the United States in the levels of endorsement of the items concerning interpersonal relationships in general (Table 4.1). We continue to find some differences in Table 6.4, where we examine the structure of these items as a set. The two samples are similar in that the first factor includes the items about tolerance and generosity, and the second includes the two items about connections; but they also differ in some ways. Specifically, in China the interpersonal harmony item is associated more closely with the other two items that are phrased in the traditional way, whereas in the United States the comparable "harmony" item loads (negatively) with "connections." In general, the factor structure in Table 6.4 is not nearly so "clean" for the U.S. sample as is the case with the Chinese. But this latter clarity of structure again can be explained by their shared locations in the political lexicon as targets of repeated propaganda campaigns.

Despite these differences, the two samples resemble each other in the basic content of the two factors. We might call the first factor *interpersonal kindness* to contrast it with the second factor, which is *interpersonal pragmatism*.[3] The two factors together accounted for 56 percent and 46 percent of total variance among the items in China and the United States, respectively.

In China not only is the first factor virtually "forced" on the data due to the three traditional phrases, the second factor likewise is practically preordained as both items have to do with connections. In the U.S. sample, on the other hand, there is less differentiation between the two factors. Using one's connections carries a negative connotation, in that this item loads negatively on the tolerance/generosity factor, while the interpersonal harmony item loads negatively on the connections factor. It is as if the American respondents see the use of connections as undermining "kinder, gentler" interpersonal relationships, while in China the need to use one's connections is more a fact of daily life; one does not have the moral options that might seem to be open to Americans. We should also note that the first question in the U.S. survey referred to a fairly circumspect course of action: the statement was that one *should* go through *normal* channels before "using connections." This wording might have by contrast delegitimized the next item, on actually "using" connections, as a mode of conduct. It is reasonably clear from Table 6.4 that there are commonalities between at least two sets of items that are similar enough

TABLE 6.4　Factor Analysis of Value Items Related to General Interpersonal Relationships (Principal Components with Varimax Rotation)

	China Survey		U.S. Survey	
Value Items	I	II	I	II
Importance of connections (*Important*)		.81		.53
Using connections to solve problems (*Yes*)		.80	-.50	.45
Tolerance, propriety, and deference (*Proud of*)	.65		.72	
Harmony is precious (*Proud of*)	.75			-.75
Generosity and virtues (*Proud of*)	.71		.71	
Percentage of variance	30.2	25.8	25.7	23.0
Eigenvalue	1.5	1.3	1.3	1.2

Note: The measures in the U.S. surveys used a five-point Likert scale. Cases with missing values were excluded from the analysis. The resulting sample size for the U.S. sample is $n=1554$. For simplicity, factor loadings below .30 are not shown.

between the two countries that we can justifiably use them in parallel fashion as dependent variables in later regression analyses (Chapter 7).

Constructing Value Indices

Compared with the results in the two previous chapters, the factor analyses reported in Tables 6.1 through 6.4 produced some striking similarities between the two cultures. The two cultures in general share similar underlying dimensions of the values measured in each of the four domains. Some specific differences were also shown, and differences that seem to indicate the unique cultural and social conditions in the two nations: In China, the repeated propaganda campaigns have forced the values signified by traditional Confucian phrases into a shared compartment. Whenever these symbolic representations are mixed together with the more behavior-oriented measures, the traditional phrases in China reduce the comparability of the value configurations between China and the United States. But what comes across more strikingly are the similarities revealed by Tables 6.1 through 6.4.

Cross-cultural equivalence means that we can conduct cross-cultural comparisons of cultural values at a higher level of abstraction. For example, we can compare the two cultures in terms of their "traditionalism in male-female sexual relationships" or "rigidity toward divorce" instead item-by-item. Our data appear to lend themselves to summary interpretations, which will make multivariate analysis much less cumbersome.

For this purpose, we constructed nine two-item indices of cultural values based on the factor analysis results. Index construction involved a balancing of the semantic similarities between items with the empirical evidence from factor analysis. For index construction in the domain of male-female relationships, two ambiguous items were eliminated: equal pay for equal work for men and women and chastity for women. These items did not relate consistently in the two countries to other items in the male-female domain (Table 6.1), nor to demographic items (Chapters 4 and 5). In the domain of general interpersonal relationships, the item on interpersonal "harmony" was eliminated from index construction based on the evidence in Table 6.4; the Chinese respondents seem to have revealed equivocal feelings about this item, which refers to a generally desirable state but in politically undesirable wording. Other than these three items, none showed sufficient empirical discrepancies in the factor structures here to warrant their being omitted from index construction.

All together, then, eighteen value items were combined into nine indices of cultural values, two items per index.[4] With only two items in an index, reliability could not be assessed. We can, though, evaluate the internal consistency of the indices by examining the patterns of correlation among the items (see Appendix 2 for the data). When we compare the correlations (underlined) between the items *within* each index with the other, *between*-indices, correlations in the table, we can see that there is a reasonable degree of validity to our groupings. Only 4 percent of the between-indices correlations are greater than the mean of the nine Tau-b coefficients within-indices for the China sample (below diagonal in Appendix 2); for the U.S. sample, only 2 percent of the 144 between-indices correlations are greater than the mean of the 9 within-indices correlation coefficients.[5] The logic of this test is that of discriminant and convergent validation developed by Campbell and Fiske (1959).

Overall, the correlations among the value items are very low, suggesting that there is not a single dimension of cultural values in either China or the United States. The China correlations are notably lower than those for the United States, partly due to the use of different statistics and also due to response scales with more limited variance in the China questionnaire. The Chinese correlations may also be truncated due to those respondents being the target of multiple forces for cultural change over the years (Whyte 1989), plus discrepancies between the Confucian value phrases used in the questionnaire and the more general ideas signified by these phrases.

For most of our nine indices, the component items correlated between one another much more strongly than they do with the items in other indices. In the domain of male-female relationships, for example, the two items measuring traditionalism in sexual relationships ("family losing face" has been reversed) correlated at .22 in the China sample and .17 in the U.S. sample. The two items measuring traditionalism in women's status correlated at .25 in the China sample and .44 in the U.S. sample. All these coefficients are significant at .01 level. The mean correlation between items that we placed in these different indices, within the male-female domain, was .16 in the U.S. sample and .03 for the Chinese respondents. This discriminant validation is important to our later purposes. We may say, though, that the two-index structure is not as clearcut in the United States as it is in China; some Americans responded to questions involving both sexual relationships and gender equality according to a single value premise.

There is also solid convergent-discriminant validity for two of the three indices in the domain of family relationships: permissiveness toward divorce and obligations toward aging parents. For these two indices, the internal correlations were .22 and .20 respectively in the China sample and .58 and .31 respectively in the U.S. sample. These coefficients were higher than any other associations involving these items within their respective samples. However, the items in the third index, traditional kinship ties, did not correlate so strongly as we had expected. In the China sample, the correlation between them was negligible and was exceeded by several other correlations in the matrix that involve the item on "a house full of children and grandchildren."[6] In the U.S. sample, the within-index correlation was significant, but the item "benevolent fathers and filial sons" was more strongly related to several other value items, such as the conformity-related questions about pleasing superiors and submission to authority. The index of traditional kinship ties is thus a weak one for later empirical analyses.

In the third domain, hierarchical relationships, neither index met our minimal criterion of higher internal than external correlations. The index for the seniority hierarchy has internal correlations of .10 and −.02, respectively, in the China and U.S. samples. The index for the authority hierarchy seemed to be more coherent in the U.S. sample with an internal correlation of .32, but it does not appear acceptable in the China sample, with an internal Tau-b of only .05.

The domain of general interpersonal relationships was also ambiguous. In the China sample, the two items measuring interpersonal pragmatism ("connections") were strongly correlated (Tau-b=.30), but the corresponding within-index figure for the Americans was a correlation of .07, probably for reasons we noted in discussing Table 6.4. The interpersonal virtues (tolerance, generosity, and the like) items were correlated at acceptable levels: .18 in the China survey and .22 in the U.S. survey. As noted earlier in this section, we had already discarded some items, such as the virtue of "harmony," which seem to evoke ambiguous meanings.

Testing the Value Indices

Another way of validating these nine indices is to test their ability to distinguish between the U.S. and China samples. This procedure is based on a simple assumption. That is, given the large differences in value prevalence between the two cultures shown in the previous chapters, similar differences at the index level would indicate consistency between items and indices. This procedure will also place all the value indices together in one analytic framework so that some comparisons can be made as to which indices account for the largest U.S.-China differences. Based on the results in Chapter 4, we would expect large differences in male-female relationship indices, with China more traditional than the United States, and in interpersonal relationships, with the Chinese respondents tending to reject the Confucian values. We would not expect significant cross-national differences in the indices concerning divorce and parental care.

The statistical tool for research of this sort is discriminant analysis. In this procedure, we use nation as the grouping variable and the nine value indices as the discriminating variables; all the discriminating variables are forced to enter the equation simultaneously. Because there are just two groups to be separated, there will be one discriminant function. The question is, how strongly do the various indices load on this function, which is a statistical construct that represents the greatest possible separation between groups on a single dimension. The result is reported in Table 6.5.

The power of the discriminant function in this case is quite high, as it should be, considering all the between-nations differences we have noted through Chapters 4 and 5. The canonical correlation *(eta)* is .77, compared to a maximum possible value of 1.00. Interpreted in terms of the square of the correlation coefficient, this means that more than 59 percent of the between-nations separation is accounted for by variance in the discriminant function that is composed of the nine indices.

This does not mean that all nine value dimensions contributed equally,

TABLE 6.5   Discriminant Analysis of Value Indices Between Two Cultures

	Correlation Coefficients	Standardized Coefficients
Traditionalism in male-female sexual relationship	−.64	−.76
Interpersonal kindness	.50	.45
Submission to authority	.38	.34
Traditional kinship ties	.31	.20
Respecting seniors	.28	.29
Lower status for women	.11	.07
Rigidity toward divorce	.06	.15
Importance of connections	.05	.01
Obligations to care for aging parents	.01	−.07
Canonical correlation	.770	
Wilks' Lambda	.407[a]	
Group centroids:		
China	−.975	
United States	1.490	

Note: The first column shows the pooled within-group correlation coefficients, which are analogous to factor loadings, indicating strengths of relationships between the indices and the discriminant function. The second column shows the standardized discriminant coefficients, which may be interpreted as standardized regression coefficients, indicating the relationships between indices and the discriminant function if the function were considered a dependent variable. The variables are ordered by size of the correlation coefficients. The number of cases: $n = 1655$ in the China sample and n = 1083 in the U.S. sample.

[a]$p < .001$, based on approximate χ^2 test, df=8.

however. In Table 6.5, these value indices are listed in descending order in terms of their contributions to distinguishing between the two nations. The most powerful discriminating variable, that is, the one that sets the Chinese and American samples farthest apart, is the levels of traditionalism in male-female relations, a value on which the United States is much lower than China. The next several indices, however, are traditional Confucian values on which the United States seems to rank above China: interpersonal kindness, submission to authority, traditional kinship ties, and respect for seniors. All of these differences have been encountered before (Chapter 4), and many of them we ascribed to negative influences on Chinese respondents of ideological propaganda against traditional Confucian values. Nonetheless, it is worth noting that in most respects we have found a general pattern of Americans giving the more traditional responses on most of our measures.

The four other value indices were not capable of separating the two samples. That is, the Americans and Chinese did not differ significantly in their values regarding the status of women, divorce, connections, or obligations to aging parents.

We can safely conclude from this and prior evidence that the Chinese are more rigid than Americans in their approach to sexual relationships, especially toward women's sexual conduct (Hsu 1981). Beyond that, though, our findings here would seem to conflict with earlier observations. Chinese, it is often remarked, are notably obedient to authority and respectful toward seniors; they emphasize interpersonal tolerance and harmony, and they value kinship ties. But our survey evidence here and in Chapter 4 would seem to indicate the opposite. Taken together with other facts that we know about recent changes in China, there does indeed seem to have been a pattern of departure from several traditional Confucian values. But other factors have been at work too. Perhaps more surprising is the extent to which many traditional values are endorsed in the United States, contrary to what many observers have presumed to "know" from other kinds of studies.

We turn next to examination of relationships between these indices. In previous chapters, we found some odd patterns of cross-cultural variation that might be due, at least in part, to different meanings of the words used in the Chinese and American questionnaires. Summing pairs of items that seem to imply approximately the same value is a way of neutralizing such extraneous influences on the data. More generally, summing items to create indices should tend to cancel out random error and thus improve the reliability of our measures. The inter-index correlations in Table 6.6 should be relatively free of these kinds of error, at least in comparison with the inter-item correlations. Further, the inter-index correlations also provide a more parsimonious way of comparing the config-

TABLE 6.6 Correlations Among the Value Indices

	1	2	3	4	5	6	7	8	9
1. Traditionalism in male-female sexual relationship		.29[a]	.17[a]	-.07	.18[a]	-.01	.19[a]	-.06	-.06
2. Traditionalism in female status	-.01		.12[a]	.04	.24[a]	.01	.34[a]	-.05	-.13[a]
3. Rigidity toward divorce	.13[a]	.11[a]		.06	.02	-.01	.05	-.05	.02
4. Obligation for parent care	.11[a]	.03	.06[a]		.16[a]	.18[a]	.05	-.04	.16[a]
5. Traditional kinship ties	.04	.16[a]	.03	.10[a]		.11[a]	.28[a]	-.09[a]	.18[a]
6. Acceptance of seniority hierarchy	.04	.01	.08[a]	.07[a]	.03		.28[a]	-.09[a]	.18[a]
7 Acceptance of authority hierarchy	.05	.18[a]	.16[a]	.07[a]	.22[a]	.02		-.02	.13[a]
8. Interpersonal pragmatism	-.08[a]	.04	-.06[a]	.03	.10[a]	-.07	.03		.01
9. Interpersonal kindness	.04	.02	-.10[a]	.01	.19[a]	-.01	.15[a]	.03	

Note: The lower half (below the main diagonal) shows the coefficients for the China sample, while the upper half shows the coefficients for the U.S. sample. The cases with missing values were excluded from the analysis. For the U.S. sample, the resulting sample size is 1074.

[a]$p < .01$.

urations of values between China and the United States. Despite the gain from examining the summative indices rather than item components, the relative differences between the two surveys should remain, though; that is, the greater reliability we have attributed to the U.S. survey, with its more finely graded measurement, should produce higher correlations, all told. The results for the American sample are shown above the diagonal in Table 6.6, and those for China are below the diagonal. The entries for the U.S. survey are, as expected, on the whole somewhat higher than those in China, but this is offset to some extent by the larger sample size in China that is available for this analysis.[7] As a result, eighteen of the thirty-six entries in Table 6.6 are significant (p<.01) in China, and nineteen of the thirty-six in the U.S. survey. This rough equivalence will be important to us when we attempt to make comparisons between the two samples in terms of what is correlated with what.

The purpose of this correlational analysis is to help us in envisioning the *structures* of the value systems in the two cultures. There is a good deal of structure in each and a good deal of commonality between the two countries in the shape of the data in Table 6.6. There are also some notable exceptions, where the structure of the indices in China differs from that in the United States. We will discuss the commonalities of structure first.

Of the seventeen correlations in Table 6.6 that are significant in China, ten are also significant in the U.S. survey. One of these, however, is in the opposite direction in the United States, so we discuss it below. The most centrally interconnected of the indices in the nine instances of common correlations is the value of traditional kinship ties. (This is also, however, one of the two indices for which the U.S. and China correlations are significant in opposite directions.) Traditional kinship values are most strongly correlated with acceptance of the authority hierarchy, traditional status for women, the values of interpersonal kindness, and acceptance of traditional status for women. This is a fairly tight knot of what are unmistakably Confucian values. The status of women index also correlates significantly, in both countries, with acceptance of the hierarchy of authority, which in turn is correlated equally with the interpersonal kindness index in both surveys. Hence there is a common structure underlying the values in both countries, and it clearly revolves around a set of traditional values. This finding, or more exactly this set of at least six interrelated findings, validates our ongoing assumption that by operationalizing Confucian values in the survey research setting we are indeed tapping a broader system of related values that represent a traditional viewpoint in any society.

That said, we must also examine the particulars in instances where the structures do not conform to this central pattern of traditionalism. These include pairs of items that are intercorrelated in both surveys, but that do not form part of the web of items noted in the previous paragraph; cases where a correlation is significant in only one of the two countries; and the single instance where we found opposing, significant correlations.

Rigidity toward divorce accounts for two common correlations, being positively related to traditionalism in male-female relationships and the index representing traditional status of women. These are wholly understandable, and probably universal, patterns of intercorrelation. All that is really surprising is that the divorce and openness scales do not correlate with any of the other traditional scales in Table 6.6 in a consistent way. They are not unrelated, however, just related in different ways. In the United States, sexual rigidity is positively related, as we might expect, to traditional values regarding female equality, kinship ties, and the authority hierarchy. Rigidity regarding divorce, though, is not correlated with any of the more general traditional value dimensions, that is, those that are not explicitly about male-female relationships. In China, on the other hand, the divorce index is significantly correlated with almost every value in the survey, while the sexual rigidity scale is much less sensitive to the broader set of traditional value measures. Without making too much of the contrast,[8] we may venture to say that divorce is such a well-established practice in the United States that it is not closely associated with one's value structure, whereas in China it is a new and challenging idea for many people, testing their traditional beliefs strongly.

The other set of commonalities in Table 6.6 involves the index representing obligations to one's aging parents. This scale is correlated significantly, in both countries, with two traditional value scales: kinship ties and the seniority hierarchy. This is an obvious overlap of meaning, since one's parents are of course both senior and kin. We could consider the parental obligations scale a part of the traditional set, but it is worth noting that its other correlates are somewhat different in the two countries. In China, obligations to one's aging parents seem to be part of a structure of values that also involves acceptance of authority; that is, caring is something one is *supposed* to do. In the United States, on the other hand, the other strong correlate of the parental obligation scale is the set of traditional values we have called interpersonal kindness; this could mean that Americans take on an obligation to care for their aging parents if they *want to* do so. Such an interpretation would accord with our general assumption that the Confucian value system is built more on universal obligations, while Western traditional values are more individualistic--that is, they are values that a person can adopt or not, whereas in the Chinese tradition there was not this sense of option. This speculation goes well beyond the capacity of the data we have here to provide any clear guidelines. Still, the structures of values in the two countries are not in all respects similar, and we should attempt to learn as much as we can from their differences.

The only truly significant anomaly between the two countries in Table 6.6 is found for the correlation between the interpersonal pragmatism ("connections") scale, which is not itself a traditional value, and the very central traditional value of kinship ties. This correlation is positive in China, but negative in the United States. We suspect this simply represents differences between the two countries in the kinds of connections that people use. That is, it is not really a matter of values, but of practice. In China, the connections one traditionally used were in fact kinship ties. These were the necessary reciprocal of kinship obligations; if you are obligated to help your brother's child, so is your uncle obligated to help you—and therefore available if asked. This practice remains one of the most visible facts of Chinese life, but it is increasingly less indicative of the Confucian value system. This is shown by its significant negative correlations in other domains: sexual traditionalism and rigidity toward divorce. In the United States, the meaning of "connections" is quite different; to judge from the other significant (negative) correlate of this scale, using connections means to Americans finding a way around the seniority hierarchy, which is to say, skirting the normal channels for doing business. There is no hint in Table 6.6 that our American respondents connected "connections" to traditional values, whereas for the Chinese there is at least a suggestion of that linkage through the correlation between the "connection" value index and kinship ties.

The differences we have remarked upon here were amplified by a second-order factor analysis of these value indices (results not shown). While there were similarities as we have noted, this procedure yielded very different factor structures between the two countries. We may conclude both that there is a common core of traditionalism that cuts across the two very different societies we are studying—and that they are indeed different in a number of important respects.

A Brief Summary

The analyses reported in this chapter were aimed at questions of (1) cross-cultural comparability of the value measures and (2) cross-cultural value configurations in the four domains of social relationships. We have been able to identify some value measures that are fairly comparable across cultures, both semantically and empirically, and to eliminate a few measures that did not meet minimal standards of comparability in both senses. But it is not possible to adduce definitive evidence of cross-cultural equivalence given the measures here. It remains an assumption, if perhaps a less shaky one than when we began our analyses in Chapter 4.

The evidence presented in this chapter suggests greater similarities than differences in the underlying dimensions of values *within* each of the domains of social relationships. In addition, the evidence also suggests some cross-cultural similarities in the interconnections among various value indices across different domains, with a central core of traditional values that relate to one another coherently both in China, where "traditional" means Confucian, and in the United States, where that is not the case. But there are also some important differences in the relationships among the value indices *across* the four domains of social relationships, and we should proceed only gingerly with our cross-cultural comparisons, keeping the various indices separate—while bearing in mind that they are connected to one another in certain ways in each culture.

We move to the next stage of our analysis with the understanding that there is a core of traditional indices, but there are also amendments to be made to that list that are peculiar to each society. If indices that we think of as functionally equivalent for purposes of representing traditional values turn out to have similar correlates in multivariate analysis, we will then be in a much stronger position to propose thinking about them as a set.

Notes

1. Conceptually, these two factors should be positively correlated. But empirically we found that the two factors produced by oblique rotation are correlated at −.09 in the Chinese sample and −.17 in the U.S. sample.

2. We tested this "propaganda effect" interpretation of the co-variations in the China survey through a factor analysis of *all* the traditional Chinese value items. Two relatively clean factors emerged. One factor consists of all the traditional Confucian phrases that have received severely critical treatment over the past forty years. The other factor was composed of the remaining phrases, which either had ambiguous ideological connotations (e.g., respecting tradition) or which remain acceptable today (e.g., submission to authority).

3. The second factor, involving "connections," may mean somewhat different things in the two cultures. Using connections for problem solving in China today is regarded as a sign of official corruption. Synonyms for connections include "back door" and "privileges," for example, associated with favoritism and bribery of Party and government officials. In the United States, connections can mean using people in powerful positions (as in China), but often too the term simply evokes well-placed, experienced family friends and colleagues who know how the system works and how to get things done. In other words, connections in the United States tend to be more advisory, in China more instrumental. We did not, though, find many effects on these items (in Table 4.2 or Chapter 5), either of demographic variables or of their interactions with the culture in question.

4. The scoring for the item on "a couple live together before marriage" was reversed, because it was negatively related to its companion item in the index. This procedure assures that the resulting index on male-female sexual relationship follows a traditional direction. The correlation matrix for all these items is presented in Appendix 2. We have underlined the correlations for the items that were then summed in index construction. These items had generally loaded on the same factors in the two surveys and appeared to be similar in their manifest meanings. Since each index consisted of only two items, a simple average of the two was taken as the index score. Simple summation of scores is a crude method of creating indices. Differences in scales between the component items were not taken

into consideration, and possible differences in measurement errors in the paired items were not estimated empirically. We have in effect weighted each item in each pair relative to its variance, since the scores were summed without first being standardized. In an exploratory study of this type, one would be hard put to offer a clear theoretical basis for transforming scales or weighting component items according to an a priori scheme.

5. Kendall's Tau-b was used here because most of the measures in the China questionnaire used ordinal scales, and this statistic does not assume equal-interval scale properties. In some ways, Tau-b is not the optimal statistic for estimating the strength of relationships among these items, due to (1) fundamentally dichotomous measurement, (2) diffused meaning of rank order on the truncated ordinal scales, and (3) narrowing of the range due to many ties (Siegel 1956). These disabilities of the coefficient are similar throughout the below-diagonal entries in Appendix 2, however, so that comparisons among the Tau-b coefficients are meaningful. To an extent, the patterns of relationships here provide a validation check on the earlier factor analyses, which were based on Pearson correlation coefficients.

6. Notice that these two relatively higher coefficients involved two other traditional Chinese phrases that have been repeatedly attacked during the propaganda campaigns: "differentiation between men and women" and "three obediences and four virtues." It is likely that the common fate of these traditional phrases during the propaganda campaigns brought them together despite the fact that they represented values in different cultural domains.

7. Due to missing data on some items, a number of cases in the U.S. sample could not be used in this exercise, creating summed indices. Hence $N=1074$ in the U.S. survey, and the standard error for significance tests is .03. In China, $N=1655$, and the standard error is .025.

8. Although we are in this section comparing correlations, and using their significance as an indicator of which ones to compare, we are not literally testing each of them against each of the others. Each has simply been tested against zero, and then the significant coefficients are the ones we consider strong enough to merit discussion. There would be 630 pairwise tests to consider in each sample, for Table 6.6, if we were to run them separately.

7

Communication Influences and Individual Differences

THE ANALYSES TO THIS POINT indicate many aggregate similarities and differences between the United States and China, but they do not examine the sources of differences in cultural values at the individual level. A first step in that direction was presented in Chapter 5, where we examined demographic groups within each nation, one variable at a time. This chapter carries cross-national comparisons several steps further. We examine individual-level differences as a set rather than piecemeal, and we examine communication influences alongside demographic factors. This chapter, then, is an attempt to identify the most important sources of social value differences in each general domain in each country.

Our central interest is social change, which implies temporal movement. But we have only cross-sectional data, which by definition cannot provide direct evidence of change across time. Temporal shifts can, however, often be inferred from cross-sectional variables that themselves represent results of change over time. The most obvious example is age, although age is an ambiguous index of social change. While one grows older a great deal of history may be occurring too; certainly that has been the case in China during the lifetimes of the respondents in this survey.

Comparisons of urban vs. rural areas often indicate patterns of change, because social innovations (including, presumably, shifts in cultural values) tend to occur earliest in urban centers and then diffuse gradually to outlying rural areas (Rogers 1983). Education is another indirect indicator of change; more-educated persons tend, like those in cities, to be on the cutting edge of social change—as we saw in Chapter 5. Education is, though, confounded with many factors, not least with variations in what is being taught in the schools a person attends in a given time or place. Too, many countries have experienced a gradual historical rise in educational levels, so that age and education tend to be negatively correlated—even though their separate effects on some cultural values might point in the same direction (Chaffee 1991:62–72).

Put a slightly different way, temporal changes often leave their traces in cross-sectional variations as a result of uneven development across various sectors of society—sectors defined by characteristics that are tied to the speed of adopting new ideas, values, and practices. Based upon the premise of monotonic development from traditional to modern society (Lerner 1958), we should expect wider acceptance of traditional values among rural residents, compared with urban, and among older cohorts, compared with the younger people in our samples.

Mass media influences, like education, have complex functions. Media use and education do not simply indicate the speed with which cultural change might reach a person; they are also indicators of intellectual development, which means that they enable people to change, to seek change, and to change again, as circumstances warrant. The educated person, and the person who is in continuous contact with the society at large via mass communication, may be more adaptable to political shifts that have implications for expressions of cultural values. These factors might operate very differently in China from the way they do in the United States.

Education and communication are both catalysts that facilitate social change; that is, they foster a readiness for innovation (Rogers 1983; Lerner 1958; Ball-Rokeach et al. 1984). In the normal course of events we should expect both these variables to be negatively associated with traditional values. But in China, political campaigns directed at cultural values may have shaped the informed person more than the uninformed, and it is no sure bet that education will be associated with antitraditional values. At the time of our survey, the Chinese government had relaxed somewhat in comparison with its tight controls during the Cultural Revolution, but that intensely anti-Confucian campaign might still have held considerable influence over the values of less-educated respondents and those not following the shifting political climate closely via the media. Thus it is possible that variables that are normally associated with antitraditional patterns of change will nevertheless be positively correlated with traditional values in the China survey; better educated citizens will be more aware of recent political changes that render traditional values more acceptable than in the recent past.

Mass communication, we should stress, is not all of a piece. The mass media in different countries convey very different messages. Channels that stress news may have quite a different impact on cultural values from channels that mostly provide entertainment. Entertainment too may be subdivided. In China, exposure to Western entertainment media, such as imported films and television programs, can undermine cultural values that channels carrying traditional Chinese forms of communication might be supporting. We need to take account of these content variations in our analyses of sources of values.

This chapter represents an attempt to predict an individual's values from a set of media-exposure and demographic variables related to change: urban/rural residency, age, and education. Gender is also included in these equations because of the centrality of male-female relationships to some of the value measures. People have different sex-role experiences in the two countries, so we expect to find differences between the sexes on values regarding male-female and family relationships. These interactions may be complex, though, and require careful interpretation. The analytical strategy in this chapter is to fit parallel regression models to the China and U.S. data separately, so that we can make direct comparisons between the two samples.

Overview

Before proceeding with detailed empirical analyses, we should consider what these analyses tell us overall. As will be seen, the total variance explained within each regression equation is quantitatively modest, usually in the range of 5 to 10 percent. This low range of predictability is partly attributable to low reliability of measurement of the dependent variables. Cultural values are necessarily vague; they are not anchored in concrete actions, nor can they be located on well-defined scales of mental intensity. Further, these values do not cluster together into a single package that one might call "traditionalism." Each index we attempt to explain here is based on only two items. So we have to be satisfied with accounting for *some* degree of variation in each dimension that we have identified.

On the other hand, each of the eighteen regression equations reported for the samples representing the two countries is statistically significant. That is to say, we are able to explain some individual differences in values by simple demographic factors and media habits. This bespeaks a degree of validity for our overall procedure, even though it is statistically unimpressive.

Perhaps more important for comparative purposes, the predictive equations for the U.S. sample are almost as high as are those for China. The mean R-square for the nine equations representing the China data is 7.09 percent, while the analogous value for the U.S. survey is 6.27 percent. This similarity in terms of predictability suggests that the basic assumption of comparability of the two countries on the cultural values measured in these surveys is reasonably valid. The conceptual starting point for the entire project was an interpretation, in survey research format, of the traditional Confucian value structure, a distinctively Chinese system of social thought. No initial consideration was given to American culture, and indeed we have in this survey ignored distinctively Western values.

And yet we find that our ability to account empirically for variation in the dependent variables is almost as great in the United States as it is in China. Hence, even though the empirical power of prediction here is rather low, the pattern of evidence encourages us in the assumption that the comparisons we are making have some degree of validity.

Media Exposure Indices and Predictions

Our first step is to introduce the media exposure measures for each country. Obviously, the two nations differ greatly in their mass media systems; we cannot consider media exposure a universal construct that has the same meaning in China as in the United States. When we examine mass media influences on values in the two nations, we are evaluating different social forces. Our operationalizations of media exposure in the two countries have more in common than do our conceptions of media use behaviors or their implications for cultural values.

All three major sources of influence in contemporary China—traditional Chinese orthodoxy, Marxism and Maoism, and Western influences—operate via mass media (Whyte 1989). In contemporary Chinese media, Western entertainment shares the stage with traditional Chinese entertainment (e.g., folk songs, vernacular dramas, and Peking operas), and with Communist government propaganda presented as news and editorials. Each of these bodies of content has its distinct ideological orientation. On the values we are concerned with here, alliances sometimes occur. Government propaganda, for instance, is consonant with traditional entertainment on questions of male-female sexual relationships, but it is more in line with the implicit Western "message" where social equality of women is concerned.

After more than forty years of ideological indoctrination campaigns (see Chu and Hsu 1979), much of China's traditional value structure has been removed from the surface of daily life (Chu and Ju 1993). But relaxation of party control over mass communication in recent years has revitalized both traditional cultural forms and the importation of cultural materials from other countries (Link 1986). We would expect diverse values to follow from this diversification of media content, to the extent that individual Chinese are exposed to varying channels of communication.

There are reasons to expect strong media effects in China.[1] First, the Communist Party controls the messages presented by the media (L. Chu 1986; Liu 1982; Whyte 1989), and alternative sources are not serious threats to this monopoly. Diversity in media content amounts to only limited variations in the media diet prescribed by the Party. Second, China has for forty years experienced mostly transition periods, punctuated by an occasional hiatus of relative stability. The reform period that began in 1979 has been characterized by deep social changes and economic and political uncertainties. As a rule, uncertain conditions heighten people's reliance on mass media (Ball-Rokeach and DeFleur 1976; Ball-Rokeach et al. 1984).

In the United States, conditions are quite different. The political and economic system in general remains stable, and the media are open to many competing sources. The government neither controls the media nor conducts pervasive long-term campaigns aimed at changing fundamental cultural values. Political administrations in the United States attempt, if anything, to *appeal to* existing value structures to achieve more specific goals in waging wars on poverty, drugs, or, occasionally, other nations.

Still, we do expect mass communication to affect American values, and there is some evidence that it does (*e.g.*, Ball-Rokeach et al. 1984). Certainly the content of the U.S. entertainment media bears upon cultural values; there have, for instance, been changes in male-female and family relationships over the past thirty years of prime-time television (Taylor 1989). American television programs feature families with divorced parents, teen sex and pregnancy, and other issues that challenge traditional values (Lichter et al. 1988). At the same time, prime-time television drama and comedy characteristically rely upon traditional sex roles, depicting women as victims of violence, as sex symbols, and as subordinates to male superiors (Greenberg 1980; Gerbner et al. 1986). Whether heavy exposure to television reinforces or undermines traditional values is a question for empirical study. We can add only slightly to that body of research with the measures available to us here.

News media also often address traditional cultural issues. News in the United States is frequently defined in terms of social problems, which include high divorce rates, female single parents, and problems of senior citizens who live alone. We have found no systematic content analyses to guide us in making clearcut predictions about differential effects of U.S. news vs. entertainment programming, although we suspect the contrasts in content are considerable. One well-established difference is that news shows are intended to be true, while entertainment programs often take dramatic license to highlight a social issue. This is important because television that is perceived as real has considerably stronger effects on social learning than is the case with perceived dramatizations (Feshbach 1972).

American television is highly diverse in content, and what a viewer acquires from it is determined by a complex interaction of predispositions (e.g., one's basic values), psychological factors (e.g., arousal, identification with characters), and content (e.g., justification and consequences for actions). Scholars long ago learned better than to make strong unidirectional predictions about TV's social effects; most also recognize the fallacy of attempting to infer effects from even a careful examination of television content per se (Comstock, Chaffee, Katzman, McCombs, and Roberts 1978).

Still, there is good reason to expect differential results from exposure to entertainment vs. news in the United States. These types of programs not only differ in content and its presumed reality, they have different audiences and their audiences bring different motivations to the viewing experience (Blumler and Katz 1974). The motivations that attract the audience for a given program genre, we might guess, are roughly the same in China and the United States. That is, the same kinds of people are likely to watch news, even though the news available to them is quite different in the two media systems. There is some reason to expect that individuals who are attentive to news programs in the two countries will vary predictably in values from those who do not pay much attention to news—even though the news programs in China and the United States may differ markedly in the cultural value messages these media and their sponsors intend to convey.

Because the media structures differ so sharply between the two countries, we adopted different strategies in developing mass media exposure indices for the two samples. The main differences have to do with entertainment media, which in China are much more identifiable in terms of cultural value implications than is the case in the United States.

For the U.S. sample, different sets of media-exposure measures were used in the six different surveys (see Table 7.1). The six U.S. surveys used not only different questions, but also somewhat different response scales. Hence, explicit comparisons of specific measures across the six U.S. sites would be difficult to justify. What we have done is first to draw a broad conceptual distinction between two major types of media content, news and entertainment. All the available media exposure measures in each of these two categories were averaged *within each site*, to create comparable indices (cf. McLeod, Rucinski, Pan, and Kosicki 1988). All of the within-site indices yielded acceptable reliability coefficients, as reported in Table 7.1.

After constructing multi-item media indices within each sample, we calculated within-sample standardized scores for each of the two types of content. These locally standardized scales were then merged into the pooled U.S. sample data; it is these merged standard scores that are represented in the multivariate analyses of this chapter. It is important to note, though, that this standardizing procedure removes between-site differences that might be due to different local conditions in media structure; some U.S. locales are indeed more "media-rich" than others. It also removes from the analysis between-site differences in the mean level of

TABLE 7.1   Components of the Media-Use Indices in the U.S. Survey

	Range	Alpha
California Survey		
Exposure to hard news		.76
Days per week reading a newspaper	0–7	
How often read national news	1–5	
How often read local news	1–5	
How often read international news	1–5	
Days per week watching TV local news	0–7	
Days per week watching TV national news	0–7	
Exposure to entertainment		.30[a]
Hours per day watching TV	0–10	
Days per week watching daytime soap operas	0–7	
Cleveland Survey		
Exposure to hard news		.75
Days per week reading a newspaper	0–7	
How often read national news	1–5	
How often read local news	1–5	
How often read international news	1–5	
How often watch PBS programs	1–5	
How often watch TV local news	1–5	
Exposure to entertainment		.51
How often read entertainment news	1–5	
Hours per day watching TV	0–15	
How often watch TV soap operas	1–5	
How often watch TV game shows	1–5	
Connecticut Survey		
Exposure to hard news		.77
Days per week reading a newspaper	0–7	
How often read national news	0–10	
How often read local news	0–10	
How often read international news	0–10	
How often watch TV national news	0–10	
How often watch TV local news	0–10	
Exposure to entertainment		.60
How often read entertainment news	0–10	
Hours per day watch TV	0–24	

(Continues)

TABLE 7.1   *(Continued)*

	Range	Alpha
Days per week watch TV game shows	0–7	
Days per week watch TV sitcoms	0–7	
Days per week watch TV crime shows	0–7	
Days per week watch TV adventure shows	0–7	
Florida Survey		
Exposure to hard news		.77
Days per week read a newspaper	0–7	
How often read national news	0–10	
How often read local news	0–10	
How often read international news	0–10	
How often watch TV national news	0–10	
How often watch TV local news	0–10	
Exposure to entertainment		.68
How often read entertainment news	0–10	
Hours per day watch TV	0–16	
How often watch TV soap operas	0–10	
How often watch TV crime shows	0–10	
How often watch TV sitcoms	0–10	
How often watch TV game shows	0–10	
Texas Survey		
Exposure to hard news		.81
Days per week reading a newspaper	0–7	
How often read national news	1–5	
How often read local news	1–5	
How often read international news	1–5	
Days per week watching TV local news	0–7	
Days per week watching TV national news	0–7	
Exposure to entertainment		.32[a]
Hours per day watching TV	0–15	
Days per week watching daytime soap operas	0–7	
Wiconsin Survey		
Exposure to hard news		.70
Days per week read a newspaper	0–7	
How often read national news	0–10	
How often read local news	0–10	

(Continues)

TABLE 7.1 *(Continued)*

	Range	Alpha
How often read international news	0–10	
How often watch TV national news	0–10	
How often watch TV local news	0–10	
Exposure to entertainment		.60
How often read entertainment news	0–10	
Hours per day watch TV	0–14	
How often watch TV soap operas	0–10	
How often watch TV crime shows	0–10	
How often watch TV game shows	0–10	
How often watch TV talk shows	0–10	

[a]Pearson correlation coefficient.

media use by individual respondents and differences in the variances around those local means. Our central goal in this study is to compare China with the United States; possible variations among our six U.S. sites are of little direct interest here, and the evidence would at best be confounded with variations in measurement.

Measurement in the China survey was identical at all sites. It included a rich set of indicators of exposure to diverse types of media content that became available during the reform period. Table 7.2 lists nineteen measures of the frequency of various media behaviors. These were included in the China questionnaire based upon further conceptual divisions beyond the conventional news-entertainment distinction that guided the U.S. analysis. We preliminarily divided entertainment into three categories: traditional Chinese entertainment, contemporary Chinese entertainment, and foreign entertainment. Similarly, conventional news was distinguished from government propaganda. These distinctions preserve the forces we have assumed act independently of one another in shaping cultural values in China.

As Table 7.2 indicates, a five-factor model was fitted to the correlation matrix of media-exposure variables. The results are mostly consistent with our expectations. The five factors are: hard news (e.g., national or international news), government propaganda (editorials and news on special topics), traditional entertainment (vernacular dramas), Western entertainment (Western music, movies, dance), and general contemporary Chinese entertainment (music, films, dance). Statistical tests indicate that this five-factor model fits the data reasonably well (see details at the bottom of Table 7.2). All the validity coefficients (factor loadings) were highly significant.

TABLE 7.2   Dimensions of Mass Media Use Among the Chinese (Confirmatory Factor Analysis with Maximum Likelihood Estimates)

	Range	*I*	*II*	*III*	*IV*	*V*	*R²*
How often read national news	1–5	.42				.35	.45
How often read local news	1–5	.18				.49	.36
How often read international news	1–5	.68			.43		.61
How often watch TV national news	1–5	.40				.19	.28
How often watch TV international news	1–5	.55			.31		.38
How often listen to vernacular dramas on radio	1–5		.83				.69
How often watch vernacular dramas on TV	1–5		.89				.80
How often watch Chinese films on TV	1–5		.30	.23			.16
How often listen to Chinese music on radio	1–5			.67			.44
How often watch Chinese dance on TV	1–5		.09	.61			.38
How often listen to Western music on radio	1–5				.79		.63
How often watch foreign movies on TV	1–5				.62		.37
How often watch music shows on TV	1–5			.62	.23		.62
How often watch Western dance on TV	1–5			.12	.62		.50
How often go to Western movies	1–12				.55		.30
How often read newspaper editorials	1–5					.59	.35
How often read science news	1–5					.52	.27
How often read court news	1–5					.56	.31
How often read economic news	1–5					.60	.37

Correlations among the factors

Factor 1: Exposure to hard news	1.00				
Factor 2: Exposure to traditional entertainment	.00*	1.00			
Factor 3: Exposure to contemporaneous entertainment	.16	-.07*	1.00		
Factor 4: Exposure to foreign entertainment	-.07*	-.33	.64	1.00	
Factor 5: Exposure to propaganda	.52	.04*	.46	.33	1.00

Notes: Fitness statistics: $\chi^2=593.0$, df=129; GFI=.958; AGFI=.938; $n=1438$. The correlated errors are not shown. All coefficients (except the ones marked by *) are three times larger than their corresponding standard errors.

The five factors were allowed to correlate freely, and the correlations among these factors provided additional evidence concerning their meanings (see Table 7.2). Exposure to hard news correlated highly with exposure to government propaganda, which is inescapable given that in Chinese media news and propaganda are often mixed together. The correlation is, however, far from total; the propaganda factor is also strongly correlated with two other factors (contemporaneous entertainment and foreign entertainment), whereas the news factor is not.

The correlations among the factors in Table 7.2 also indicate a sharp differentiation between traditional entertainment and Western entertainment in the media. These two types of media use are negatively correlated with one another, which is to say they attract quite different audiences. Our distinction between two types of contemporary entertainment, Chinese vs. Western, is not so clear; Table 7.2 shows that these two factors are highly correlated with one another and with exposure to government propaganda. Apparently the media audiences for these three types of content overlap to a great extent. In regression analysis employing indices that represent the factors in Table 7.2, these correlations between factors will reduce the power of each index to explain unique variance in cultural values.

Table 7.3 presents the correlation coefficients between the media-use indices in each country and the demographic variables that we will be using in our multiple regression analyses. For the most part, these media-use habits are distinct in their demographic roots. Put another way, these different types of media content appeal to audiences with different demographic profiles. The exception to this general conclusion is the overlap we have noted between the index representing contemporary Chinese entertainment and both foreign entertainment and Chinese government propaganda. Because of its lack of empirical differentiation from the latter two measures, each of which we have hypothesized contributes in a distinct way to cultural values, the index of exposure to contemporary Chinese entertainment will not be used in our multiple regression analyses.

A few other comparisons in Table 7.3 are worth noting as well. One might expect that certain general classes of content would appeal to demographically similar audiences in each country, but this does not seem to be the case. For news, gender and education are strong predictors in China, but not in the United States, where age and income are the important factors. For entertainment, the strongest correlates in China (for both domestic and foreign programs) are education, youth, urban location, and labor occupation; none of these is an important predictor of entertainment consumption in the United States. To the extent that we find similar effects of a given type of media exposure in the two countries, then, it will not be a likely artifact of mere demographics.

TABLE 7.3   Relationships Between Demographic and Media-Use Variables

	China Survey (N=1503)					U. S. Survey (N=1975)	
	News	*Trad.*	*Cont.*	*West.*	*Prop.*	*News*	*Ent.*
Sex	−.21[a]	.20[a]	−.02	−.09[a]	−.15[a]	−.06[a]	.16[a]
Age	.09[a]	.14[a]	−.21[a]	−.28[a]	−.09[a]	.31[a]	.02
Education	.14[a]	−.32[a]	.33[a]	.41[a]	.28[a]	.06[a]	−.08[a]
Income	.06[a]	−.02	.04	.05	.04	.13[a]	−.13[a]
Agriculture	−.12[a]	.18[a]	−.24[a]	−.27[a]	−.18[a]	−	−[b]
Labor	.01	−.11	.16[a]	.19[a]	.06	−.04	−.01
Service	−.01	−.08[a]	.09[a]	.11[a]	.04	−.03	.05
Professional	.07[a]	−.09[a]	.07[a]	.08[a]	.08[a]	.04	−.16[a]
Managerial	.10[a]	.00	.03	.02	.12[a]	.02	−.09[a]
Under-30 cohort	−.11[a]	−.11[a]	.15[a]	.22[a]	.04	−.26[a]	.05
30–49 cohort	.07[a]	−.01	.04	.00	.06	.02	−.10[a]
50–65 cohort	.03	.12[a]	−.20[a]	−.22[a]	−.11[a]	.18[a]	.01
Urban	.09[a]	−.22[a]	.22[a]	.31[a]	.10[a]	−.02	.02
Rural	−.13[a]	.24[a]	−.26[a]	−.33[a]	−.15[a]	−	−[c]

[a]p<.01.
[b]The agriculture category was not used in the U.S. surveys.
[c]The town category in the China sample is not shown here. The U.S. samples are dichotomized into urban and rural represented by a single dummy variable.

The demographics and media-exposure indices in Table 7.3 are the independent variables for the remaining analyses in this chapter. We will examine systematically the influence of this set of predictors on each of nine indices that represent clusters of cultural values, as established in previous chapters. We first examine results of the nine total-sample regression analyses within each nation and compare the two countries in terms of the weightings of predictor variables in these equations. As will be seen, for most of the cultural value domains we are analyzing, age is a strong predictor—sometimes virtually the only independent variable of consequence. Given our concern with cultural *change*, this is a most important finding. It encourages us to look in more detail at the influences on values of the other independent variables *within* each age cohort. A final section of this chapter is given over to that within-cohort regression analysis.

While the tables in this chapter represent separately the nine dependent variables, we will look across this set of tables in discussing the results in the text. That is, we will interpret the results separately for each *independent* variable across all nine value variables. This serves two purposes. First, it maintains our focus on traditional cultural values as a set and on the specific concern of this chapter with evaluating each potential source of these values. Second, this format enables us to maintain comparisons in parallel with the bivariate results in Chapter 5.

The cell entries presented in Tables 7.4 through 7.12 are correlations, standardized regression coefficients (betas), and incremental R-squares. The raw correlations are reported mainly for completeness of information; our interpretations will be based on the betas and R-squares, which are the tests that take into account the other variables in multiple regression. The betas in these tables are taken from the final equations that include all predictors. Each incremental R-square, however, represents the proportion of variance accounted for by the specific block of variables after subtracting the variance attributable only to previous blocks. These two summary statistics serve quite different purposes. The R-square is useful primarily in judging whether a given block of variables has added significantly to the predictive power of a particular equation in one country. The betas provide us with an estimate of the relative size of the effect of each variable, which can be compared within an equation to the other predictors. Although comparing the parallel standardized regression coefficients across nations requires the additional assumption of equal variances in the United States and China, this assumption becomes irrelevant if the comparisons are made in terms of *relative importance of predictors in parallel equations* across nations. This is exactly the type of comparison we intend to make with these regression analyses.[2]

In reviewing the regression equations, we will not discuss the effects of occupation, which we have tested. The reason for this omission is simple: We did not find any significant relationships, even though we tested for possible differences based on three distinct categories: laborers, professionals, and managers. Only six of the fifty-four raw correlations between these three dummy variables and the nine value indices in the two countries were statistically different from zero—and those three relationships were accounted for by the other variables in our regression equations. Each of the other independent variables we examined, however, did produce some significant relationships in multiple regression.

Effects of Urbanism

Urban residence is theoretically related to cultural values not only cross-sectionally—we expect rural residents in any time and place to be more traditional in most respects—but also in the context of the linear evolutionary model shown in Figure 4.1. That is, we expect *change* to occur earlier, and to proceed faster, in urban settings. Earlier we did find less traditionalism in certain values, comparing rural to urban areas. But this was not a general pattern that held for all dependent variables, and the bivariate relationships lacked controls for other variables that might have explained the differences we did find.

In Tables 7.4 through 7.12, urbanism in China is represented by two dummy variables, since there are three levels: urban, town, and rural. In the United States, the coding is dichotomous, urban-rural, and we show only the one dummy variable. This procedure makes between-country comparisons easy to visualize, as the first line of each table shows the effect of the dummy variable for urban residence in each country. Because all nine dependent variables in these tables are coded in the direction of the traditional response, a negative sign for the correlation coefficients and beta weights in the first line of each table indicates that the data conform to our general expectation that rural residence will be associated with traditional values.

Of the nine value clusters represented in these tables, seven are significantly affected by urbanism in China, but only two are significantly affected in the United States. Three of these significant relationships in China are found for the raw correlations only; the beta weights are not significant, when all the other variables are added to the equations. Each of these effects in both countries is in the direction hypothesized, that is, rural residents hold more traditional values. The only instance of replication between the United States and China, however, is found in Table 7.10; in both countries rural residents are more accepting of the authority hierarchy.

The first two tables deal with aspects of male-female relations. Table 7.4 shows that the American sample produced the expected correspondence between urban residency and openness in male-female *sexual relations*, but no such relationship was found among the Chinese respondents. For *women's status*, by contrast, Table 7.5 shows a significant effect of urbanism in China but not among the American respondents. Similarly, Table 7.6 indicates that urbanism makes a difference in values related to *divorce* in China, but not in the United States.

The lack of urbanism effects regarding sexual relationships in China is

TABLE 7.4   Traditionalism in Male-Female Sexual Relationships: Multiple
Regression Analysis

	China Survey		U.S. Survey	
Predictors	Corr.	Beta	Corr.	Beta
Block 1: Areas				
Urban	.02	.01	−.13[a]	−.12[a]
Rural	−.01	−.02	–	–
Incremental R² (%)	.05		1.57[a]	
Block 2: Demographics				
Age	.20[a]	.13[a]	.29[a]	.33[a]
Sex (female)	.12[a]	.13[a]	.01	−.04
Education	−.06	.04	−.09[a]	−.06
Income (standard units)	.01	−.02	−.05	−.03
Occupation:				
Labor	−.05	.01	.00	−.02
Professional	−.02	−.04	−.02	.00
Managerial	.06	.05	−.01	.00
Marital status:				
Single	−.18[a]	−.03	−.08[a]	.10[a]
Married	.16[a]	.05	.06	.12[a]
Incremental R² (%)	7.57[a]		9.64[a]	
Block 3: Media exposure				
China survey measures				
News	.05	.00	–	–
Traditional entertainment	.13[a]	.01	–	–
Western entertainment	−.21[a]	−.18[a]	–	–
Government propaganda	−.02	.07	–	–
U.S survey measures				
News	–	–	.01	−.08[a]
Entertainment	–	–	−.01	−.01
Incremental R² (%)	2.08[a]		.64[a]	
n =		1476		1926

Note: The dependent variable is an index combining two items: family losing face
if teenage girl gets pregnant before marriage and all right for a man and a woman
to live together before marriage. Incremental R²s are expressed in percentage of
variance accounted for by the corresponding blocks. Betas are the standardized
regression coefficients in the final model when all the variables are entered.

[a]p < .01.

TABLE 7.5   Traditionalism in Female Status: Multiple Regression Analysis

Predictors	China Survey		U.S. Survey	
	Corr.	Beta	Corr.	Beta
Block 1: Areas				
Urban	−.13[a]	−.11[a]	−.03	−.02
Town	−.02	−.09[a]	–	–
Incremental R^2 (%)	2.76[a]		.09	
Block 2: Demographics				
Age	−.15[a]	−.15[a]	.06	.09[a]
Sex (female)	−.08[a]	−.10[a]	−.20[a]	−.25[a]
Education	−.09[a]	−.05	−.25[a]	−.17[a]
Income (standard units)	−.08[a]	−.03	.06	−.05
Occupation:				
Labor	.04	.05	.17[a]	.05
Professional	−.04	.03	−.17[a]	−.07
Managerial	−.02	.01	−.04	−.01
Marital status:				
Single	.01	−.02	.01	−.02
Married	.02	.04	-.05	-.02
Incremental R^2 (%)	2.78[a]		12.94[a]	
Block 3: Media exposure				
China survey measures				
News	−.09[a]	−.01	–	–
Traditional entertainment	−.01	.01	–	–
Western entertainment	−.03	.03	–	–
Government propaganda	−.11[a]	−.12[a]	–	–
U.S. survey measures				
News	–	–	−.11[a]	−.12[a]
Entertainment	–	–	.08[a]	.08[a]
Incremental R^2 (%)	1.15[a]		1.55[a]	
$n =$		1483		1248

Notes: The dependent variable is an index combining two items: differentiation between women and men and three obediences and four virtues. See Table 3.1 for the wording differences between the China and U.S. survey instruments. The incremental R^2s are expressed in percentage of variance accounted for by the corresponding blocks. Betas are the standardized regression coefficients in the final model when all the variables are entered.

[a]$p < .01$.

due to contradictory results for the "family loses face for pregnant teen-age girl" and "premarital cohabitation" items. As reported in Chapter 4, we found a negative correlation between urbanism and "losing face" but a positive correlation between urbanism and the premarital cohabitation item; these canceled each other out when the two were used to form a single index. If we consider premarital cohabitation only, there is a positive relationship between urban residence and openness: The standardized regression coefficients were .06 for township residence and .08 for urban residence (both $p < .05$).

Traditional Confucian values with regard to kinship, seniority, and family obligations are affected by urbanism among the Chinese respondents, but not for their American counterparts. There is a weak effect of urban and township residence on traditional obligations of adult children to take care of their aging parents (Table 7.7). But we find strong urbanism effects in China both for values concerning kinship ties (Table 7.8) and traditional seniority hierarchies (Tables 7.9 and 7.10). Chinese rural residents were more likely to accept the traditional values of "benevolent fathers and filial sons" and "a house full of children and grandchildren" than were their compatriots living in urban and township areas.

In neither area of interpersonal relationships (Tables 7.11 and 7.12) was there a clear effect of urbanism in either country. The only possible exception is that Chinese urban residents seem to prize the traditional values such as "tolerance, propriety, deference, harmony, and generosity and virtues" more than do their rural compatriots; this correlation is not significant when other variables are added to the full equation, however.

Overall, it appears that despite the heavy counter-structuring campaign of Chinese government propaganda, many rural Chinese retain some traditional Confucian values: lower status accorded to women, less receptiveness toward divorce, the importance of parent-child relationships, and deference toward seniority and authority. The general hypothesis that rural areas are more traditional than urban locales is supported in China, but not, by and large, in the United States. (This may be due to limited sampling of rural residence, which was a feature only of the Florida subsample in the United States.) Our finding that rural Americans are less open regarding sexual relationships, and more deferential to authority, scarcely constitutes a general pattern. In general, we can say that we have found much greater diversity in cultural values between urban and rural areas in China than in the United States.

Effects of Age

The first variable listed in the second block of each equation in Tables 7.4 through 7.12 is the respondent's age. As expected from our earlier bivariate findings, age is a most powerful predictor of cultural values, producing at least one significant correlation or regression coefficient in every table except 7.12. This is important to our analysis, because age is a variable that implies temporal movement, even though it confounds social change with individual aging.

While age is consistent in its sheer predictive power, it is not at all consistent in the pattern of its relationship with traditional values, nor is it consistent in the patterns it produces in the two countries. If one harbors an image of older people as holding more traditional values of all sorts, in both the United States and China, there is little support for that stereotype in our data. A negative view of premarital sex is the only topic on which we find older people in both countries clearly in agreement (Table 7.4).

The other two indices involving male-female relationships show opposite results in the two countries, and they are in different directions for the two measures. Table 7.5 shows that younger Chinese are more traditional than their older compatriots in accepting traditional views of the superiority of men and wifely obedience. In the United States the opposite relationship is found, that is, older Americans are more likely to endorse this traditional view of male-female differentiation, when other factors are controlled in the final equation. But on the question of divorce (Table 7.6), the two samples diverge in the opposite fashion, if we interpret divorce as a nontraditional institution. In China, age is negatively related to openness toward divorce; in the U.S. sample, older people are more accepting of divorce—although the beta in the final equation does not reach statistical significance.

The samples from the two countries are in accord on the obligation of adult children to take care of their aging parents (Table 7.7), but in both cases it is the *younger* respondents who are more likely to endorse this traditional Confucian precept. As for the traditional Confucian value of children and filial sons, it is the older Americans who are more likely to endorse these items (Table 7.8). In China, the younger respondents support this view much more than older people do.

On the remaining values examined here, age effects are much smaller in one or both samples, so it is difficult to draw general inferences. Regarding the seniority hierarchy (Table 7.9), older Chinese are more traditional than their younger counterparts, but there is no age effect on this value in the U.S. sample. By mild contrast, the traditional authority hier-

TABLE 7.6 Rigidity Toward Divorce: Multiple Regression Analysis

Predictors	China Survey		U.S. Survey	
	Corr.	Beta	Corr.	Beta
Block 1: Areas				
Urban	−.15[a]	−.14[a]	.01	.02
Town	−.03	−.11[a]	−	−
Incremental R^2 (%)	4.20[a]		.02	
Block 2: Demographics				
Age	.10[a]	.09[a]	−.10[a]	−.06
Sex (female)	.01	−.01	−.09[a]	−.07
Education	−.27[a]	−.15[a]	.02	.01
Income (standard units)	−.02	−.01	−.01	−.02
Occupation:				
Labor	−.05	.02	.06	.04
Professional	−.10[a]	−.02	.03	.02
Managerial	−.04	−.02	.00	.00
Marital status:				
Single	−.10[a]	.05	−.01	−.04
Married	.10[a]	.07	.07	.09
Incremental R^2 (%)	5.94[a]		2.40[a]	
Block 3: Media exposure				
China survey measures				
News	−.02	−.01	−	−
Traditional entertainment	.18[a]	.05	−	−
Western entertainment	−.24[a]	−.09	−	−
Government propaganda	−.10[a]	.02	−	−
U.S. survey measures				
News	−	−	.10[a]	.08[a]
Entertainment	−	−	.07	.05
Incremental R^2 (%)	.86[a]		.90[a]	
$n =$		1466		1585

Notes: The dependent variable is an index combining two items: a couple having difficulties should get a divorce if they (1) do not have children or (2) even if they have children. The incremental R^2s are expressed in percentage of variance accounted for by the corresponding blocks. Betas are the standardized regression coefficients in the final model when all the variables are entered.

[a]$p < .01$.

TABLE 7.7 Obligation to Care for Aging Parents: Multiple Regression Analysis

Predictors	China Survey		U.S. Survey	
	Corr.	Beta	Corr.	Beta
Block 1: Areas				
Urban	−.09[a]	−.05	−.01	−.01
Town	−.01	−.06	−	−
Incremental R^2 (%)	1.30[a]		.00	
Block 2: Demographics				
Age	−.14[a]	−.14[a]	−.24[a]	−.25[a]
Sex (female)	.02	.02	−.07	−.03
Education	−.06	−.05	.10[a]	.05
Income (standard units)	−.09[a]	−.05	.06	.02
Occupation:				
Labor	.03	.03	.01	.01
Professional	−.04	.01	.06	.04
Managerial	.02	.04	.04	.03
Marital status:				
Single	.03	−.04	.04	.03
Married	−.02	−.02	.05	.06
Incremental R^2 (%)	2.16[a]		7.38[a]	
Block 3: Media exposure				
China survey measures				
News	−.01	.00	−	−
Traditional entertainment	.06	.05	−	−
Western entertainment	−.01	−.01	−	−
Government propaganda	.02	.03	−	−
U.S. survey measures				
News	−	−	.01	.07[a]
Entertainment	−	−	-.02	.01
Incremental R^2 (%)	.31		.40	
n=		1447		1913

Notes: The dependent variable is an index combining two items: aging parents should be cared for by children and when aging parents have financial difficulties, they should ask their adult children for help. The incremental R^2s are expressed in percentage of variance accounted for by the corresponding blocks. Betas are the standardized regression coefficients in the final model when all the variables are entered.

[a]$p < .01$.

archy (Table 7.10) is valued more by older Americans, but no age relationship is found in the China sample.

The scale representing interpersonal pragmatism or "connections" (Table 7.11) is negatively related to age in both countries. In China age is the strongest predictor of this index, but the relationship is much weaker in the United States, and it is not significant in the final equation. No age effect is found on the interpersonal kindness index in either of the two samples (Table 7.12).

In summary, our comparative analyses reveal as many similarities as differences in age effects on the nine cultural value indices. The two samples show similar age effects on values concerning premarital sexual relationships, caring for aging parents, and interpersonal pragmatism. Of these three, though, only one is in the traditional direction; the others are either antitraditional (regarding aging parents) or irrelevant to the Confucian tradition (pragmatism regarding connections). In the China sample, older respondents are progressively more traditional with regard to sexual relationships, divorce, and seniority. But greater adherence to traditional values is found among *younger* Chinese in the areas of women's social status, caring for aging parents, and traditional kinship ties. Overall, the U.S. sample indicates a more consistent pattern of traditionalism in decline as we move from older to younger respondents than does the survey in China.

Effects of Education

There are good reasons to expect that a person's education will relate strongly to adherence to cultural values (Hyman and Wright 1978). Education is itself highly valued in the Confucian tradition. At the individual level, extensive education represents the accumulation of knowledge and greater cognitive sophistication and analytical abilities. Moreover, the content of education is closely tied to the dominant ideological orientations in each culture. Greater education in China has also meant heavy exposure to either communist ideology or traditional literature, or both. This complication makes it difficult to predict effects of education in China, but it also makes comparisons between China and the United States more valuable. They may show the different implications of education in differing social systems. Earlier we found a number of bivariate correlations between years of schooling and various value items.

Our high expectations for education as a predictor variable are not encouraged, however, by the findings reported in Tables 7.4 through 7.12. While thirteen of the eighteen within-nation correlations between educa-

TABLE 7.8   Traditional Kinship Ties: Multiple Regression Analysis

Predictors	China Survey		U.S. Survey	
	Corr.	Beta	Corr.	Beta
Block 1: Areas				
Urban	-.13[a]	-.16[a]	-.06	-.05
Town	-.07[a]	-.17[a]	–	–
Incremental R^2 (%)	4.19[a]		.40	
Block 2: Demographics				
Age	-.24[a]	-.23[a]	.15[a]	.14[a]
Sex (female)	.02	.03	.01	-.01
Education	-.06	.03	-.09[a]	-.07[a]
Income (standard units)	-.07[a]	-.01	-.05	-.03
Occupation:				
Labor	.04	.03	.05	.03
Professional	-.08[a]	-.03	-.04	-.01
Managerial	-.02	.01	.01	.02
Marital status:				
Single	.05	-.15	-.08[a]	.04
Married	-.05	-.10	.07[a]	.10[a]
Incremental R^2 (%)	4.74[a]		3.60[a]	
Block 3: Media exposure				
China survey measures				
News	.01	.02	–	–
Traditional entertainment	.04	.02	–	–
Western entertainment	.03	.04	–	–
Government propaganda	.05	.04	–	–
U.S. survey measures				
News	–	–	.06	.03
Entertainment	–	–	.04	.02
Incremental R^2 (%)	.47		.11	
$n =$		1470		1670

Notes: The dependent variable is an index combining two items: a house full of children and grandchildren and benevolent father and filial sons. The incremental R^2s are expressed in percent of variance accounted for by the corresponding blocks. Betas are the standardized regression coefficients in the final model when all the variables are entered.

[a]$p < .01$.

TABLE 7.9 Acceptance of Seniority Hierarchy: Multiple Regression Analysis

Predictors	China Survey		U.S. Survey	
	Corr.	Beta	Corr.	Beta
Block 1: Areas				
Urban	−.10[a]	−.21[a]	−.06	−.06
Town	−.02	−.13[a]	−	−
Incremental R^2 (%)	1.76[a]		.36	
Block 2: Demographics				
Age	.02	.12[a]	.02	.02
Sex (female)	.01	.04	−.01	.00
Education	−.09[a]	−.03	.06	.04
Income (standard units)	−.02	−.02	.01	−.01
Occupation:				
Labor	−.01	.04	−.04	−.01
Professional	−.06	−.03	.03	.03
Managerial	−.02	−.02	.04	.04
Marital status:				
Single	−.01	.11	.03	.06
Married	.01	.07	−.02	.00
Incremental R^2 (%)	.93		.74	
Block 3: Media exposure				
China survey measures				
News	.09[a]	.07	−	−
Traditional entertainment	.10[a]	.04	−	−
Western entertainment	−.04	.03	−	−
Government propaganda	.09[a]	.08	−	−
U.S. survey measures				
News	−	−	.07[a]	.06
Entertainment	−	−	.02	.04
Incremental R^2 (%)	2.18[a]		.48	
$n =$	1501		1490	

Notes: The dependent variable is an index combining two items: expressing own opinions when disagreeing with a senior and young people respecting older people. The incremental R^2s are expressed in percent of variance accounted for by the corresponding blocks. Betas are the standardized regression coefficients in the final model when all the variables are entered.

[a]$p < .01$

tion and a value index are significant, only five of these remain significant when the other variables are controlled in multiple regression. All five of these significant betas are in the negative direction, which is to say that education seems to undermine traditional values to some extent.

The fact that our regression equations "account for" most of the correlations between education and the value indices also suggests that we have included some of the important explanatory variables in our full model. We will not explore here the possibility that certain of these "control" variables are themselves explained by education, which may operate indirectly via consequent individual differences (such as media-use habits) that education fosters.

The most consistent results are found in Table 7.10, for the traditional value of respect for authority. In both countries, the more-educated respondents are more likely to reject the value of authority, and this pattern holds up in the final equation. Indeed, education is the strongest predictor of the questioning of authority in China, and it is the second strongest (after urbanism) in the U.S. sample.

Most of the other negative effects of education on traditional values have to do with male-female relationships. As Table 7.5 shows, the less-educated respondents in both samples are more likely to adhere to traditional views of female inferiority and the obedient wife; this effect is significant in the final equation only among the American respondents, for whom it is the second-strongest predictor (after gender) of this value index. Table 7.6, on the other hand, shows that education is an important predictor of openness toward divorce in China but makes no difference in the United States.

The only other significant effect of education that survives our multiple regression tests is found in the U.S. sample in Table 7.8, for values concerning "benevolent father and filial sons" and "a house full of children and grandchildren." The beta weight in this instance is a weak one, although statistically significant. In both samples, the positive correlation of education with use of connections and interpersonal kindness is no longer statistically significant after we control for other variables in regression.

The net effect of education, overall, is not as strong as one might expect based on a conception of education as a catalyst for social change. Schooling probably entails absorbing some traditional cultural values, even as it undermines others, and these tendencies would cancel one another out in a quantitative survey analysis. The limited education effects that do reach statistical significance are in a direction consistent with expectations. That is, increased education is related to decreased

TABLE 7.10   Acceptance of Authority Hierarchy: Multiple Regression Analysis

Predictors	China Survey		U.S. Survey	
	Corr.	Beta	Corr.	Beta
Block 1: Areas				
Urban	−.13[a]	−.10	−.16[a]	−.14[a]
Town	.01	−.06	–	–
Incremental R^2 (%)	2.25[a]		2.43[a]	
Block 2: Demographics				
Age	−.05	−.05	.09[a]	.07[a]
Sex (female)	.08[a]	.05	−.01	−.03
Education	−.19[a]	−.14[a]	−.15[a]	−.11[a]
Income (standard units)	−.05	−.01	−.06	−.01
Occupation:				
Labor	.03	.05	.08[a]	.05
Professional	−.08	−.01	−.03	.04
Managerial	−.06	−.03	.03	.06
Marital status:				
Single	−.03	−.13	−.08[a]	−.01
Married	.01	−.10	.05	.03
Incremental R^2 (%)	3.38[a]		3.25[a]	
Block 3: Media exposure				
China survey measures				
News	−.08[a]	-.04	–	–
Traditional entertainment	.12[a]	.07	–	–
Western entertainment	−.06	.04	–	–
Government propaganda	−.06	.01	–	–
U.S. survey measures				
News	–	–	−.05	−.08[a]
Entertainment	–	–	.11[a]	.11[a]
Incremental R^2 (%)	.56		1.42[a]	
n =		1452		1683

Notes: The dependent variable is an index combining two items: pleasing superiors and submission to authority. The incremental R^2s are expressed in percentage of variance accounted for by the corresponding blocks. Betas are the standardized regression coefficients in the final model when all the variables are entered.

[a]$p < .01$.

TABLE 7.11 Interpersonal Pragmatism: Multiple Regression Analysis

Predictors	China Survey		U.S. Survey	
	Corr.	Beta	Corr.	Beta
Block 1: Areas				
Urban	.04	.03	.02	.01
Town	−.03	−.03	–	–
Incremental R^2 (%)	.18		.00	
Block 2: Demographics				
Age	−.21[a]	−.19[a]	−.08[a]	−.05
Sex (female)	.01	.02	−.09[a]	−.07
Education	.08[a]	.03	.08[a]	.04
Income (standard units)	−.08[a]	−.06	.10[a]	.10[a]
Occupation:				
Labor	.13[a]	.07	.02	.04
Professional	−.02	−.01	.06	.05
Managerial	−.05	−.02	.03	.03
Marital status:				
Single	.07	−.03	.06	−.05
Married	−.05	.01	−.08[a]	−.13[a]
Incremental R^2 (%)	6.55[a]		3.42[a]	
Block 3: Media exposure				
China survey measures				
News	−.04	.09	–	–
Traditional entertainment	−.10[a]	−.01	–	–
Western entertainment	.15[a]	.15[a]	–	–
Government propaganda	−.03	−.18[a]	–	–
U.S. survey measures				
News	–	–	.09[a]	−.02
Entertainment	–	–	−.01	.04
Incremental R^2 (%)	1.64[a]		.12	
$n =$		1492		1483

Notes: The dependent variable is an index combining the endorsement of two items: Importance of connections in society and using connections to solve problems. The incremental R^2s are expressed in percentage of variance accounted for by the corresponding blocks. Betas are the standardized regression coefficients in the final model when all the variables are entered.

[a]$p < .01$.

traditionalism. And among the limited number of significant education effects, the two nations exhibit more similarities than differences.

Effects of Gender and Marital Status

Neither gender nor marital status is a variable that carries implications for change. But both are closely connected to some of the cultural values in this study, specifically those involving male-female relationships, marriage, and family. We do not consider that being either female or a married person should tend to impel a person toward traditional values in general, but there is good reason for individuals in these demographic conditions to hold specific views on particular items that affect them—views that might otherwise be construed as indicators of a traditional value structure.

The purpose of this section is almost as negative as it is positive in our approach to hypotheses. We do expect women to differ from men with respect to male-female issues, and we expect married respondents to differ from others when the question directly relates to the value of marriage and children. Otherwise, however, these two demographic variables should *not* be related to traditional values. If that turns out to be so, then we will be in a stronger position to infer that the relationships we have found between value items and other, more change-implicated, predictors are indeed evidence on behalf of general processes of cultural change.

Our regression equations in Tables 7.4 through 7.12 are quite encouraging in this respect. Of the nine dependent variables in these tables, none is significantly related to married status in China. In the United States only two of the eight indices that might represent Confucian values are significantly related to being married, and each of these is readily explanable on its face: opposition to premarital sex (Table 7.4), and emphasis on the value of children and grandchildren, and on intergenerational relations (Table 7.8). (We have no particular explanation for the endorsement of "connections" by our married American respondents, but it is not in any event a traditional Confucian practice.) If we assume that values are enduring within the person, the fact that changing marital status does not affect them is an encouraging sign of the general validity of our approach.

All of the significant gender differences in the regression analysis are to be found in Tables 7.4 and 7.5, which deal directly with male-female relationships. In both countries, women respondents are clearly more

TABLE 7.12   Interpersonal Kindness: Multiple Regression Analysis

Predictors	China Survey		U.S. Survey	
	Corr.	Beta	Corr.	Beta
Block 1: Areas				
Urban	.14[a]	.10	.01	.00
Town	−.06	−.01	–	–
Incremental R^2 (%)	2.09*		.00	
Block 2: Demographics				
Age	.01	.01	.02	.02
Sex (female)	−.01	−.01	.04	.05
Education	.13[a]	.07	.10[a]	.06
Income (standard units)	.01	−.03	.05	.01
Occupation:				
Labor	.04	.02	−.10[a]	−.06
Professional	.04	.00	.06	.02
Managerial	.00	−.02	.02	.00
Marital status:				
Single	.07	−.02	.02	.07
Married	.06	−.05	.01	.03
Incremental R^2 (%)	.88		1.96[a]	
Block 3: Media exposure				
China survey measures				
News	.08[a]	.01	–	–
Traditional entertainment	−.02	.03	–	–
Western entertainment	.10[a]	.02	–	–
Government propaganda	.12[a]	.07	–	–
U.S. survey measures				
News	–	–	.10[a]	.09[a]
Entertainment	–	–	−.03	−.04
Incremental R^2 (%)	.81		.70	
$n =$		1451		1255

Notes: The dependent variable is an index combining three items: having tolerance, propriety, and deference; harmony is precious; and generosity and virtues. See Table 3.1 for wording differences between the China and U.S. survey instruments. The incremental R^2s are expressed in percentage of variance accounted for by the corresponding blocks. Betas are the standardized regression coefficients in the final model when all the variables are entered.

[a]$p < .01$.

likely to reject the traditional prescription of deferential status for women (Table 7.5). This finding is virtually face-valid and requires no recourse to a theory of long-term change in broad cultural values for its explanation. Whether women in a truly, thoroughgoing traditional society would accept second-class status below men we cannot determine. Suffice to say that neither U.S. nor Chinese women today can be described as accepting of that rigid gender hierarchy—whether they ever were. Indeed, the marginal results we reported earlier indicate rejection of the traditional gender hierarchy by most respondents of both sexes in both countries.

The other significant finding with regard to gender does not generalize from the one country to the other. Women in China are, as Table 7.4 indicates, less accepting of premarital sex than are Chinese men; there seems to be no gender difference on this issue in the United States, however. (It is possible that in China females were simply less prone to express support for the rather un-Chinese practice of premarital sex, which operates to the detriment of the woman more than the man involved.) The remainder of our tests of gender and marriage effects on cultural values yield nothing of significance, statistically speaking. We consider this substantively significant in a negative sense, though; there is no reason within the context of our general model of cultural change to have expected any relationships between these variables.

Effects of Mass Media

We did not conduct direct bivariate comparisons of media effects across the two nations in earlier chapters, because the U.S. and Chinese media systems are so different. Both their contents and the social forces they represent are specific to each country. Further, we have no clear basis, in theory or prior research, to hypothesize directional media effects on values in the United States.

But while the U.S. analysis reported here is exploratory, we have clear expectations insofar as China is concerned. In China, the mass media have served mainly as an agency of the Communist government in its counter-structuring propaganda campaigns. And to the extent that other forms of mass communication reach people, they are thought to represent competing traditional or Western ideological orientations. We do expect each of these countervailing channels to influence people's values concerning social relationships in predictable directions.

In China, exposure to traditional media sources should predict traditional values, and exposure to Western sources should predict nontraditional values, if the effects of these media are detectable by our methods.

Exposure to government sources, whether news or propaganda, should predict the holding of specific values that represent goals of these government campaigns; these goals have varied over the decades, so we can make no uniform prediction.

In the United States, we distinguish only between news and entertainment media. Either of these broad classes of mass communication might stimulate its audience's concern for certain traditional values. The audiences for news and entertainment tend to be different, though, so we do expect to find opposing results between the two media indices in the United States. Americans who are heavy consumers of media entertainment tend to be less favorably situated in the social structure (e.g., less educated, lower income) than are those who follow news closely (Comstock, Chaffee, Katzman, McCombs, and Roberts 1978). Our multivariate equations control for these demographic factors to a large extent.

The multiple regression analyses in Tables 7.4 through 7.12 show only scattered media effects on the nine value factors in the two samples. Less than 10 percent of the 108 beta weights tested in these tables are significantly different from zero, and only one-half of the eighteen increments to R-squared add significantly to the base equations. The other variables in our predictive model account for a good deal of the variance that might be mistaken for media effects in a less rigorous analysis.

To some extent, between-nation differences are attributable to differences in the number of media variables in the predictive equations. For example, in the China data five of the increments to R-squared are significant for the four-media block as a whole, but in only two instances does a specific beta weight differ significantly from zero (Tables 7.4 and 7.5). The several media factors were inter-correlated, often competing for the same variance in a model, and we will take their collective import seriously here even when no one medium stands out in the regression equation.

In the U.S. analysis, by contrast, there are two significant beta weights (both involving the news exposure index) that do not generate significant increments to R-squared (Tables 7.7 and 7.12). Because our analysis of media influences is exploratory, and unique in the empirical literature comparing the two countries, we will examine each of these significant findings even though the statistical import may be slight in some instances.

Most of the significant effects of mass communication are to be found in the three tables dealing with values in the male-female domain (Tables 7.4, 7.5, and 7.6). The increment to variance explained by the media block is significant in each country in each of these hierarchical analyses. The most consistent finding is that exposure to news in the United States predicts less traditional values of all three kinds, even when all demographics and entertainment exposure are controlled in the final equation. Only for the index representing traditional status of women (Table 7.5), however, do we also find a significant opposing influence of entertainment media exposure. That is, heavy consumers of entertainment media are more likely than other Americans to endorse gender inequality in social status. The news audience, by contrast, not only rejects this value, but it also tends to be more accepting of premarital sex (Table 7.4) and of divorce (Table 7.6) than are those who do not watch news frequently.

In China the picture is, inevitably with so many forces operating simultaneously, more complex. Exposure to Western entertainment predicts less traditional views of premarital sex and (marginally) of divorce, in effect replicating the U.S. findings. Traditional media sources seem to operate in the opposite (i.e., traditional) direction on both these dependent variables, although they do not produce significant betas in the final equation when all other variables have been controlled. These results are in the directions expected. Official propaganda (and possibly news) has its clearest influence on values concerning the equal status of women, a theme that has been featured by the Communist government for many years (Table 7.5). We see in Table 7.6 evidence of alignment of ideological forces concerning divorce, in that exposure to Western entertainment and government propaganda both predict greater openness; in the final equation, neither influence is significant although the overall contribution of the media block is.

The only other clearcut influence of mass communication is found in the United States, with regard to the authority hierarchy (Table 7.10). In this instance, the effect of news is to erode the value accorded to authority, while the effect of entertainment is contrarily to reinforce this value. There is in China a similar pattern of raw correlations (comparing news to traditional entertainment), but these are accounted for in the final equation by controls for demographic variables, particularly education.

These findings might seem to encourage the notion that media news contributes to an erosion of traditional values, but that is not the conclusion we draw from the remainder of these analyses. In the United States, news exposure is a *positive* predictor of two traditional values, the obligation to care for one's aging parents (Table 7.7) and endorsement of kindness in interpersonal relationships (Table 7.12). We found an echo of this latter effect of news in China as well (Table 7.12). Similarly, in Table 7.9 news in China makes a minor but positive contribution to a significant block of media variables in support of the traditional hierarchy based upon seniority. On balance, then, exposure to news in both countries seems to have an antitraditional influence on people's views of male-female relations and on deference to authority, but in some other domains news reinforces traditional values. One would need much more extensive data on the content of news programs in each country, and on the interpretations people make of news that emphasizes crises and challenges to traditional values, before drawing any major conclusions about the influences of mass communication.

The only other significant media effects in these tables appear in the China data in Table 7.11. The media variables as a set influence people's views regarding interpersonal pragmatism. Acceptance of "connections" as a way of conducting business is greater among those who are more exposed to Western entertainment and less among those heavily exposed to government propaganda. Use of connections, a time-honored Chinese practice but certainly not a traditional Confucian principle, has been the object of a concerted government campaign against using the "back door" and government corruption. This campaign's influence on people's views appears to have been eroded by incursions of Western entertainment in the media of China.

We are somewhat surprised to note in Table 7.12 that exposure to traditional entertainment in China is not correlated with principles that were championed in traditional Chinese culture: tolerance, propriety, deference, generosity, and virtues. Despite the fact that almost all traditional operas and stories dramatize the values embodied in the idea of *li*, exposure to these entertainment shows in the media is not related to acceptance of these values. The evidence even suggests that exposure to government propaganda may be related to these values, although the findings lack statistical significance in the context of our demographic controls.

Overall, the evidence of media effects in the two countries is mixed and difficult to sort out. In China, we have an indication that those who are most exposed to Western entertainment are more open in male-female sexual relationships. This empirical relationship is not a spurious one due to age, education, or urban residency, all of which we controlled. We also have a clear indication that exposure to government propaganda reinforces the principle of equality of men and women. This is consistent with our understanding of official communist ideology.[3] These results lend a considerable degree of construct validity to our study as a whole and to the measures that have entered into these empirical relationships.

There is support for our expectation that traditional and Western entertainment in China work as opposing forces, at least with regard to sexual values (Table 7.4). Western media content seems to ally with government propaganda regarding openness to divorce; traditional entertainment propagates the opposite orientation (Table 7.6). But traditional entertainment and government propaganda share a tendency to reinforce the traditional seniority hierarchy (Table 7.7). Hence there is no clear pattern, except that we have found no value domain where western and traditional Chinese media influences impel values in the same direction.

The evidence concerning media effects in the United States is even more difficult to interpret, which is not surprising given the lack of a theory regarding media effects on these cultural values in the United States. We have simply presented the evidence here as we found it for comparison with the more complex swirl of influences in China. Overall, though, we can say that we find no clear indication that American mass media are undermining traditional values. In the areas of authority and male-female relations, news exposure may have this kind of effect, but the entertainment media tend to have a countervailing influence. And news exposure is positively associated with several traditional values, contrary to what some critics of American mass communication might suggest.

Cohort Differences

One way to capture social changes that have been deposited in a population over time is to examine differences across age cohorts. Two approaches can be used: use of age as a predictor variable or as a segmenting variable. In Chapter 5 we described different cohorts as being more or less traditional in their value orientations, and in the multiple regressions just reported we noted that age is a strong linear predictor of values. In this section, a different criterion is employed: We examine variation across cohorts in the ways media exposure and demographic variables are related to the nine value indices. That is, we repeat the analyses we have just reported, but this time we use age to segment the samples into cohorts that shared common historical experiences at roughly the same period in their lives.

Although estimates of cohort effects are always confounded somewhat with effects of aging, the form of analysis of this section frees us from one stringent assumption we have been making about the nature of age—linearity across the entire life cycle. We divide each sample into three age segments: young (under 30), middle-aged (30–49), and older (50–65). These groupings represent life experiences associated with growing up in three different historical periods. Those under thirty in China have lived their entire lives under the Communist regime; the same cohort in the United States has come to maturity in an era when equality for women, among other challenges to traditional values, was a major cultural issue. Those over fifty, by contrast, were ushered into adulthood during a decidedly more traditional era in China, and at least a comparatively more traditional society in the United States. There is reason, then, to assume that the factors that explain individual differences could vary from one cohort to another in each country.

We will describe the results of these segmented regression analyses, but for simplicity of presentation we will not show the results in detailed tables. We also streamlined the regression models for this analysis; each within-cohort equation includes only those variables for which we found effects in the full-sample analyses. Hence, income, occupational categories, and marital status were not included. Also, all the independent variables for each within-cohort equation were entered simultaneously; the purpose is not to evaluate sequential blocks of predictors, but rather to identify interactions between age and other variables.

As in the previous section, we will discuss what we found in these simplified regression equations as a single set, taking each independent variable separately. Overall, the equations accounted for a little more than 4 percent of the variance in each dependent variable, a statistically significant but not especially impressive degree of predictability. This reduced variance is due to the restricted variance in age, which was one of the strongest predictors in the full-sample models.

In China, the strongest equations tend to be those for the youngest cohort, age below thirty (median R-square=5.8 percent); in the United States the opposite pattern is found, in that the highest R-square (median=4.25 percent) is found in the oldest cohort, those aged fifty to sixty-five. While we should not make too much of slight statistical tendencies, these may be the cohorts that, in their respective countries, have undergone the greatest pressures toward cultural change during their lifetimes. There seems to be more effect of demographic and communication variables on cultural values in China on those whose entire life experiences have been dictated by the shifting tides of Communist propaganda, while in the United States the greatest individual differentiation is found among the older citizens, who have seen the greatest shifts in cultural values during their lifetimes. These speculations give us a useful point of departure for examination of the particular equations that follow here.

Effects of Urbanism

Urbanism might affect values at different time points, defined both in terms of life-cycle stages of individuals and in terms of historical eras. The results in the within-cohort regressions, however, offered little evidence of this kind of process. The only fully consistent effect of urbanism is its tendency to undermine the authority hierarchy in the United States; each of the negative beta weights in the three age cohorts was significant. If we set aside statistical significance and examine only the consistency of signs (positive vs. negative betas), two other urbanism effects were consistent across age cohorts in both countries: the negative influences on traditional kinship ties and on respect for seniority.

Most of the strong effects of urbanism within specific cohorts involve these same dependent variables, the hierarchies of authority (in the United States) and seniority and filial parent-child kinship relations (in China). There was evidence of an erosion of these traditional values in the urban setting, an effect that was not particular to any age cohort.

The other coefficients worth noting in this analysis mostly involve male-female relations, and here we did find some cohort-specific differences. In China, the effect of urbanism on rigidity toward divorce was weakest in the youngest age cohort. In the United States, it was the oldest cohort in which urbanism was most strongly predictive of less traditional views on premarital sex and equality for women. These are not simply mirror-image findings; the linear effect of age is opposite in the two countries for both equality of women (Table 7.5) and rigidity toward divorce (Table 7.6).

Because the China sample was broken down into three residential categories (urban, town, and rural), there were some relationships that are best described as "ruralism" effects, that is, dependent variables where the dummy variables for urban and town residence produce about the same coefficients in regression equations. There was in China a consistent ruralism effect in all age cohorts against openness toward divorce and toward traditional kinship ties and acceptance of the seniority hierarchy. All these influences were in the direction of persistent traditionalism in rural settings, which would accord with the general notion of modernization originating from the cities.

Two interactions between ruralism and age cohort were suggested by the China data. One was that the obligation to support one's aging parents is most characteristic of rural residents in the oldest age group; these are people who may well foresee a time when they will need to be cared for themselves. The other interaction involves the value of equality for women; rejection of this change from the traditional status hierarchy was strongest in rural areas among those in the *middle* cohort, aged thirty to forty-nine. This group includes mostly people whose sex-role socialization was underway, but probably not complete, at the time the Communist government began to campaign for equal status of women. Being in a rural area may have insulated people somewhat from the influence of this counter-structuring effort. We do not wish to make too much of slight statistical tendencies, though; suffice to say that this was one of the very few indications of a nonlinear interaction of age with urban-rural location in all our analyses.

The other interaction involved the seniority hierarchy. While ruralism was correlated with maintaining respect for seniors in every cohort (especially in China), this effect was significant only in the middle-age (30–49) cohort. This is probably not mere statistical coincidence. These people were in their key formative years during the Cultural Revolution of 1966–1976, and in the cities especially they would have experienced many challenges to the tradition of concession to one's elders. As the middle cohort today, those in the cities are squeezed between elders who hold on to good jobs and younger people who have more systematic training for these same positions.

Effects of Age

Even though we segmented the total sample from each country into age cohorts, we retained age as a linear predictor within each equation. This is problematic because of the truncated variance in the age variable, and it asks a somewhat different question than do the tests for age effects in the total sample. One purpose is to sort out cohort vs. aging effects; if age remains significant in a within-cohort regression, its effect is less likely due to common experiences and more likely to an aging process. There might also be nonlinear effects of age that show up within a specific cohort. For example, in China we might expect age differences among those who were educated during the Cultural Revolution (1966–1976), that is, those now in our sample's middle-aged cohort.

Of the fifty-four regression coefficients we tested for age effects within cohorts, only seven were significantly different from zero. This is more than would be expected by chance, but it suggests that overall the effects of age that we found earlier are accounted for by those linear analyses. There were some interesting reversals in the within-cohort analyses, though, particularly on traditionalism regarding extramarital sex. Here, the linear effect of age within the youngest cohort was toward more openness in the United States, but in the more traditional direction in China. In other words, Chinese respondents in their late twenties were less open to premarital sexual relations than were those who are even younger. In the United States, as young people age from their early to late twenties they seem more approving of extramarital sex. This reversed itself in the next age group, though; there was less approval for such behavior as Americans moved through their thirties and forties.

The other significant within-cohort age effects in China were found for the pragmatism measure. Age was associated with greater approval for use of connections among those in their twenties, but in the two older cohorts this practice decreased in approval as people aged. The one other significant age effect was found in the United States, a tendency (wholly understandable) for people over fifty to become increasingly positive about children and grandchildren, and filial intergeneration relations, as they grow older. Neither of these findings seems to require a general pattern of change in traditional cultural values for its explanation.

It is also instructive to compare the age effects in the within-cohort tests with those found for the entire samples. The negative age effect on openness in male-female sexual relationships in the U.S. sample remained in two of the cohorts and was in the same direction in the third. In the China sample, however, there was a nonlinear component to the relationship between age and sexual values, notably a high level of openness among the very youngest Chinese.

In the China sample, the significant age effect on traditionalism in female status observed in the total-sample regression essentially disappeared in the within-cohort regression analysis. Similarly, all five of the significant relationships with age in Tables 7.6 through 7.9 were well accounted for by cohort differences.

Effects of Education.

We found very little evidence of differential effects of education between age cohorts. Of the significant education effects in the total-sample regression analyses, about one-half of the betas remained significant in the partialed analyses across cohorts and all were in the same direction. Education's antitraditional effects on, for example, traditionalism in female status in the U.S. sample, and openness toward divorce in the China sample, were roughly constant across age cohorts. Education's effect of undermining the authority hierarchy, found in both countries, persisted across age cohorts in both countries, although it was most evident in the middle age groups.

Education had a significant positive effect on the index of traditional interpersonal kindness, among the Chinese who were fifty and older; no effect was found in the two younger cohorts. It is worth noting that the three Chinese phrases that formed this value index were taught in elementary school textbooks until the early 1950s, as the proper manner of dealing with interpersonal relationships in the Chinese gentile class. The anti-Confucian counter-structuring program of the intervening decades seems not to have eradicated these precepts in this older cohort.

Effects of Sex

In the previous section, we found that the respondent's sex made very little difference apart from values related to male-female relationships.

The segmented regression analyses produced only limited evidence of differential effects of gender across the age cohorts. Each of the significant regression coefficients for sex in Tables 7.4 through 7.12 held up at least in terms of direction, and usually at a significant level, when we controlled for cohort.

American women's rejection of traditional female status, for example, was strong and significant in comparison with men's views in every cohort. The results were in the same direction (albeit weaker) in every cohort in the Chinese sample as well. On premarital sex and divorce, the gender differences in China held up across cohorts. There was one age-specific sex difference in the American sample: Women thirty and older were more likely than their male age-mates to accept divorce as a solution to marital problems; in Table 7.6, no significant gender effect was found in the total-sample regression.

The significant tendency of American males more than females to approve of use of connections held up in every age cohort in about equal degree; this finding is probably peculiar to the U.S. social structure and has little to do with traditional values. The only other age-specific gender effect in these analyses was found in China, where the older women were more likely than older Chinese males to accept the traditional authority hierarchy. This isolated result could easily be a result of chance fluctuations in the data, given the large number of betas representing sex differences that we examined.

Media Effects

In the previous section, we presented evidence showing some significant media effects in each sample. Media effects in China were particularly interesting because they represent influences of three distinct social forces that have been at work in contemporary China. Now, we ask the question: "Did mass media affect people's value holdings differently in different age cohorts?"

In male-female relationships, there was very limited evidence of differential media effects. The positive effect of Western entertainment on openness in male-female sexual relationships remained in each age cohort in the China sample. The parallel effect on divorce, however, occurred mainly in the middle-age cohort. We were not surprised to find traditional communication influencing traditional views on divorce among the youngest Chinese adults. News exposure was unrelated to any of the values in the male-female relations domain in China.

In the U.S. sample, however, we found that the antitraditional effect of news exposure on the three male-female indices was age-specific. For none of the three indices (premarital relations, traditional status for women, and openness toward divorce) was the effect of news exposure significant for the under-thirty Americans; all six of the corresponding betas were larger in the older cohorts, and four of the six were significant. It seems plausible that news does in general have a liberalizing influence on this domain of values in the United States, but that among young adults there are many other influences that override this influence. The opposing tendency of entertainment media use in the United States was found mainly in the middle-age cohort.

In the domain of hierarchical relationships, only the Americans had shown significant media effects in the total-sample analyses: a negative effect of news, and a positive effect of entertainment, on acceptance of the authority hierarchy. These two effects remained in the within-cohort regression models, with some shifts in magnitudes. In the China sample, we uncovered two additional significant effects specific to an age cohort. Exposure to government propaganda was related to greater acceptance of the seniority hierarchy among Chinese respondents under thirty years of age; among Chinese between thirty and forty-nine, exposure to Western entertainment had a similar effect.

The effects in China of both Western and government media on the index concerning interpersonal pragmatism turned out to be limited to the under-fifty age cohorts. In the middle-age cohort, news as well as Western entertainment seemed to encourage approval of "connections." Exposure to government propaganda had the opposite effect.

Overall, our partitioning of the samples on age tended to demonstrate the robustness of our earlier findings more than to locate cohort-specific effects of demographic or media variables. The idea that we would find in specific cohorts evidence of a particular cultural influence persisting from an earlier time did not gain much credence from this segmenting exercise.

Summarizing Media Influences

Given our original interest in cultural change in China, we should take a more comprehensive look at the major communication influences that have seemingly been directed against traditional values in that country. Overall, the influence of Western entertainment is, as expected, antitraditional. But the relevant correlations are significant for only three of eight value domains, and in only one of these domains—male-female sexual relations—is the beta weight significant or consistent across age cohorts. The remaining regression coefficients (ignoring the "connections" measures) in Tables 7.4 through 7.12 are mostly near-zero. In the segmented cohort analyses, the middle-age cohort more often produced betas that were positive (i.e., pro-traditional) than negative. The influence of Western media, then, seems to be localized, fostering openness regarding extramarital sex but not extending to a more general assault on the traditional Chinese value structure.

We might entertain several conclusions from this lack of evidence of a broad erosion of traditional Chinese values due to Western media incursions. One possibility is that Western entertainment is not particularly antitraditional. Indeed, we note in the U.S. sample that exposure to media entertainment is most often *positively* associated with traditional values, in some instances significantly so. A second possibility is that the effects of Western media have been limited due to neutralizing influences within China. There is some evidence of this in our results.

One indigenous influence we have examined consists of traditional Chinese media forms, and in four of the eight value domains we find evidence that traditional values are indeed correlated with exposure to traditional media. But none of these correlations remains significant when other variables are controlled in multiple regression. With the exception of engendering resistance to divorce among those under thirty, traditional media did not exercise a detectable influence on Chinese values as represented in this study.

Government propaganda is a bit more powerful, particularly in reversing the traditionally lower status of women. But otherwise where we find correlations that might indicate propaganda influence in China they lie in the direction of *supporting* traditional values. This is true for the seniority hierarchy and the Confucian virtues of interpersonal kindness, although in neither case is the beta weight significant, and in both cases the effect seems to be limited to the youngest Chinese adults. We cannot, then, conclude that the propaganda campaign waged by the Communist government has eroded the broad range of Confucian values, at least not in the sense that at the individual level heavier exposure to this kind of communication implies that pattern of value change. In some respects, exposure to government propaganda instead seems to have counteracted antitraditional influences from Western media.

Finally, individual differences in news exposure in China have no significant relationships with traditional values in the multiple regression analyses, either for the total sample or within any age cohort. In the United States, news exposure is a significant predictor of antitraditional values in male-female relationships and the authority hierarchy, but of *traditional* values regarding parents and virtues of kindness. Hence, where heavy consumption of media news is correlated with values, which is to say in the United States, those values are about as likely to be traditional as antitraditional.

Media influences may not be captured effectively by the methods used here. Exposure is difficult to measure accurately by self-report methods, especially where no universal metric can be offered to the respondents. Media content is not all of a piece, in either country, and the values represented are often implicit rather than straightforward teachings. Individual differences within a country say nothing about structural differences between countries. Our measures are doubtless weak in reliability, which attenuates the observable correlations. And we have exercised stringent statistical controls on our tests, entering all our demographic variables before examining any media indices, and then controlling for all media simultaneously as we tested the influence of each.

Thus we consider the significant beta weights and increments to R-square reported in this chapter to represent serious influences, powerful enough to withstand a number of barriers to acceptance of the inference of media effects. They are few, and those few deserve to be taken seriously in theorizing about the processes of value change in China, or for that matter in the United States.

Notes

1. The adjective "strong" is used here in a relative sense in the context of the "limited media effects" model that once prevailed in the United States (Klapper 1960). Even today, some scholars have reservations about the exact nature and magnitude of media effects (e.g., McGuire 1986). The hypothesis of media effects in China is based on the media dependency model: Because of the continuous social changes over the past forty years and because of the Party monopoly of media in China, there may be a greater level of media dependency in China.

2. Use of standardized regression coefficients is also based on empirical considerations. First, the different surveys used very different response scales, so it is difficult to compare the indices with the original metrics. Second, we have no conceptual basis for "appropriate" units for those value scales.

3. For example, one often quoted statement by Mao claims that women "support half of the sky" under the socialist system.

8

Macroscopic Comparisons:
Taiwan and Korea

THE COMPARISONS OF CULTURAL VALUES in China with those in the United States have indicated a number of differences, but many similarities too. We have attributed these similarities mainly to assumed processes of change in China, although it must be kept in mind that values have been changing in the United States as well. Cross-sectional data, though, cannot directly indicate change. We have relied upon our understanding, from prior scholarship, of Chinese culture at earlier times. In this chapter we take an entirely different approach by comparing these two countries to two others: Taiwan and Korea.

The addition of Taiwan and Korea to our comparisons of value prevalence does not literally solve the problem of *observing change*; in none of these countries can we work from baseline data from an earlier historical era on the measures in question. But Taiwan and Korea can be very useful points of comparison for purposes of *inferring change*. Each of these countries shares to some extent the Confucian tradition, which emanated from China to neighboring lands in East Asia over many centuries of cultural diffusion.[1] While far less anthropological effort has been devoted to Taiwan, or even to Korea, in comparison with the documentation on China dating from the early twentieth century, these countries carry distinctly Confucian reputations.

Taiwan and Korea are intended to serve in this chapter as—in a very loose sense of the term—"control groups." That is, given our central purpose of comparing China with the United States, and our underlying interest in cultural change where we cannot directly observe historical changes in the variables we have measured, we require additional context. With this in mind, parallel surveys were undertaken in 1990 in both Taiwan and Korea; the same value questions we have been analyzing in our previous chapters were asked of large and heterogeneous samples. The marginal results from those two surveys have been published, and we will make use of their findings in this chapter.

We should not stereotype or simplify the intricate cultures of Taiwan and Korea any more than we would those of China and the United States. A full-blown comparative analysis of the four countries, doing justice to their unique histories in which many people and cultural traditions have been blended, is far beyond our scope or intention in this chapter. What we do assume is that, whatever their other differences, the peoples of Korea and Taiwan shared with the Chinese a common core of Confucian values earlier in this century. We cannot know with certainty how widespread this cultural influence was in either country. Certainly Korea has from early in its history incorporated cultural (including linguistic) traditions of more northerly peoples, and Taiwan has been home to a Pacific Islander culture that dates to a time long before the influx of Chinese. These factors would tend to produce results in Taiwan and Korea that are counter to our general assumption, which is that these countries today are *more* Confucian than China.

If Confucian values turn out to be more prevalent in Taiwan and Korea than in China, that will be evidence relevant not only to questions of change and what has changed, but of the *sources* of that change. An issue we raised in the previous chapter concerns possible external influence, particularly of Western media, on cultural change in China. We did find some evidence of this external influence, particularly in the domain of male-female relationships. The alternative hypothesis is that change in China has been mainly a matter of *internal* dynamics, and this is where Taiwan and Korea can provide especially useful comparisons.

If Western media influence accounts for the erosion of traditional Confucian culture, then this influence should be far more evident in Taiwan and Korea than in China. These two countries have been closely aligned with the United States, and with the West in general, since approximately the time of the Communist Revolution in China. American military forces have been stationed in Korea for four decades, and U.S. media have been plentiful there throughout that period. Taiwan has been a major importer of made-in-the-U.S.A. media products (among other things American) for some decades too.

It is a basic article of faith among critical theorists of the "Media Imperialism" persuasion (e.g., Schiller 1976) that the introduction into a traditional society of mass media cultural artifacts inevitably destroys the indigenous culture and its traditional system of social obligations and relationships. If that hyperbolic account is accurate in even a modest degree, the process it describes should have by this time rendered both Taiwan and Korea decidedly less Confucian than they might have been in the absence of Western influences. We cannot test that proposition, as we lack baseline data for these countries.

A related proposition that we can test here is that Taiwan and Korea have, as a result of heavier infusions of Western media, become less Confucian than China. China has during the Communist era permitted only minor incursions of Western media in comparison with the wholesale importations that have been evident in Taiwan and Korea. If Western influences were the major force working toward cultural change in China, dominant over that country's own internal dynamics, we should see in our surveys much greater adherence to Confucian values in China than in Korea or Taiwan. Put more comparatively, we should according to the Western Cultural Imperialism model find more similarities in values between the United States and either Korea or Taiwan than between the United States and China.

We have, however, been stressing throughout this study the alternative view, that cultural value change in China has been mostly an internal process, force-drafted by the Communist government through its counter-structuring programs. These have involved media propaganda, to be sure, but in Chapter 7 we found that exposure to government propaganda is only a minor predictor of individual differences in specific values. In this chapter we are looking at cultural values in a much more macroscopic sense, comparing whole nations as if each were a single entity. We also look at the cultural values as a set, not just as a series of individual measures. If our inferences about China's cultural change, and the sources impelling toward it, are valid, we should see a greater breaking away from the Confucian tradition by the Chinese than by the Korean or Taiwanese respondents in these parallel surveys. More specifically, we should find that the Korean and Taiwanese value structures are more similar to one another than either is to that which prevails in China.

The comparative status of the United States in this context is somewhat ambiguous. We began this analysis with a conventional stereotype (based on anthropological observers' accounts) of American culture as the antithesis of the Confucian tradition. But we have found many areas in which American values are, while not Confucian in any literal sense, indistinguishable from the cultural values we associate with the Confucian tradition. This is especially true in the areas of family pride and individual virtues. American culture is more traditional than many have suggested, including many American leaders who get themselves elevated to positions of power by warning of the erosion of these traditional values. These values seem not to have eroded in the broad population, which is perhaps what makes them rhetorically useful in America. Still, we must consider the United States as an opposite pole from traditional Confucian culture, to the extent that such an opposition is empirically to be found somewhere in the world. Thus our expectations need to be cast in comparative terms again. We anticipate that the cultural values of the U.S. sample will differ from those of all three Asian countries in this chapter, China, Korea, and Taiwan.

That said, what would the two processes of cultural change in China, that is, Western influence and internal dynamics, lead us to predict in macroscopic comparisons across these four countries? The Western influence model is fairly straightforward, predicting more "Westernized" (that is, non-Confucian and nontraditional) values in countries where Western media have made their greatest incursions. This would mean that people in either Korea or Taiwan (we have no basis for fine distinctions between the two in terms of Western media) would produce value structures that resemble that of the U.S. sample more than would the comparable measures for the Chinese sample.

The theory of indigenous origin, that is, that China's value structure has moved away from the Confucian tradition more than has that of either Korea or Taiwan, does not necessarily predict greater similarity between China and the United States. Certainly the Communist government has not sought to Westernize, nor to Americanize, the Chinese people; quite the contrary. There is no reason to expect that a result of counter-structuring and propaganda from Beijing would be to create values among the Chinese that resemble those of the United States more than they do those of Korea or Taiwan. All three of these countries have been treated as enemies of China throughout the Communist period.

Still, if there has been change away from Confucian values in China due to the Communist restructuring efforts, it would in a survey such as this (where we limit ourselves to measures of values that were central to the old Confucian tradition) have the following inadvertent result: The value structure of the Chinese would be more like that of Americans than would the value structures in either of the two countries that have been overtly aligned with, and in cultural contact with, the United States, that is, Korea and Taiwan.

To these contrasting accountings of cultural change we must add a third model that has been referred to repeatedly in this study: modernization. There has been, throughout this century at least, a long-range trend in all these societies (and elsewhere) toward "modern" social practices such as greater gender equality than one finds in most "traditional" cultures. But as we have repeatedly pointed out in our analyses, the process of modernization is not one of smooth, linear, inexorable, and universal transition. Cultural change occurs spasmodically, in one venue or another, from time to time, as a result of extraordinary or at least novel ideas and social forces.

Communication between cultures is one factor that enhances modernization, and internal efforts directed toward change is another (Schramm 1964). Some modernization may be virtually inevitable in what we usually characterize as "modern" times: universal public education, industrialization, and urbanization. Changed lifestyles and practices associated with these "megatrends" may erode Confucian values in such areas as female status, family and kinship ties, and interpersonal deference and propriety. If this is the operative force, it should tend to obscure differences between the samples under study here that are due to country-specific indigenous forces. More specifically, it means that there would be some departure from traditional values in these nations, corresponding to their respective levels of "modernization." This reasoning would place the Chinese sample at the most traditional end of the scale, compared with the other three countries in our study.

Taiwan and Korea Surveys

The sample surveys conducted in Taiwan and Korea were designed as part of the larger project on communication and cultural change in East Asia directed by Godwin Chu. Efforts were made in the Taiwan and Korea surveys, therefore, to provide cross-cultural comparability of the survey questions. The data from these two surveys are still being analyzed by other members of Chu's research team for separate reports. In this study, only the published marginals involving the eighteen traditional Chinese phrases are used (Wang, Chung, and Chu 1991; Chu, Lee, and Kim 1991).

The Taiwan survey, conducted in 1990, interviewed 960 randomly selected individuals from four districts, covering Taipei, a city and a town in the Taipei suburbs, and a village. The same instrument used in the China survey was used in Taiwan.

The Korea survey was also conducted in 1990. The sample respondents were selected from among the adult residents of Seoul, the capital of Korea, and other cities, towns, and villages. Of 584 respondents interviewed, 530 provided complete data. The part of the survey we use here involved the eighteen traditional phrases used in the China survey. Most of these Chinese phrases have corresponding expressions in Korea; several were paraphrased into Korean idiomatic expressions. The researchers conducting the survey consulted a Chinese studies expert for the adequacy of the Korean idiomatic expressions in representing the ideas expressed in the Chinese phrases. A small pretest was conducted to test the adequacy of the Korean version of these Confucian ideas.

In the analysis reported in this chapter, we treat each nation as a unit of analysis and the eighteen Confucian value measures as attributes selected from the universe of cultural values in each culture. We examined the percentage of people in each sample endorsing each of the value measures. To measure the geometric distances between the four cultures, we took the difference between the percentage endorsing a value and the percentage rejecting the same value, and then calculated correlations between the four series of percentage differences. By this procedure, we took into account not only people who had a clear idea concerning each value measure but also those who were ambiguous or ambivalent toward an item. The U.S. survey contained the English expressions of only thirteen of the eighteen Confucian value items. Therefore, in the analyses that involve the U.S. data, the N was 13, while the comparisons between China, Taiwan, and Korea are based on the full eighteen items.

Findings

There are two ways of comparing empirical relationships between these four countries. One is to calculate a standardized coefficient that indicates the similarity between each pair in terms of the *pattern of responses* to the value items in our survey. The second is to calculate the *absolute distances* between pairs of countries on specific items. In this chapter we perform both kinds of tests. It is important to note that these do not test the empirical similarity between a pair of countries in the same sense. It is quite possible for two countries to be far apart in absolute locations on a value scale and yet to hold the same relative priorities among these values and thus to produce high positive correlations. In this case, however, the two methods produce very similar conclusions.

First we calculate the Pearson product-moment correlations between countries based on paired scores for the same items. These scores take into account both the percentage of respondents endorsing an item and (by subtraction) the percentage rejecting that item. These analyses are summarized in Table 8.1. Second, we present in Table 8.2 and in the bar charts that follow the absolute percentages in each country who endorsed each item. The differences between any two countries can be readily seen in these displays.

Imagine a universe in which we can place the four nations we are comparing. We might imagine that at one time there would have been a cluster of the three nations that share the Confucian heritage, with the United States isolated, far away from this three-nation cluster. But a quick look at Table 8.1 indicates that this is not the case. This table shows the correlations between each pair of countries. The data show that the common cultural heritage among China, Taiwan, and Korea does draw them together in that there are significant positive correlations between these three nations. In addition, a greater similarity is shown between China and Taiwan than between China and Korea, suggesting special commonalities between the two Chinese cultures. But Taiwan and Korea

TABLE 8.1   Correlations of Confucian Values Between Cultures (Percentage Endorsement minus Percentage Rejection)

	China	Taiwan	Korea
Taiwan	.73[a]		
Korea	.58[b]	.88[c]	
United States [d]	.69[a]	.47	.32

Note: The cell entries are Pearson correlation coefficients, based on the differences between the percentages of endorsement and rejection of the eighteen Confucian value items.

[a]$p \leq .01$
[b]$p \leq .05$
[c]$p \leq .001$
[d]The coefficients are based on the English translations of thirteen of the Confucian value items.

are more similar than China and Taiwan, indicating the possibility that something shared by Taiwan and Korea is no longer shared by China.

As we expected, the United States is not significantly correlated with Taiwan or Korea. But China is a different story. It seems that despite their shared cultural heritabe, China and Korea are less similar than are China and the United States. Saying this in another way, China is closer to the United States at the level of aggregate value prevalence than it is to Korea, and the correspondence in values between China and the United States is almost as strong as that between China and Taiwan.

The data suggest that if we use Taiwan and Korea as anchors to locate the contemporary remains of Confucian values, China is farther away from them than one might have expected. We should hastily add that the United States is more similar to these two anchors of Confucian values than conventional wisdom might have predicted. Even though the correlations between the United States and either Taiwan or Korea do not reach significance with $N=13$ values, they are nevertheless positive and of moderate strength.[2] The data can also be examined from a different direction. If we use the United States as the anchor for the antithesis of the Confucian values, we find that China is much closer to it than one would have expected. The correlations seem to embed different forces of influences in these four nations. To account for them, we must look at the data in more detail.

The raw data are shown in Table 8.2. In this table, we show the four

TABLE 8.2   Acceptance of Confucian Values in Four Countries (in percentages)

	China	Taiwan	Korea	U.S.A.
Tradition and Heritage				
Long historical heritage	93	70	81	n.a.
Respect tradition	55	61	82	73
Loyalty to state	77	72	82	92
Familial Relations				
Benevolent fathers, filial sons	63	93	97	74
Glory to ancestors	19	63	83	n.a.
A house full of children and grandchildren	21	27	16	54
Social Relations				
Way of the Golden Mean	5	69	58	n.a.
Generosity and virtues	59	89	92	92
Harmony is precious	49	89	97	24
Tolerance, propriety, deference	47	83	88	94
Submission to authority	53	83	80	56
Pleasing superiors	7	26	8	59
Discretion for self-preservation	8	44	92	n.a.
Roles of Women				
Chastity for women	32	59	80	31
Three obediences and four virtues	8	50	67	30
Differentiation between men and women	10	39	30	13
Work Ethic and Economic Status				
Diligence and frugality	90	93	82	81
Peasants high, merchants low	11	11	16	n.a.

Sources: Godwin C. Chu and Yanan Ju (1993). "Statistical tables for The Great War in Ruins—Communication and Cultural Change in China," Honolulu: East-West Center. Georgette Wang, Chung Wei-wen, Godwin C. Chu (1991). "Cultural value survey in Taiwan," *Journal of Communication Arts* 12, 71–80. Godwin C. Chu, Jae-Won Lee, and Won-Yong Kim (1991). "Perceptions of traditional values in South Korea," *Journal of Communication Arts* 12, 81-90.

Note: For the first three samples, cell entries are percentage "proud of" each item as a cultural element. For the U.S. sample, cell entries are percentage who agree with the statement.

nations side by side, and we present only those value items that have been classified into the four domains of social relationships examined in this book: male-female, family, authority and seniority hierarchy, and general interpersonal relationships. To facilitate comparisons, we also used bar charts, each depicting the data concerning the value prevalence in the four nations in one of the four domains. The bar charts help to visualize the relative emphases in the four nations within each value domain.

Figures 8.1 through 8.4 reveal one distinct common feature: With a single exception, the Taiwan and Korea respondents are more likely to endorse the Confucian values in all four domains than are those in China. (With a few exceptions, Taiwan and Korea also stand more on the side of Confucian values than does the U.S. sample.) China appears to be different from all three nations in different ways.

Figure 8.1 shows that on male-female relations, the Taiwan and Korea samples consistently gave higher endorsement to the Confucian viewpoint. The China sample was similar to the U.S. sample on two of the three items. On obedient wife (i.e., "three obediences and four virtues"), there was almost unanimous rejection among the Chinese respondents, while this value was still endorsed in Taiwan and Korea.

Figure 8.2 shows a similar picture in the family relations domain, with some small variations. On "glory to the ancestors" and "benevolent fathers and filial sons," the Taiwan and Korea samples gave much higher levels of endorsement than the China sample. The three samples are similar, however, on the phrase "a house full of children and grandchildren." All three Asian samples gave lower levels of endorsement of this item than did their American counterparts.

This pattern of homogeneity among the three East Asian samples, compared with the U.S. sample, showed up again on the item "pleasing superiors" (Figure 8.3). While the U.S. sample reported nearly 60 percent endorsement, the levels in China and Korea fell to single digits. In the Taiwan sample, the corresponding number was 26 percent—higher than those in the China and Korea samples, but much lower than that in the U.S. sample. On submission to authority, Taiwan and Korea are on the side of strong endorsement, while the United States and China go together on the low side. Figure 8.3 also shows that the United States, Korea, and Taiwan were similar on the value of respecting tradition. In China, a large number of respondents had reason to reject this Confucian value.

Figure 8.4 shows China lowest overall in endorsement of the Confucian values concerning interpersonal interactions. The Taiwan and Korea samples produced similar levels of strong endorsement on three of the four value phrases. Even though they differed somewhat on the phrase "Way of the Golden Mean," the Taiwan and Korea respondents were much more favorable than the China sample, which unambiguously rejected this traditional teaching. Compared with China, the U.S. sample seemed more approving of two of the three value phrases asked about: generosity and virtues and tolerance and deference. The U.S. sample, similar to Taiwan and Korea, showed high proportions of people endorsing these two value phrases. Removed from their Confucian context, of course, these items may sound like simple truisms to most Americans.

Interpretation

How to interpret the findings? Returning to the alternative expectations that guided this analysis, we find that our first assumption is basically confirmed. On a majority of these value phrases, the Taiwan and Korea samples are more "Confucian" than the U.S. sample in terms of the aggregate levels of prevalence. By and large, though, the data presented here also lend support for one basic conclusion of Chapter 6: The English expressions of the traditional value phrases were meaningful to the U.S. respondents. These items were able to locate the U.S. respondents correctly on the less "Confucian" side in comparison with Taiwan and Korea.

It is the China data that defy standard expectations, from either a "Westernization" or a "modernization" theory of change. Although China was sometimes close to Taiwan and Korea, the value structure in China also exhibits a significant positive correlation with the U.S. data. The four figures show that on a number of values, notably the three items on male-female relationships, the "benevolent fathers and filial sons" item in the family relationships domain, the "submission to authority" value in the hierarchy domain, and the "interpersonal harmony" item, the Chinese were much closer to the U.S. respondents than to the two samples drawn from cultures with the same Confucian heritage. This pattern indicates two things for us to consider in more detail.

One is that something unique to China, not shared by Taiwan and Korea, has forced the Confucian values out of their historical prominence in the culture. And this force is unlikely to be Western influences, even though at the individual level, those with more exposure to Western influences showed less support for Confucian value expressions (Chapter 7). The generally low levels of endorsement of Confucian values in China indicate only the rejection of those values, *not* replacing Confucian values with Western values. The acceptance of distinctly Western cultural values in China (or in Korea or Taiwan) is a subject for another study.

The other point that the data lead us to consider is where we would place the United States on the value ideas expressed in these items. Based

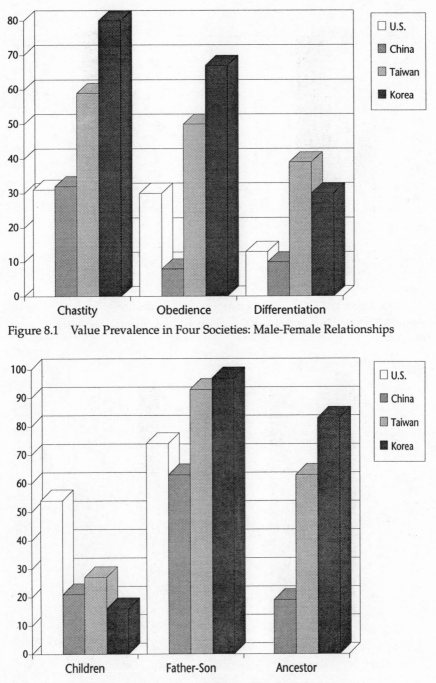

Figure 8.1   Value Prevalence in Four Societies: Male-Female Relationships

Figure 8.2   Value Prevalence in Four Societies: Family Relations

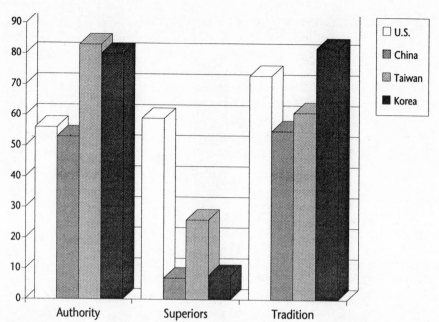

Figure 8.3   Value Prevalence in Four Societies: Authority and Seniority Hierarchies

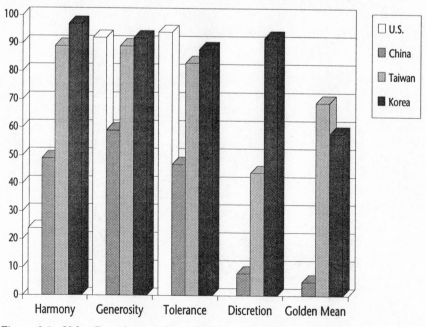

Figure 8.4   Value Prevalence in Four Societies: Interpersonal Relations

on a common-sense perception of the United States and China as two cultures located at the two ends of an East-West spectrum, one would expect an almost consensual rejection among American respondents of many of the value expressions taken straight from Confucian teachings. Our data show that this is hardly the case. In fact, quite a few of the value ideas taken from Confucian teachings were readily acceptable to many American respondents, often more so than to Chinese.

Conclusions

When Americans are asked about a series of values that to a Chinese appear to be Confucian, they accept many of them. These individual items, taken out of the context of a traditional body of teachings, often seem unexceptionable. The U.S. respondents, then, appear on some items to be *more* Confucian than the Chinese. This we think would be an erroneous reading of our data. The Americans were definitely less Confucian than were the Chinese in Taiwan or the Koreans. But because of their experiences with the massive counter-structuring campaigns under Mao, the people in China were further removed from Confucianism in their value expressions than were the Americans.

As the analyses of this chapter make clear, the Confucian tradition is alive and well—even if it is undergoing some changes—in both Taiwan and Korea. These countries are much more like one another than like China in both their absolute endorsements of cultural value items and in their configurations of responses across the Confucian values in these surveys. The United States is even less like these countries in the overall configuration of values indicated by the correlation coefficients, although on some specific questions the American responses are more favorable than are those of the Chinese. In China these instances mostly involve rejection of Confucian phrases. This does not mean that China is becoming more like the United States. It simply means that China under communism has departed dramatically from traditional Confucianism and bears little resemblance to either Taiwan or Korea.

Notes

1. It would be pretentious to suggest a degree of past homogeneity among the three nations. The current population in Taiwan consists predominantly of Han people who speak the same language as people in mainland China, as well as

very small segments of indigenous people whose culture is being assimilated by the Han Chinese. Korea is an independent nation that has shared common cultural roots with China throughout its long history. Confucianism was the official state ideology of the Yi dynasty in Korea for more than five hundred years (1392–1910). The Chinese language was used as the official Korean language for centuries until the adoption of *han'gul*. While sensitive to the differences and originality of those cultures,most observers hold that both Taiwan and Korea share the Confucian heritage (Tu 1991; Chu, Lee, Kim, and Ju 1993).

2. We keep in mind that the correlation coefficients involving the U.S. data are based on thirteen items. Significance level is affected by the smaller sample size.

9

Summary and Looking Ahead

CULTURES CHANGE. Indeed, even as we write about the two cultures we have surveyed and analyzed, they are changing. It was an interest in the *changing* Chinese culture that brought us to this study originally. We added the U.S. survey as a way of contextualizing the data from China, because of the difficulty of inferring change from cross-sectional evidence. The Taiwan and Korea studies were initiated for the same reason. But in all, we must admit that we have only snapshots at one point in the long history of each nation, insofar as the traditional values we have measured are concerned. This will not prevent us from drawing inferences about change, but we should be properly wary.

Our evidence is unavoidably deficient in a second respect. We have asked people what values they endorse, and they have answered our questions in terms of the options they were offered. These kinds of survey data are useful, but not always to be taken literally. We know what people say they value, but neither we nor any other scholars using self-report data can determine what people really value. Our evidence is, then, one kind of indicator of what people think about cultural values, a tool for making judicious inferences that inevitably go beyond the data per se.

For purposes of assessing change, the results of this study can be quite useful to future researchers, for whom we have provided benchmark data. A replication of this study in the next few years could reach much firmer conclusions about change than we can draw at this point. We view these surveys as analogous to Godwin Chu's 1964 interviews in rural Taiwan, which became clearly interpretable after he replicated the same survey in the same villages fourteen years later (Chaffee and Chu 1992). But there is no analogous way of our looking back in time from the surveys reported here, and we will have to be content with less than comparable evidence when we consider processes of change.

We emphasize these caveats because our data have provided us with many surprises and findings that we consider quite substantial. We began with an assumption that there existed in China at least the remnants of an integrated structure of values corresponding to the traditional teachings of Confucius. This we did not find. Not only were there rather feeble endorsements of major Confucian precepts, but the key cornerstones of Confucian teachings, such as the way of the Golden Mean, were actually rejected by a majority of the Chinese respondents. There were weak correlations across the various items representing traditional values in China, a pattern that we had expected (and also found) in the United States.

There was, then, no overall Confucian value structure evident in our data. At the best, we were able to pair up items that shared some content and were positively correlated, to reduce eighteen single items to nine value indices. This represents a simple exercise in scale construction, not to be taken as evidence of a sustaining body of what used to be a highly integrated system of Confucian values in traditional China. Quite the contrary, the factor structures were about the same in the United States, a country little touched by Confucian doctrine and one that has classically been contrasted with China. There were in both countries some intercorrelations between a few of these factors, which do indicate that these value domains are not isolated from one another. But these intercorrelated factors do not extend to the full breadth of our value measures; they mostly involve status hierarchies and have no clear implications for either male-female relations or personal virtues, for instance.

The image of these two countries as repositories of opposing tendencies in cultural values has similarly been shattered by our findings. On some key values, contemporary China resembles the United States more than it does the two other Asian nations we examined here, Taiwan and Korea. The latter two are much more clearly Confucian in their general support for most of the traditional value items in the questionnaires. China seems to be in a transitional state, not so much moving in the direction of the West (as represented here by the United States) as in its own direction. This is not surprising, of course; it was Communist China's stringent internal programs of class struggle aiming at cultural change that gave rise to this study, and we have certainly found evidence of the effects of those counter-structuring campaigns.

Given that history, and this evidence, we will not shrink from interpreting our results in terms of change. This will to some extent include the United States as well. The U.S. survey reported here was conducted at a time when power in Washington, D.C., had been placed in ideologically very conservative hands. The women's movement, which dates back to the suffragette era of the turn of the century, had foundered in the 1980s after the defeat of the Equal Rights Amendment to the U.S. Constitution. Proselytizing churches that champion large families (e.g., Mormon) and oppose birth control (e.g., Roman Catholic) reached new heights of influence. Thus our snapshot of America may not have caught that country in a typical pose.

Nonetheless, in commenting upon our findings in the United States we will offer inferences not only about what American values are, but also about how we think they got that way—and where we think they are headed. That is, we intend in our synthesis here to maintain the spirit of parallelism that has guided us throughout this book, although admittedly our primary focus has from the outset been China.

It is clear to us that *internal dynamics*, rather than either foreign influences or a linear process of modernization, hold the key to explanation for most cultural change. We have repeatedly noted this in our analyses, as we tested each of these general models against the survey evidence and against one another. This we suspect is true for almost any country; the forces that produce cultural change tend to be primarily indigenous in origin even though they may be reacting to external influences. Specifically, our most general inference is that today's predominant cultural values in both China and the United States are the product of the particular histories of those countries. Accordingly, our attempts to explain change in either country should focus mainly on its history. But we are not historians and this is not a historical study. To the extent that we refer to historical events, they will be major ones—and they will mostly be events that marked major transformations in China. It is there that forces have been mobilized on behalf of cultural change in recent decades, and it is there that our study began and will conclude.

Value Differences and Similarities

This analysis focused first on twenty-three measures of cultural values that we considered comparable across the two cultures. Of the twenty-three items, eighteen were chosen, on the basis of empirical evidence of cross-cultural equivalence, to create nine value indices in four domains of social relationships. To help us interpret the Sino-U.S. comparisons, we also considered data from Taiwan and Korea, which may be regarded as would-be levels of Confucian values that might have been expected in China without the Communist revolution.

The results suggest that there have been some fundamental changes in Chinese values regarding these social relationships. Some of these shifts amount to no less than the annihilation of the Confucian value system, particularly in terms of traditional value expressions that were once widely accepted in China and are still widely accepted in Taiwan and Korea.

The Sino-U.S. comparisons also show that American culture houses many values that are equivalent to the Confucian precepts signified in those Chinese value expressions. This is not to say that we have found

America to be a Confucian society. Rather, what we have seen in this study are two characteristics about Americans. First, the English expressions of the traditional Confucian values posed no particular difficulties for American respondents. These value statements were *meaningful* to them in that they responded to these statements in a fashion similar to their Chinese counterparts. This point is clearly illustrated by the factor analysis results shown in Chapter 6. Second, albeit with some variations, a large number of American respondents found the English expressions of traditional Confucian values *acceptable*. And in general, the within-nation patterns of acceptance conform with the general dualism of traditionalism vs. modernity. That is, the United States remains in many respects a traditional society in terms of cultural values, and it is "modernizing" like other traditional societies.

With the exception of Hsu (1981), no one has compared American and Chinese cultural values from a traditional Chinese perspective. Relying on his cultural anthropologist's perceptiveness, Hsu noted major differences between American and traditional Chinese cultures. Analyzing lay persons' self-reports of their values in the two countries, we have found more similarities than Hsu noted. While differences may excite people of one culture about the other, similarities may help people of one culture to appreciate the other.

Comparisons at such a general level may, however, miss some concrete cultural contexts and interpretations of the value statements in them. We need to examine specific value items at more concrete levels and to synthesize the bits and pieces of evidence we have accumulated.

Let us look first at each of the four general domains we have concentrated upon in this study and then look at the structure of values across these domains. We conclude with a discussion of the dynamics of cultural change, mainly in the context of Communist China, both during the decades prior to our survey and in the foreseeable future.

On Male-Female Relationships

The domain of most clarity is male-female relationships. In general, the Chinese respondents held a more restrictive posture than did the Americans concerning *male-female sexual relationships*. There was less acceptance of equal status for males and females among the Chinese respondents (although in both the Chinese and U.S. samples, equal pay for equal work was approved by overwhelming majorities). The two samples were quite similar, although perhaps for different reasons, in their rejection of the notion of lower female status and of chastity for women. In all these respects, the United States and China stand fairly close to one another, and far below Taiwan and Korea, in traditionalism.

Compared with what we know of traditional Confucian values in this area (see also Chaffee and Chu 1992), and from Taiwan and Korea, the findings from China indicate remarkable changes in cultural values. Many fewer Chinese respondents endorsed such values as chastity for women and wifely obedience, compared with Taiwan and Korea. Contemporary Chinese culture embraces a much broader acceptance of male-female equality, compared with what we know of the Confucian value system.

Several factors might explain these changes in China. The proclamation of the New Marriage Law in the early 1950s marked the beginning of an end to the practice of placing women in an inferior state. The new marriage law prescribed equal status for Chinese women via a set of legal rights, including the right to seek a divorce. Universal employment under Communist rule brought women into the labor force; in nearly every Chinese family, both the husband and wife are employed, each earning an independent wage. The value changes induced or accompanied by these social changes are in the same direction as change that has been promoted by the government's ideological campaigns, so it is impossible for us to disentangle the two sources of changes. But they have been powerful.

In this same era women have struggled for equality in the United States as well. There have been many legal provisions, such as affirmative action and equal-pay laws, toward this general end. The result in the United States seems to be about the same as in China, which is to say general (but not unanimous) acceptance of equality for women. Chastity, a concept built upon a double standard that exempts men, still has its adherents in both countries (although not nearly so many as in Korea and Taiwan), but economic equality between the sexes has become the rule in both the United States and China.

The two countries diverge where sex itself enters the picture, the Americans being much more permissive in their views on premarital relations. On the other hand, the American respondents were much more likely to endorse the traditional Confucian teaching of wifely obedience than were the Chinese.

On Family Relationships

Values concerning family relationships are directly related to daily routines of life. In China, the family is still the basic unit of consumption, housing, child-care, and welfare. In rural areas, families are even the basic units of production to some extent. This is clearly not the case in the United States. Although there are still some family farms in America, agriculture represents only a small percentage of the labor force. In an industrial society where information work is expanding rapidly (Machlup 1962; Porat 1977; Nass 1986), increasingly more social functions have been assumed by other social institutions. Considering the comparative centrality of the family, we expected the Chinese to emphasize traditional family values more than American respondents.

There is some evidence supporting this expectation, but most of our findings point in the opposite direction. A slightly higher proportion of Chinese endorsed the obligation to take care of aging parents. But a significantly higher proportion of Chinese respondents expressed readiness to accept divorce when children were not a consideration. More American respondents endorsed the English equivalents of such traditional Confucian values as "benevolent fathers and filial sons" and "a house full of children and grandchildren."

The relatively low acceptance of the Confucian value of "benevolent fathers and filial sons" in China, in comparison to its nearly universal acceptance in Taiwan and Korea, is rather clear evidence that such experiences as the Cultural Revolution have had a deep impact. During that period, some children were urged to condemn in public their "reactionary" parents, a practice explicitly denounced by Confucius (see Spence 1993).

In the United States, where this reciprocal Confucian relationship had to be expressed in a double-barreled question, more than two-thirds of our sample agreed that "Fathers should be kind to their sons, and sons should be devoted to their fathers." While many respondents may have mentally divided this item into two propositions and found each reasonably acceptable, their overall reaction is clearly more in line with traditional familial obligations than are the results from the China survey.

In the United States there was much wider endorsement of the value of "a house full of children and grandchildren" than was found in any of the three Asian countries. China ranked about midway between Korea (which was lowest) and Taiwan on this item. Obviously Americans value children and hence family, which suggests that this value is not peculiarly Confucian but rather a universal feature of life. It is somewhat traditional, in the extreme phrasing, though, an inference supported by the fact that in both the United States and China this item is negatively correlated with education and professional occupational status, and in China it is more popular in rural areas.

Real-life circumstances may indicate rejection of the value of children and grandchildren in the Asian countries. We note that *married* Americans are, as one might expect, more likely to endorse this item, but in China that is not the case. The effect of age is also opposite in the two countries: older Americans are more likely to endorse the "children and grandchildren" item, but the older Chinese are less supportive.

A major factor affecting this value could be public communication campaigns. Family planning has been widely promoted throughout Asia in recent decades, perhaps no less in Korea or Taiwan than in China. In the United States, on the other hand, the administration of the 1980s had drawn back from support of family planning programs at home and abroad, and the dominant church voices were promoting large families (although decrying teenage pregnancy and births out of wedlock). This difference in official policy could help to explain why Americans endorsed the traditional large family much more than did the Chinese.

In China, people's life experiences under the current system appear to be a more potent determinant than the moral influences of erstwhile Confucian teachings. Family life today is drastically different from the rural China of a century ago. In contemporary China, the basic social unit is no longer the extended family, in which a family elder functioned as the enforcer of authority. Today, nuclear families with a working father and mother are much more typical. Villages are headed by individuals selected not by family elders based on kinship ties but by the Party based on ideology. In cities, individuals are closely tied to work units (factories, schools, agencies, or institutions) that have no bearing on kinship ties. In the past, children were helping hands for family operation of production; now, children are more considered mouths to be fed. As these new life experiences supersede the social and economic functions of the extended family, the Confucian teachings on behalf of the extended family are weakened too.

The breakdown of Confucian values concerning families was not brought about solely by the Communist revolution. A more likely starting point was the Japanese invasion of 1937, when millions were forced to leave their homes and separated from their families. The land reform of the early 1950s, which stripped land holdings from millions of landowners, and the collectivization movement, which took the production function away from families, completed this transformation.

The demise of the extended family is reflected also in the low value placed on ancestors in Chinese life. In the world depicted by Hsu (1949), ancestors were a source of inspiration and power for Chinese people. But in our survey, only about one Chinese in five approved of the item regarding glory to the ancestors, whereas in Taiwan and Korea approval was in the 70 to 90 percent range.

The enduring force of life experiences in Chinese family relations can be seen in two specific findings. Chinese females were more likely than males to endorse obligations for taking care of aging parents. The reality in contemporary China is that married women still assume the role of a traditional daughter-in-law by taking responsibility for housekeeping. The other observation is that when children were involved, nearly half of those who would accept divorce as a solution to problems between a couple instead rejected divorce. Parental commitment to the next generation, a central component of the Confucian value system, remains deeply rooted. What has changed, compared with the "old China," is the concept of family that used to include not only several vertical generations and ancestors, but also several horizontal layers of relatives. Now, a family in China means a couple with their immediate children and perhaps the grandparents. That is, the boundary of one's "family" in China is coming to resemble that in the United States.

On Hierarchical Relationships

On the surface, the Chinese and American respondents do not differ much in their values concerning authority and seniority hierarchies. In both samples about 50 percent accepted submission to authority. Both samples evinced a broad consensus of respect toward older people. When it comes to expressing one's disagreement with an older person, however, the Chinese were less prepared to breach tradition than were Americans. On the other hand, the Chinese were also less likely to attempt to please superiors. If we attribute some variation to wording and context, this set of results can be viewed as roughly a tie between these two supposedly contrasting countries on those manners of traditionalism.

Submission to authority is a value that lies at the heart of the Confucian value system (Hsu 1981). It was presumably taken for granted in traditional China and is still accepted by more than 80 percent of people in both the Taiwan and Korea surveys. We cannot resist the conclusion that significant changes have taken place concerning people's view of authority in China (Chu and Ju 1993).

There are well-defined historical events to account for the undermining of the Confucian hierarchy of relationships. The land reform in the early 1950s eliminated the traditional authority in rural China, the landlord class. Similar activities were carried out in the cities against factory and shop owners in 1956. About a decade after the local Party bosses were established as the new authorities, the Cultural Revolution specifically aimed at removing them. This process laid bare the transitory nature of authority in contemporary China, breaking down the traditional orientation of unquestioned submission to authority.

However, there appears to be a lingering presence of the Confucian value of authority, as illustrated by a scene in Tiananmen Square on April 20, 1989. A large crowd of college students and their supporters gathered, not to worship an authority figure, but to express their discontent. But the means of their expression was to commemorate a symbol of reform—a figure of authority—the former Communist Party chief, Hu Yaobang, and to kneel on the steps of the People's Great Hall to present their petitions to the Party authority. Clearly, these young Chinese were not willing to submit themselves blindly to any authority, an unmistakable indication of departure from the past; but they chose the symbolic act that was a traditional display of the authority hierarchy for their political protests (Esherick and Wasserstrom 1992).

Erosion of the authority hierarchy has approximately the same demographic roots in today's China as it does in the United States. The strongest adherents to this tradition tend in both countries to be rural, less educated, and followers of media entertainment (but not news). Americans seem to be willing to submit to those who have power because of what they can *do*, rather than because their authority is perceived as legitimate and inherent. That is, status is achieved in the United States, whereas in a traditional hierarchy, such as China in the past, it is ascribed. Contemporary China appears to be moving away from the traditional orientation to authority and adopting a more instrumental or situational view than would have been advised by a Confucian teacher of bygone times.

This change is probably not so much a product of what the Chinese have been taught, as what they have *learned*, largely from events during the Cultural Revolution. The more orderly regimes of Taiwan and Korea, while they have, to say the least, been heavy-handed at times, have not impressed on their people the latent lesson that those in authority can be humiliated and summarily ousted. While political change continues apace in all four of the countries we compared in Chapter 8, it has been much more mercurial in China than in the others. Elsewhere, existing local power structures tend to be left in place even when there is a shift away from centralized authoritarian power (as in Taiwan) or toward it in recent times. In China, the restructuring has been much more thoroughgoing, and the result—no doubt unintended by those who have intermittently seized or transferred power—has apparently been to discredit the authority hierarchy itself.

This process is far from a complete one, however. Submission to authority, which at some level is necessary within any society, is in China about as widespread as in the United States. The exact nature of authoritative relationships in the two countries eludes detailed analysis given the data at hand here, but our general expectation for the future is that a kind of equilibrium will be reached such that China will resemble the United

States more than it did in this empirical analysis—and much more than it had in the past.

On General Interpersonal Relationships

The domain of general interpersonal relations produced little evidence of uniform differences or similarities between Americans and Chinese. A significantly higher proportion of the Chinese agreed on the traditional value of interpersonal harmony, but endorsement of this idea in China is much lower than in Taiwan and Korea. Striving for interpersonal harmony to the extent of "yielding to others' wishes," as the question was worded in the U.S. survey, was not among the favored ideas of American respondents.

In both societies, personal connections were considered quite important, which in fact they are for many people. But a much higher proportion of Chinese respondents, compared with the U.S. sample, said personal connections are "very important." Chinese more often than American respondents said they were willing to use connections for problem solving. These patterns indicate a stronger pragmatic orientation in China, probably a continued influence from China's past. In traditional China, networking was a very important part of life (King 1991), a point clearly illustrated by the traditional notion of "five sames" (wu tong)— that is, same ancestral origin, same kinship clan, same native place, same career affiliation, and same school. People with any one of these "sames" would treat one another with affection and special consideration (Chu 1979). A pale version of this obligation is the Anglo-American tradition of the "old school tie." Still, Americans find connections quite helpful in getting jobs and other valuable situations, as in Granovetter's (1973) study of "the strength of weak ties."

In other areas of interpersonal relationships, the evidence suggests a surprisingly low incidence of Confucian values in China. Few Chinese respondents said they accepted the Confucian view of benign human nature. (A majority regarded human nature as neither benign nor evil, a view consistent with Chinese Communist doctrine.) Fewer than half of the Chinese respondents were proud of the Confucian value of "tolerance, propriety, and deference." Chinese traditions heavily valued the virtues stated in this phrase and the mannerisms they embodied (Chu and Ju 1993; Hsu 1981). The much lower approval of this concept in China compared to the U.S. data could be an artifact of wording in translation. But that will not account for the overwhelming endorsement of the same ideas in Taiwan and Korea (Figure 8.4). We think the difference in China is real, and it signifies a major change from the past.

Being generous to others and being tolerant of people with different beliefs are not exclusively Confucian norms by any means. Most Americans in our survey agreed with both ideas, which express universal humanistic principles. Accepting them does not mean that the United States is more traditional than China, but that those concepts have in China been invested with a negative connotation by past ideological campaigns. This evidence supports our argument that rejecting Confucian values in China is not primarily a result of Western influences. But it does not mean that the Chinese people are themselves less generous or tolerant with others; we suspect that they will behave very much in accordance with these principles if they find them rewarding. They shy away, however, from according to these traditional virtues the normative status that used to be honored in traditional China.

On Dimensionality

Compared with differences in value prevalence, value dimensionality is an area of striking cross-cultural similarity between China and the United States. In the area of male-female relationships, in each sample two dimensions, male-female sexual relationships and female social status, were clearly distinguished. In family relationships, both cultures grouped values along three dimensions, divorce, caring for parents, and kinship ties. The two cultures also were similar in differentiating the seniority and authority hierarchies, as well as in separating interpersonal pragmatism and interpersonal kindness.

These similarities indicate a degree of conceptual equivalence of the value measures across the two cultures. That is, the measures seem to have meant the same things to respondents in both cultures. If that is so, we may more confidently attribute the observed differences in values to cultural differences and the observed similarities in values to cultural similarities. That has been our assumption here.

We should, however, also note an important difference between the two cultures in the way respondents might have interpreted specific value measures. That is, although the U.S. sample showed clear dimensions parallel to the China data as we just noted, the Chinese survey revealed an additional dimension: there was a decided separation between behavior-specific value indicators and the traditional-phrase measures.

Two factors helped cluster the traditional phrases together. First, these phrases originated from or are present in the writings of Confucian scholars and literature. Second, all of them were targets of propaganda campaigns in China over the years. These common origins and cultural meanings can explain the correlations among them, even when they refer to quite distinct realms of personal relations. Although we have no direct empirical evidence, the commonalities among these phrases, and especially the extent to which they were viewed negatively in China alone, can be taken to reflect the effectiveness of Communist indoctrination.

Value Variations and Cultural Change

It is, as we have said, risky to draw inferences of cultural change based on cross-sectional data. Two procedures can help us to reduce that risk. One is to explicate cross-sectional sociological characteristics that relate to processes of change, including urban and rural residency, age, and educational levels. The second is to make use of our indigenous knowledge of the historical movement of the two cultures.

Urban and Rural Plurality

Urban and rural differences are often time-dependent in the developmental sense. When looking at cultural values that persist from the pre-industrial past, differences between urban and rural areas tend to indicate a pattern of change: innovations are most often first urban, then rural. This is at least the case in the developmental model based on the experiences of industrialization and agricultural modernization (Rogers 1983).

We might then say that more changes in cultural values took place recently in China than in the United States, because we found larger urban versus rural value differences among the Chinese than American respondents. Although the U.S. sample did show a few urban-rural differences (Chapter 4), these differences were largely explained by correlated differences in education, age, and other demographic characteristics of the urban and rural residents (Chapter 7). Only the rural Americans' more restrictive orientation regarding male-female sexual relations cannot be accounted for by other variables in the multivariate models.

Overall, Chinese rural residents, compared with city dwellers, were much less open toward male-female premarital cohabitation; more traditional in their views toward "equal pay for equal work"; more inclined toward the notion of an obedient wife; less agreeable to divorce; and more willing to take care of aging parents. These tendencies are consistent with the general view that rural residents in China remain more traditional than their urban counterparts. But Chinese rural residents were also less likely to consider premarital teen pregnancy a "family shame" and less concerned about "chastity for women." Chinese rural residents were also less supportive of "benevolent fathers and filial sons" and of such traditional Confucian values as interpersonal harmony, "tolerance, propriety, and deference," and "generosity and virtues." Taken as a whole, these differences cannot be simplified into a claim that rural residents are more "traditional" than urban dwellers, even in China.

China is obviously at an earlier stage than the United States in national development, which can readily account for the larger urban-rural differences in China. In American society, whatever differences in lifestyle existed in the past between urban and rural areas, they have disappeared in recent decades due to easy transportation, saturation of mass media coverage (especially television), and nationwide distribution of common goods and services. This has not been the case in mainland China. For decades, the Chinese Communist Party has included urban-rural differences as one of the "Three Big Divides"*(sanda chabie)* to be eliminated. But its policy has been concentrated on industrializing the urban economy, in effect squeezing the farmers. Rural China is still characterized by a low standard of living, limited availability of information, and difficult transportation. In short, these were the conditions of a traditional society, and we should not be surprised to find traditional values persisting there as well. What our study offers is a more particular view. Rural traditionalism in China is not all of one piece. We find a more Confucian orientation in male-female relationships, which were largely untouched by the rural land reform, but at the same time we note changes in other types of social relations, including father-son relationships, authority patterns, and seniority hierarchies, which were once grounded in extended families.

Age Differences

Age is a "natural" variable that can represent several theoretical constructs (Chaffee 1991), such as growth, socialization, and history. All of these involve change. When different age groups in a population demonstrate prevalent values that are so dissimilar as to be unlikely results of maturation and aging, we should be encouraged in making inferences about cultural change even in the absence of longitudinal data.

Our results showed significant age differences in cultural values in both nations. The two samples exhibited a few similarities in age effects that are consistent with the linear model of diminishing traditional orientations among the younger cohorts. Specifically, in both samples, younger respondents were more open to the idea of premarital cohabitation, less likely to accept family shame for unmarried pregnant teens, more accepting of the idea of equal pay for equal work, more likely to choose love (a

Western value) as the most important criterion for mate selection, and less concerned about "frugality and diligence." While these cohort differences probably will not all remain stable as those individuals grow older, we can say that both cultures seem to be becoming less traditional in these specific value domains.

But there are limitations to the linear model of cultural change as indexed by age. In both nations, younger respondents were more likely to accept obligations for taking care of and offering financial assistance to their aging parents. If we assume that fulfilling one's obligations for the welfare of one's parents represents a traditional value (certainly a Confucian value), this result is inconsistent with the linear model.

The two samples reveal some intriguing differences related to age cohorts. Young and middle-aged Chinese respondents were, compared with their American counterparts, less likely to accept the principle of "equal pay for equal work." More Chinese than American respondents in the 50–65 age cohort endorsed the idea of adult children taking care of aging parents, while more American than Chinese respondents in this age cohort accepted "benevolent fathers and filial sons." The notion of "a house full of children and grandchildren" was more prevalent among older Americans, as one might expect, but also more prevalent among younger Chinese (perhaps due to resentment against the one-child policy, which affects primarily young adults). Probably the most striking difference between the two samples is the age pattern on chastity for women. The youngest Chinese cohort cared about chastity for women as much as the oldest American cohort, and the oldest Chinese cohort cared about it as little as the youngest American cohort. Such interactions suggest that, while the age-related value differences in the United States conform to the linear model reasonably well, the Chinese respondents reflect the erratic differences in life experiences among the different age cohorts during their formative years.

Some age differences have to do with each cohort's unique life experiences and expectations. For example, the "1960s generation" in the United States came to maturity in an era of social conflict, questioning of authority, and liberal egalitarianism. Searching for meaning in life and experimenting with different lifestyles is characteristic of this cohort, who were mostly in our middle age (30–49 years) group. Compared with that generation, the younger Americans socialized in the Reagan era are more conservative. These differences show up in our aggregate analyses (Table 5.2) on items related to these cultural themes. Similarly, in China, those in their late thirties and forties experienced the Cultural Revolution more intensely and hence may have become more disillusioned with the Communist doctrines. They tend to produce some slight curvilinear patterns in our analyses. If we used finer-grained age divisions, it may well be that

America's 1960s generation and China's youth of the Cultural Revolution ended up adopting a distinct set of rather similar values. The commonalities, while statistically weak, are substantively striking. In both countries the middle age cohort is less deferential to authority and places greater emphasis on the traditional personal virtues. The Little Red Book of Chairman Mao was popular reading for American university students during the Vietnam War era, and this may represent a subtle influence of Chinese cultural change on one cohort in the United States.

Social Influences via Education and Media

Age differences are in China an indication of value volatility, that is, the lack of coherence or stability in value orientations. They are not the only indication, however. Early in this book, we presented Whyte's (1989) typology of three distinct types of value orientations in China: orthodox traditionalism, Communist propaganda, and Western cultural input. Those influences contribute greatly to value volatility in China.

Chapter 7 shows that heavy exposure to Western entertainment in China is related to greater openness in male-female sexual relationships and to divorce; exposure to government propaganda predicts lower acceptance of traditional values concerning women's status. Some media-exposure effects differ across the age cohorts. In the sensitive 30-to-49 age cohort, for example, higher exposure to government propaganda predicts less openness toward divorce while exposure to Western entertainment seems to have the opposite effect.

On male-female sexual relationships, traditional Chinese programs and Western entertainment operate as opposing forces. These Western programs seem to be consistent with government propaganda in increasing openness toward divorce. But a different alignment is found where seniority is concerned; traditional entertainment and government propaganda exposure both reinforce the traditional seniority hierarchy. No parallel findings are observed in the United States, where the media are not so readily distinguishable in terms of Confucian value implications. It remains to be shown that television in America is as homogeneous with regard to the dimensions we have measured here as it seems to be in some other respects (Gerbner et al. 1986; Greenberg 1980).

Another variable that conveys various influences on cultural values is education. Education, when used as a tool to enforce the hegemonic ideology, may prevent change from occurring. But in general, one expects that increased education produces a person who is more accepting of equality and openness in value orientations and of change in general. To a limited degree, this expectation was supported by the data. In both samples, people with lower education were more likely to accept the more traditional status accorded to women. At least in China, increased education was related to greater openness toward divorce.

In China, there were also indications that education might function as a mediating factor. Education seemed to reinforce the traditional values regarding "chastity for women," "benevolent fathers and filial sons," and "interpersonal harmony." But in other areas, education weakened traditional influences. For example, higher education was related to greater acceptance of divorce and to lower approval of "a house full of children and grandchildren." In sum, education may be an important factor in value changes in China, but the direction of the change effected via education is not necessarily to undermine Confucian values nor to boost Western values.

Modes of Cultural Change

Our comparisons of China and the United States can tell us a good deal beyond these specific value measures. Our larger goal in this project is to understand the dynamics of cultural change in these two nations, and to some extent in all nations—a challenging task. Any nation experiences pressures, both within and from outside, toward change and responds with internal efforts at preservation (or restoration) of cultural values of the past. This was true, at the time of our surveys, of political discourse both in Reagan-Bush America and in Communist China.

National leaders often find it meaningful to discuss the present and the future in relation to something that is vaguely understood as "traditional values." There is even some parallel between the two countries in what "traditional" means. Reference to strong family ties, male dominance, conformity, and interpersonal harmony is not limited to Confucian societies, as we have seen here.

This study provides a basis for extending our conceptual analysis to a higher level of generality. In closing, we want to consider the contours of cultural change not just in these two countries in this specific era. Our first step in that direction has been to incorporate into our analysis of cross-sectional findings what we know about historical changes in the two nations. China and the United States are changing, but in distinctly different ways. We want to conceptualize the ways in which these changes are occurring, over and above what we can say directly from the evidence presented in our many tables of data.

Change in China has been characterized by fragmentation, interruption, and cultural zig-zags. These have often been forced from the center by radical movements and the seizing of power. This is most notably a feature of the Communist Revolution, but it has also occurred, as we have noted, at earlier times in this century. The methods of cultural change in China have often been draconian, aimed at restructuring society in fundamental ways, including the breakup of families, limitations on childbearing, and other imposed social practices that ran counter to traditional teaching. A linchpin in this counter-structuring strategy has been to attack Confucian doctrine, and Confucius himself, at times. Other political seasons have witnessed an official rehabilitation of certain Confucian doctrines, but the thoroughgoing traditional ordering of life has clearly not survived these periodic assaults.

Change in the United States has been somewhat more gradual and less radical in nature. We can certainly identify periods in which American values seemed to change considerably, such as the turn-of-the-century era of muckraking and progressive reform; the national self-questioning that all Western nations underwent during the Great Depression of the 1930s; and the cultural movements of the 1960s on behalf of women and minorities, fostered both by antiwar protest and by the birth-control pill. Still, in none of these eras did the American people abandon their basic values; indeed, most of these reform movements appealed to traditional and spiritual values as their ultimate basis for acceptance (McClosky and Zaller 1984). This is probably inevitable in a democracy, where change must be accomplished by widespread assent. Americans respond to calls for "progressive" change, but the preservation of basic values must underlie almost any proposal for social reform if it is to succeed.

These different modes of change derive from the different histories of the two nations. A simple general model of change from past to future, or traditional to modern, may be a fair approximation of what is occurring in all countries over the long haul, but it is too parsimonious an approach to account for the discontinuities that one can discern in the United States, and that one cannot escape in China.

The discourse of cultural change in both countries tends to rely, however, upon such simplistic dualisms. Debate over the meaning of traditional Chinese culture in the past century has been carried out in these terms and often consisted of intense ideological clashes and polemics. A recent example is a 1988 television documentary titled "River Elegy" (He Shang). This six-part series condemned China's "yellow earth culture," that is, the traditional Confucian society associated with backwardness, weakness, closeness, and narrow-mindedness; it looked forward to a "blue ocean culture," that is, Western culture, which would presumably bring advancement, strength, openness, efficiency, and competitiveness (Su and Wang 1988). In other words, this TV series revived in China's political discourse the hackneyed image of development as an unfolding

Ideological Sphere

		Constraining	Motivating
Structural Sphere	Constraining	Stability of the status quo/ system breakdown	Political/ bureaucratic engineering
	Motivating	Suppressive instability	Dynamic evolution

FIGURE 9.1 Modes of Cultural Change

conflict between traditional Chinese culture and Western culture on a bipolar continuum (Li 1979; Pang 1988).

The parallel process in the United States tends to look in the other direction, backward to an arcadian past of high principle, family integrity, and community solidarity—even while change is in process. Because authority is derived from the electorate, American political leaders often express continuity of common values when they are seeking power (through votes or through acquiescence to change) and when they are exercising power. Presidents speak often of the Founding Fathers, of motherhood and children, of God (and of equality before Him), and of the need to sacrifice for the common good. So do candidates for all major offices. A notable example was the Republican National Convention of 1992, which featured speeches championing powerful authority (by Pat Buchanan), religious values (Pat Robertson), and family values (Marilyn Quayle), among other themes that are considered traditional in this study. Although the Bush-Quayle ticket lost its bid for reelection, that defeat is generally attributed to the economic recession, not a recession of the traditional value structure that the convention showcased (Ladd 1993:19–30). Advocates of radical socio-political change, as Barry Goldwater was viewed in 1964 and George McGovern in 1972, are usually rejected by the American electorate. The result is that cultural change in the United States tends to be evolutionary, rather than the revolutionary pattern of China.

But these dualisms do not take us very far toward understanding the complexities of cultural change in these countries, nor elsewhere. We need a framework within which to analyze different processes that derive from specific social and historical conditions of each culture. We began this study with a conceptualization of culture in which an individual is located in physical, social, and symbolic environments through interactions, both in "reality" and in the "perceptual" sphere (Figure 2.1). We have argued that culture is a dynamic process, a constantly flowing current of change and adaptation. Here we will explicate further this conception.

Our general model is outlined in Figure 9.1. In this fourfold typology, social relations in a culture are constantly adjusting to changing internal and external conditions, which may be either constraining or motivating forces, in both the structural sphere and the ideological sphere. The modes defined in Figure 9.1 are ideal types, not necessarily descriptions of the exact empirical conditions that would be found in a given country at a given time. Neither the United States nor China literally matched one of these four ideal types at the time of our surveys of cultural values. These modes describe alternative ways in which cultures might change, not what a culture is. Still, we consider that our analyses of processes of change in the two countries we have been studying intensively here can be illuminated by this typology—and vice versa.

In our framework, processes of adaptation and change by members of a society are experienced at least at two levels. At the *behavioral* or interactional level, people must cope with changing structural features of the social, economic, and political systems. And at the *cognitive* level, the members of a society strive to maintain a balance between these changes and their values and beliefs.

The forces pushing people toward behavioral and cognitive adaptation derive from various "constraining" and "motivating" elements of the social-cultural system. These two kinds of systemic forces may operate in either the structural or the ideological sphere (Chu 1989). As these systemic forces change, people adapt by modifying their patterns of behavioral interactions and their values and beliefs. Whether behavior change precedes or follows cognitive change depends upon other factors and is itself a topic for more detailed research (Ray 1973).

Cross-cutting these two dimensions generates the fourfold typology of modes of cultural change in Figure 9.1. When the structural and ideological forces are in consonance (i.e., when both function in the same way), they create contrasting patterns that correspond very roughly to what we consider to be observable tendencies in China and the United States, respectively.

When both kinds of forces function to constrain, this consonance tends inflexibly to reinforce the status quo. This condition will for a time manifest itself in ultra-stability of the existing system. But a system shaped by such a hegemonic process is unlikely to adjust itself dynamically. Changes eventually do occur, but chaotically as a result of system breakdowns, sometimes revolutionary. This mode of change, hegemonic stability punctuated by periodic violence and changes of regime (dynasties), we consider a fair description of Chinese history over the past two thousand years. We have in this volume noted many such instances in this century, especially in the latter half of it.

In contrast, when a system's structural features motivate, or at least permit, change, and when the ideology defining and legitimizing the system sets flexible parameters to accommodate change, we would expect a dynamic evolutionary pattern. This seems to have been the case throughout most of American history, with the exception of the Civil War of 1861–65. Ebbs and flows of reform and counter-reform have been the rule since that time, always within a flexible two-party political structure.

The Progressive Era prior to World War I influenced the Theodore Roosevelt and Woodrow Wilson administrations, but it was followed by a return to commercialism and "rugged individualism" in the 1920s. Leftist movements of the 1930s and 1960s were absorbed into Franklin D. Roosevelt's New Deal and Lyndon B. Johnson's Great Society, but these were followed by rightist anti-Communist swings in the 1950s and 1980s, under Republican leadership. In each of these counter-reform phases, most of the shifts to accommodate cultural values that had changed remained intact.[1] An ideology of change-with-continuity could be said to be a precept of American life, starting with the country's dogged dedication to its Constitution (by far the world's oldest such document), a system designed, many say, to bend so that it will not break.

Even the U.S. Civil War, which was fought over the issue of slavery, was formally declared to preserve the union of the states; its outcome was indeed a strengthened national unity. At the dedication of the Gettysburg battlefield site, Lincoln delivered one of the best known speeches in American history. Not a religious man, he nevertheless couched his rhetoric with religious phrasing ("consecrate," "hallow," "under God"), as well as evocations of filial relations ("our fathers brought forth") and obligations ("these dead shall not have died in vain"), and the traditional virtue of humility ("The world will little note nor long remember what we say here"). Lincoln was appealing to continuity of traditional values even while presiding over the most dramatic change in hierarchical social relations in the nation's history (Wills 1992).

These two contrasting modes of cultural change are logical outcomes of the two prototypes of social organization that Durkheim (1984) called "mechanical" and "organic" solidarities. A society whose social organization is characterized by mechanical solidarity can only change when the old system breaks down, providing room for a new system to emerge from its ruins. Organic solidarity, by contrast, is a form of social organization that enables a society to adjust its different components to change without radical restructuring.

The other two cells of Figure 9.1 point up two other possible conditions, which occur when the two forces are not consonant. Either the structural or the ideological sphere may generate incentives for change while the other suppresses and constrains change. When the structural forces generate motivations for changes that will expand beyond the boundaries of a regnant ideology, change may be accompanied by reluctance and hesitation and by authoritarian suppression. A system in this mode can be very unstable, as has been the case of China in the past few years. Following ten years of economic reform, the structural forces impelling toward change have built up while political and ideological suppression continues. It was, notably, argued on behalf of the brutal suppression at Tiananmen Square that these drastic steps were necessary to safeguard the continuation of structural changes.

Under different circumstances, a condition of dissonance between the structural and ideological forces could produce steady movement toward change after some initial hesitation. An apparent example is Taiwan, where economic development and changes in lifestyles took place haltingly, until the mid-1980s, within the old ideological regime. After grudging removal of some political obstacles to change, Taiwanese society seems to be on its way toward steady economic and political development. That is, Taiwan has brought its ideology into line with its structural motivations, and cultural change there is proceeding more as we would expect in a dynamic evolutionary mode. Suppressive instability is, then, almost by definition a temporary phase. We consider the unpredictability of contemporary China to represent such a delicate imbalance.

The fourth possibility in Figure 9.1 is that ideological forces may generate incentives for change while the structure remains constraining. We call this mode of change "political/bureaucratic engineering." That is, the political elite is motivated by an ideology favoring change, but finds it necessary to overcome social and economic barriers by mobilizing popular support behind its reform programs via political and bureaucratic means.

Change through such top-down engineering may or may not succeed, depending on the nature of the structural constraints. One common constraint in developing countries is the lack of an infrastructural apparatus, such as money market, communication and transportation systems, manufacturing capacity and skilled labor.[2] The other type of constraint is simply structural inertia, a tendency of any existing pattern of functioning to remain in place. While this systemic foot-dragging is also often found in developing nations, we might note that it is characteristic of otherwise highly sophisticated bureaucracies as well.

Structural constraints that are grounded in lack of resources and infrastructure may be overcome through carefully designed policies and programs, as in the case of Singapore and more recently perhaps Indonesia. Bureaucratic inertia is characteristic of very large systems, a notable current example being Russia. A distinct characteristic of change in this mode is reliance on a powerful center and top-down procedures for development. It too is presumably an unstable mode, eventually leading toward dynamic evolution, although if pursuit of an ideology of development lags, a system can retrogress from this mode back into alternating cycles of stability/breakdown.

These four modes of change are theoretical constructions. The primary value of our model is to understand why and how nations vary as they progress toward systemic change. Cultural change in each mode reflects adaptation to particular structural and ideological constraints. Because these are ideal types, no nation fits perfectly into any one category. And as we have made clear, these four modes of change should not be viewed as static. Because the two main dimensions of society, the structural and the ideological sphere, may change, each of the four modes is dynamic in nature. A nation may transform itself from primarily one mode of change to another. For example, China under Mao exhibited features prototypical of the stability/breakdown cycle; China under Deng may be better characterized by the "suppressive instability" mode.

Cultural Change in China and the United States

Having located the Chinese and American cultures in our fourfold typology, we can make better sense of the patterns of cultural values reported in our previous chapters. Evolutionary changes in cultural values in the United States are indicated by the variations across rural and urban areas, age cohorts, and educational levels. Our research suggests a reasonably monotonic progression from rigidity to openness, and from hierarchical to egalitarian, consistent with the notion of a traditionalism-to-modernity transition. Although we did not find many age-related differences that would suggest greater change in certain eras than in others, that is part of what one should expect from a process of dynamic evolution. That is, motivations toward change may arise in either the ideological or the structural sphere. Adaptation in the other sphere takes some time, and the swing may for a time go beyond what is necessary to adapt. That seems roughly to describe how American cultural values have been, and are, changing in the past century or so.

This stands in contrast to what we would describe as more chaotic revolutionary changes in China. There has been in the United States no era of rigid stability, nor any episode of system breakdown, to match those we associate with, for example, the reign of Mao. The United States has accomplished some major social changes in recent decades (see Bell 1973;

Inglehart 1977) and at times has appeared to be facing a systemic crisis, as in the turbulent late 1960s and early 1970s. But instead of system breakdown, forces for change were constructed to expand the basic premises of the American system (see McClosky and Zaller 1984). Most of this change was registered in the area of political attitudes; the more fundamental realm of cultural values and beliefs seems to have remained fairly stable.

Major changes in the United States have been couched in ideological terms of reinterpreting, extending, and amplifying values that go back as far as the American Revolution. This kind of oscillation between change and continuity, typical of the dynamic evolutionary mode of change, is illustrated by 1960s student activist leaders, who questioned the very foundations of "the system" (Gitlin 1980)—and twenty years later had become legislators, corporate lawyers, and university professors.

American culture has been characterized as emphasizing "rationalism," mastery of nature, and an orientation toward the future, all of which are opposite to a general conception of traditionalism (Williams 1970). Our research, though, shows that, in the specific domains of male-female relations, the family, and hierarchical relationships, Americans are still not very far from the traditional end of the scale. Some other research has indicated the same thing. Harding, Phillips, and Fogarty (1986) showed that traditional Judaeo-Christian cultural norms attribute negative values to neglect of children or aging parents, abortion, divorce, extramarital affairs, homosexuality, and so on. The United States has less need to "restore" the "traditional" values than critics and outsiders might suggest.

If internal processes of cultural change are, relative to China, evolutionary in the United States, the picture is, if anything, less dynamic with respect to *external* cultural influences. While almost every Asian society today confronts accelerating Western influence, primarily from American media and other products, the overwhelming majority of Americans are effectively buffered against exogenous cultural inroads. Very few Americans watch foreign films or television programs, for example, whereas America's own media products are well known almost everywhere. Those foreign products that are imported into the United States have been purposely designed to cater to the tastes of American customers. In the heartland of America one is unlikely to encounter alternative portrayals of family life or authority patterns of other cultures. This contrasts with all the other countries represented in this study. Indeed, Korea and Taiwan have been on the receiving end of the U.S. media industries for much longer, and in much greater volume, than has China.

Still, we do not consider China's principal source of cultural change to be external influence, from the United States or any other country. We have found only a few minor influences of exposure to Western media in this study. Further, China tends to absorb exogenous cultural influences, transforming them into Chinese interpretations rather than what was intended in the culture of origin. (We are not attributing international designs to American media, but rather the lack of any consideration of what cultural artifacts from the United States might mean to another culture that imports them.) The dominant factor in the Chinese mode of cultural change has been the repeated class struggle and propaganda campaigns against traditional Confucian values. The rather dramatic impact of such campaigns on Chinese culture was made clear in Chapter 8, when we compared China with parallel data from Taiwan and Korea.

Ideological campaigns against Confucianism were not, we should emphasize, invented by the Chinese Communist Party since 1949. The counter-structuring campaign has been a continuing feature of the Chinese intellectual scene since the May Fourth movement of 1919, which began the breaking away from the Confucian tradition. The Communist revolution was a much more massive blow, though, partly because the ideological theme of anti-Confucianism became merged with the structural power of the Communist state. The resultant series of radical programs fundamentally transformed the traditional social structure and ways of life in China (Chu 1977).

The Communist regime replaced the traditional rural social fabric, based upon land ownership and tenant leasing, with the collective commune system. Decentralized small private businesses, operating in mutual contingency between individual entrepreneurship and local resources, were replaced with state-owned factories and enterprises. The institution of these programs was accomplished not only by ideological indoctrination, which played a major role, but sometimes also by coercion and even physical elimination of landlord and capitalist owners. The new value system espoused by the Communist Party centered on Mao's "struggle philosophy," meaning confrontation as the primary mode of action. Between 1949 and 1976, cultural change in China followed an oscillating stability/breakdown mode that climaxed in the Cultural Revolution.

This revolution fostered a general rejection of the Confucian value system and widespread ignorance of the original meanings of traditional value precepts among those who grew up under the communist system. These revolutionary changes may account for some of the differences we found between the Chinese and American samples, with the Americans more often endorsing ideas such as interpersonal kindness and "obedient wife."

It remains to be seen, however, how deep the revolutionary changes have been and how long or how thoroughly they will last. For some of us who have lived in contemporary Chinese society, there is no simple answer. A few of the changes have been fundamental, and we expect them to be long lasting. For example, certain social classes have been eliminated; the Confucian value system is no longer taken for granted; traditional arts are no longer practiced; and some traditional ceremonies and rituals have been forgotten to such an extent that they could not be revived even for historical studies or tourist attractions.

At the same time, certain values have stood against time and the revolution. Strong family ties remain characteristic in contemporary China, partly because families are in rural areas once again the basic production units, and partly because the family is the primary unit for care of children and of the elderly. The traditional conception of the "five sames" (*wu tong*) and recognition of the importance of personal connections remains a cornerstone of interpersonal effectiveness. By and large, women are still expected to take primary responsibility for the family and to smooth relationships with in-laws. Although a woman no longer needs to commit suicide to demonstrate her fidelity, women are still excoriated more than men for premarital or extramarital affairs and for divorces.

Why didn't the revolution completely destroy the old and build upon its ruins, as Lenin envisioned a communist revolution? Perhaps the most fundamental reason is that cultural development does not proceed in discontinuous leaps. The cultural values examined in this study are so basic, and so directly tied to everyday life experiences, that people who are educated and socialized under traditional values will draw from them, dealing with problems in their lives in the ways they know. Even a proclaimed revolution in the cultural sphere cannot produce a clear-cut demarcation of "old" and "new." There is a constantly flowing current at the core of a culture. Its workings can be found in the routines of people's everyday lives and in collective memory in the forms of traditions, customs, conventional wisdom, proverbs, myths, and sayings.

Another consideration in China has been the complex alliance of the three ideological forces, that is, orthodox traditionalism, Marxism and Maoism, and Western culture. Alignments and conflicts among these three influences make it very difficult to construct a single model to predict cultural values or the ways they might change. With several processes operating jointly, each can lead toward a different outcome.

The linear progression from traditionalism to modernity works to transform the traditional value orientations. Some specific values recede or are abandoned, some may be repatterned, and a few may be brought back into prominence as structural and ideological factors interplay over time. Propaganda and indoctrination can, as we have seen, lead to rejection of traditional value phrases. If the values in question directly contradict the official ideology, most people would presumably abandon the values themselves, not just the phrases that represented them. An example in our data is the traditional value accorded to "a house full of children and grandchildren," which is not only Confucian but also not very practical in densely populated regions. When a traditional value is simply reiterated in new terms as part of an official ideology, it may be transformed so that its continued presence might not be detected in a survey such as ours, which relied heavily on traditional phrases for measurement. An example is "chastity for women," which is valued in contemporary China but not in the way it was traditionally expressed.

The three main cultural forces are currently interacting in China, in the context of the dissonance between the structural and ideological forces that began with implementation of the reform program in late 1978. Economic reforms liberated individual entrepreneurship and revitalized social life that relies upon families as well as individuals. The direction of these changes was unmistakably toward a broader and more mature market economy.

Despite some "thought liberation" efforts, though, ideological force still works to suppress change in China. Changes in the economic sphere, and in people's life experiences, are expanding the boundaries of the dominant ideology, but they operate only within the prescribed ideological framework. Under these circumstances, change is characterized by hesitant steps that risk authoritarian suppression, that is, the mode we call "suppressive instability." Given this uncertainty, there has been some revival of traditional, native Chinese cultural values and expressions. Western influences have been experienced mainly among younger Chinese, manifested in individualistic choices such as divorce and extramarital cohabitation.

This formulation of different modes of cultural change reflects both our observations and our conviction that cultural heritages preserve themselves, adapt themselves, and transform themselves. In looking at American and Chinese cultural values, we have made a conscious effort to distinguish two types of variance, that is, China-U.S. differences vs. past-present differences. It is critical not to mistake one for the other. In contemporary China, both "preservationists" and "Westernizers" treat the Chinese and Western cultures as an either/or choice and tend to view the two cultures as static entities. Both camps, then, fail to recognize the complex linkages between cultural symbols, values, beliefs, and knowledge, on the one hand, and changing life experiences of individuals who share these cultural elements on the other.

Our research and theory suggest that, on values that concern social relationships, the three major cultural forces in contemporary China will continue for some time to produce unstable patterns of conflict and alignment. These anomalies may become "domesticated" to some degree by real-life experiences, so that a new value system could emerge. We are tempted to hope that China has abandoned the "revolutionary mode" for good. After the current cycle of hesitation and suppression passes, the culture could move toward the mode of steady change that we call dynamic evolution. That is the global pattern that we expect to observe some years from now when a new wave of comparable data is gathered in a future China.

As for the United States, the unique value measures we designed for this study helped to locate the country on the cultural change spectrum. Our findings reveal a pattern of culture that seems better characterized by the evolutionary mode of change. But it is no simple linear progression either. There have been periodic flurries of change in certain areas, while in other respects Americans remain rather traditional in their values. This is a major finding of our study. But we must reiterate that this study was not built upon prevalent American values and quite possibly fails to capture the conflicts and tensions that are central to cultural change in the United States. Hence our proposal for future research on this side of the Pacific would not be directed so much at replication of the present survey, as toward expansion of the study to incorporate values other than those derived from our explication of traditional Confucian culture.

Major value conundrums remain for an America with a degree of social inequality that is inconsistent with the stated ideology, with many broken homes in a society that prizes the family and children, and with a subculture of violence where social harmony is for many a personal goal. How will values regarding social relationships change? With constantly increasing diversification, is fragmentation in cultural values inevitable? If television has (as it appears here) been a factor in retaining traditional values, will new "user-controlled" technologies speed the fragmenting of the population into distinct subcultures? Or will the culture reassert itself in the face of these challenges, finding new ways to provide a homogeneous symbolic environment? No one can guarantee that American society will maintain its mode of dynamic evolution, or that China will finally move into that mode. This study and this book will have been worth our while if we have helped to define the way to imagine the futures of these two great countries.

Notes

1. The cultural issues in these swings in the United States were not necessarily the traditional Confucian values represented in the present study. The discussion here is broader, having to do with the conditions governing how cultural change of all types might occur.

2. Lerner's (1958) theory of modernization laid great stress on infrastructural development including urbanization, literacy, and especially mass media institutions. In contrast to the model we present here, however, he ignored the possibility of lags in the ideological sphere.

Appendixes

Appendix 1

Chinese-English Wordings of the Traditional Value Phrases

1. Male-Female Relationships

    妇女贞节 Chastity for women

    三从四德 Three obediences and four virtues

    男女有别 Differentiation between men and women

2. Family Relationships

    子孙满堂 House full of children and grandchildren

    父慈子孝 Benevolent father and filial son

    光宗耀祖 Glory to ancestors

3. Hierarchies

    顺从尊长 Submission to authority

    迎合上意 Please superior

    尊重传统 Respect tradition

4. Interpersonal Relationships

    以和为贵 Harmony is precious

    仁义道德 Generosity and virtues

    容忍礼让 Tolerance, propriety, deference

    明哲保身 Discretion for self-preservation

    中庸之道 Way of the golden mean

5. Other

    历史悠久 Long historical heritage

    勤劳节俭 Diligence and frugality

    精忠报国 Loyalty to the state

    重农轻商 Peasants high, merchants low

APPENDIX 2   Rank-order Correlations of the Value Items Used to Create Indices

	1	2	3	4	5	6	7	8	9	10	11	12	13	14	15	16	17	18
Male-Female Relationships																		
1. A couple live together before marriage	—	.17*	-.15*	-.28*	.20*	.25*	.03	.08*	-.17*	-.09*	.11*	-.12*	-.14*	-.24*	.09*	.09*	.08*	-.09*
2. Family losing face for teenager's pregnancy	.22*	—	-.09*	-.12*	-.07*	.00	.03	.01	-.08*	-.01	-.02	-.01	-.04	-.07*	-.04	.02	.08*	.04
3. Differentiation between men and women	-.02	-.04	—	.44*	-.02	-.06	.01	-.04	.15*	.07*	-.10*	-.04	.10*	.14*	-.04	.05	-.25*	-.02
4. Three obediences and four virtues	-.04	-.03	.25*	—	-.12*	-.16*	.08*	.02	.29*	.13*	-.03	.08*	.26*	.37*	-.04	-.07*	-.19*	.03
Family Relationships																		
5. A couple should divorce if they have no children	-.06	.02	-.04	-.01	—	.62*	-.04	-.02	-.05	.01	.05	-.06	.01	-.08*	.07	.01	.03	-.06
6. A couple should divorce if they have children	-.11*	-.10*	-.04	-.06*	.22*	—	-.06*	-.03	-.08*	-.02	.04	-.06	-.02	-.08*	.06*	.02	.03	-.09*
7. Aging parents cared for by their children	.13*	.08*	-.04	.00	-.01	-.05	—	.44*	.12*	.10*	.01	.21*	.01	.07*	.02	-.06*	.07*	.12*
8. Aging parents ask their children for financial help	.03	.03	.01	.02	-.04	-.01	.20*	—	.08*	.08*	.06*	.18*	-.01	.02	.04	-.07*	.06	.11*
9. Benevolent fathers and filial sons	.03	.06	-.06	.04	.04	.01	.06	.07*	—	.16*	-.01	.22*	.22*	.27*	-.01	-.10*	.02	.16*
10. A house full of children and grandchildren	.01	-.03	.10*	.22*	.03	-.05	.04	.06	.01	—	-.03	.07*	.14*	.13*	-.02	-.08*	.03	.16*

	1	2	3	4	5	6	7	8	9	10	11	12	13	14	15	16	17	18
Authority hierarchy																		
11. Express your opinions when you disagree with a senior	-.01	-.02	-.01	-.04	-.02	-.03	.04	.01	-.04	.00	–	<u>.02</u>	-.05	-.02	.08*	-.03	.08*	.01
12. Younger people respect older people	.04	-.01	-.02	.05	-.02	-.01	.12*	.02	.08*	.03	<u>.10*</u>	–	.05	.10*	.06	-.10*	.18*	.14*
13. Pleasing superiors	-.01	-.05	<u>.10*</u>	.21*	-.04	-.14*	.08*	.02	-.08*	.21*	.01	-.01	–	<u>.38*</u>	.01	-.10*	-.06	.07*
14. Submission to authority	.08*	.03	.01	.04	-.07*	-.08*	.05	.04	.11*	.08*	-.04	.08*	<u>.05</u>	–	.01	-.14*	-.07*	.13*
Interpersonal Relationships																		
15. Importance of connections	-.07*	-.01	.02	.06	-.01	.03	.00	.03	.09*	.07*	-.02	.06*	.01	.03	–	<u>.02</u>	.08	.01
16. Using connections to solve problems	.08*	.01	-.05	-.03	-.11*	-.05	-.02	-.06*	-.06*	-.08	.09*	.07*	-.02	.03	<u>-.30*</u>	–	-.10*	-.08*
17. Tolerance, propriety, and deference	-.02	-.03	.01	.03	.04	.06*	-.01	.04	.17*	-.02	-.01	.03	-.09*	.07*	-.02	.01	–	<u>.22*</u>
18. Generosity and virtues	-.01	.02	-.02	.04	-.07*	.00	.03	.06*	.19*	.05	-.01	.04	-.01	.27*	-.07*	-.04	<u>.18*</u>	–

Note: The lower half (below the main diagonal) shows the coefficients of the China sample, while the upper half shows the coefficients of the U.S. sample. For the Chinese sample, Kendall's Tau B coefficients are calculated. For the American sample, Pearson correlation coefficients are shown here.

*p < .01.

References

Allerbeck, Klaus R. 1977. "Analysis and Inference in Cross-national Survey Research," in Alexander Szalai and Riccardo Petrella (eds.), *Cross-national Comparative Survey Research: Theory and Practice*. Oxford: The European Co-ordination Centre for Research and Documentation in Social Services, pp. 373–402.

Almond, Gabriel A., and Sidney Verba. 1963. *The Civic Culture: Political Attitudes and Democracy in Five Nations*. Princeton, NJ: Princeton University Press.

Alwin, Duane F. 1988. "From Obedience to Autonomy: Changes in Traits Desired in Children, 1924–1978," *Public Opinion Quarterly* 52, 33–52.

Ball-Rokeach, Sandra J., and Melvin L. DeFleur. 1976. "A Dependency Model of Mass-media Effects," *Communication Research* 3, 3–21.

———, Milton Rokeach, and Joel W. Grube. 1984. *The Great American Values Test: Influencing Behavior and Belief through Television*. New York: Free Press.

Bell, Daniel. 1973. *The Coming of Post-industrial Society: A Venture in Social Forecasting*. New York: Basic Books.

Bengtson, Vern L., Michael J. Furlong, and Robert S. Laufer. 1974. "Time, Aging, and the Continuity of the Social Structure: Themes and Issues in Generational Analysis," *Journal of Social Issues* 30, 1–30.

Blumler, Jay G., and Elihu Katz (eds.). 1974. *The Uses of Mass Communication: Current Perspectives on Gratifications Research*. Beverly Hills, CA: Sage.

Campbell, Donald T., and Donald W. Fiske. 1959. "Convergent and Discriminant Validation by the Multitrait-multimethod Matrix," *Psychological Bulletin* 56, 81–105.

Chaffee, Steven. H. 1991. *Communication Concepts 1: Explication*. Newbury Park, CA: Sage.

——— and Godwin C. Chu. 1992. "Communication and Cultural Change in China," in Jay G. Blumler, Jack M. Mcleod, and Karl Erik Rosengren (eds.), *Comparatively Speaking: Communication and Culture Across Space and Time*. Newbury Park, CA: Sage, pp. 252–277.

Chow, Tse-tsung. 1960. *The May Fourth Movement: Intellectual Revolution in Modern China*. Cambridge, MA: Harvard University Press.

Chu, Godwin C. 1964. "Problems of Cross-cultural Communication Research," *Journalism Quarterly* 41, pp. 557–562.

———. 1977. *Radical Change through Communication in Mao's China*. Honolulu: University Press of Hawaii.

———. 1979. "Communication and Cultural Change in China: A Conceptual Framework," in Godwin C. Chu and Francis L. K. Hsu (eds.), *Moving a Mountain: Cultural Change in China*. Honolulu: University Press of Hawaii, pp. 2–24.

———. 1985. "The Changing Concept of Self in Contemporary China," in Anthony J. Marsella, George DeVos, and Francis L. K. Hsu (eds.), *Culture and Self: Asian and Western Perspectives*. New York: Tavistock Publications, pp. 252–277.

————. 1989. *Empirical Studies of Cultural Change in Asia*, paper presented to Culture Studies Symposium, Institute of Culture and Communication, Honolulu: East-West Center.

———— and Ginyao Chi. 1984. *Cultural Change in Rural Taiwan* [Taiwan nongcun shehui bianqian]. Taipei, Taiwan: Shangwu Commercial Press (in Chinese).

———— and Francis L. K. Hsu (eds.). 1979. *Moving a Mountain: Cultural Change in China*. Honolulu: University Press of Hawaii.

————, Jae-won Lee, and Won-yong Kim. 1991. "Perceptions of Traditional Values in South Korea," *Journal of Communication Arts* (Special Issue on Cultural Change in Asia and the United States) 12, 81–90.

———— and Yanan Ju. 1993. *The Great Wall in Ruins: Communication and Cultural Change in China*. Albany: State University of New York Press.

————, Jae-won Lee, Won-yong Kim, and Yanan Ju. 1993. *Modernization and Revolution—Cultural Change in Korea and China*. Seoul: Sung Kyun Kwan University Press.

Chu, Leonard L. 1986. "Revolution Becomes Evolution: China's Communication Across 30 Years," *Media Development* 33, 8–12.

Clark, Grover. 1935. *The Great Wall Crumbles*. New York: Macmillan Company.

Coleman, James S. 1986. "Social Theory, Social Research, and a Theory of Action," *American Journal of Sociology* 91, 1309–1335.

Comstock, George, Steven Chaffee, Natan Katzman, Maxwell McCombs, and Donald Roberts. 1978. *Television and Human Behavior*. New York: Columbia University Press.

Croizier, Ralph. 1989. "Going to the World: Art and Culture on the Cosmopolitan Tide," in Anthony J. Kane (ed.), *China Briefing, 1989*. Boulder, CO: Westview Press, pp. 67–86.

Cronbach, Lee J., and Paul E. Meehl. 1955. "Construct Validity in Psychological Tests," *Psychological Bulletin* 52, 281–302.

Duncan, Otis Dudley. 1961. "A Socioeconomic Index for all Occupations," in Albert J. Reiss, Jr. (ed.), *Occupation and Social Status*. New York: Free Press, pp. 109–275.

Durkheim, Emile. 1984. *The Division of Labor in Society*. W. D. Halls (trans.). New York: Free Press.

Esherick, Joseph W., and Jeffrey N. Wasserstrom. 1992. "Acting Out Democracy: Political Theater in Modern China," in Jeffrey N. Wasserstrom and Elizabeth J. Perry (eds.), *Popular Protest and Political Culture in Modern China*. Boulder, CO: Westview Press, pp. 28-66.

Eulau, Heinz. 1986. *Politics, Self, and Society: A Theme and Variation*. Cambridge, MA: Harvard University Press.

Feather, Norman T. 1975. *Values in Education and Society*. New York: Free Press.

Featherman, David L., and Richard M. Lerner. 1985. "Ontogenesis and Sociogenesis: Problematics for Theory and Research About Development and Socialization Across the Life Span," *American Sociological Review* 50, 659–676.

Feshbach, Seymour. 1972. "Reality and Fantasy in Filmed Violence," in John Murray, Eli Rubinstein, and George Comstock (eds.), *Television and Social Behavior*, vol. 2. Washington, DC: Department of Health, Education, and Welfare, pp. 318–345.

Fishbein, Martin, and Icek Ajzen. 1975. *Belief, Attitude, Intention, and Behavior: An Introduction to Theory and Research*. Reading, MA: Addison-Wesley Publishing.

Forster, Lancelot. 1936. *The New Culture in China*. London: G. Allen and Unwin.

Frey, Fredrick W. 1970. "Cross-cultural Survey Research in Political Science," in Robert T. Holt and John E. Turner (eds.), *The Methodology of Comparative Research*. New York: Free Press, pp. 173–294.

Fudan University History Department (ed.). 1987. *Reflections on the Traditional Chinese Culture* [Zhongguo chuantong wenhua de fansi]. Shanghai: Fudan University Press (in Chinese).

Gan, Yang (ed.). 1989. *The Contemporary Cultural Consciousness* [Dangdai wenhua yishi]. Hong Kong: Joint Publishing (H.K.) Co., Ltd. (in Chinese).

Gerbner, George, Larry Gross, Michael Morgan, and Nancy Signorielli. 1986. "Living with Television: The Dynamics of the Cultivation Process," in Jennings Bryant and Dolf Zillmann (eds.), *Perspectives on Media Effects*. Hillsdale, NJ: Lawrence Erlbaum, pp. 18–40.

Giddens, Anthony. 1989. *Sociology*. Cambridge, U.K.: Polity Press.

Gitlin, Todd. 1980. *The Whole World Is Watching: The Mass Media Making and Unmaking of the New Left*. Berkeley: University of California Press.

Glaser, William A. 1977. "The Process of Cross-national Survey Research," in Alexander Szalai and Riccardo Petrella (eds.), *Cross-national Comparative Survey Research: Theory and Practice*. Oxford: The European Co-ordination Centre for Research and Documentation in Social Services, pp. 403–436.

Goldblatt, Howard. 1988. "Back Where We Started: Culture in 1987," in Anthony Kane (ed.), *China Briefing, 1988*. Boulder, CO: Westview Press, pp. 63–78.

Granovetter, Mark. 1973. "The Strength of Weak Ties," *American Journal of Sociology* 78:1360–1380.

Greenberg, Bradley S. 1980. *Life on Television: Content Analysis of U.S. TV Drama*. Norwood, NJ: Ablex.

Groves, Robert M., and Robert L. Kahn. 1979. *Surveys by Telephone: A National Comparison with Personal Interviews*. New York: Academic Press.

Hamelink, Cees. 1983. *Cultural Autonomy in Global Communications*. New York: Longman.

Harding, Stephen, and David Phillips with Michael Fogarty. 1986. *Contrasting Values in Western Europe: Unity, Diversity and Change*. Basingstoke, U.K.: Macmillan in association with European Value Systems Study Group.

Hofstadter, Richard. 1955. *The Age of Reform: From Bryan to F.D.R.* New York: Alfred A. Knopf.

Hovland, Carl I., Arthur A. Lumsdaine, and Fred D. Sheffield. 1949. *Experiments on Mass Communication*. Princeton, NJ: Princeton University Press.

Hsu, Francis L. K. 1949. *Under the Ancestors' Shadow*. London: Routledge and Kegan Paul, Ltd.

———. 1953. *Americans and Chinese: Two Ways of Life*. New York: H. Schuman.

———. 1981. *Americans and Chinese: Passage to Differences* (3rd Ed.). Honolulu: University Press of Hawaii.

Hu, Shengwu, and Cheng Weikun. 1987. "Changes in Social Customs during the Beginning Period of the Republic of China" [Minguo chuniande shehui fengshang bianhua] in Fudan University History Department (ed.), *Reflections on the*

Traditional Chinese Culture. Shanghai: Fudan University Press (in Chinese), pp. 253–284.

Hulin, Charles L. 1987. "A Psychometric Theory of Evaluations of Item and Scale Translations: Fidelity Across Languages," *Journal of Cross-Cultural Psychology* 18, 115–142.

——— and Laura J. Mayer. 1986. "Psychometric Equivalence of a Translation of the Job Description Index into Hebrew," *Journal of Applied Psychology* 71, 83–94.

Hyman, Herbert H., and Charles R. Wright. 1978. *Education's Lasting Influence on Values*. Chicago: University of Chicago Press.

Inglehart, Ronald. 1977. *The Silent Revolution: Changing Values and Political Styles Among Western Publics*. Princeton, NJ: Princeton University Press.

———. 1990. *Culture Shift in Advanced Industrial Society*. Princeton, NJ: Princeton University Press.

Inkeles, Alex. 1978. "National Differences in Individual Modernity," *Comparative Studies in Sociology* 1, 47–72.

———. 1983. *Exploring Individual Modernity*. New York: Columbia University Press.

——— and David H. Smith. 1974. *Becoming Modern: Individual Changes in Six Developing Countries*. Cambridge, MA: Harvard University Press.

Kahle, Lynn R. (ed.). 1983. *Social Values and Social Changes: Adaptation to Life in America*. New York: Praeger.

——— and Susan Goff Timmer. 1983. "A Theory and a Method for Studying Values," in Lynn R. Kahle (ed.), *Social Values and Social Changes: Adaptation to Life in America*. New York: Praeger, pp. 43–69.

Kephart, William M. 1977. *The Family, Society, and the Individual* (4th Ed.). Boston: Houghton Mifflin Company.

King, Ambrose Y. C. 1991. "Kuan-hsi and Network Building: A Sociological Interpretation," *Daedalus* 120, 63–84.

Klapper, Joseph T. 1960. *The Effects of Mass Communication*. New York: Free Press.

Kluckhohn, Florence R., and Fred L. Strodtbeck. 1961. *Variations in Value Orientations*. Evanston, IL: Row, Peterson and Company.

Kohn, Melvin L. 1977. *Class and Conformity: A Study of Values* (2nd Ed.). Chicago: University of Chicago Press.

Kraus, Sidney (ed.). 1979. *The Great Debates 1976: Ford vs. Carter*. Bloomington: Indiana University Press.

Kroeber, Alfred L., and Clyde Kluckhohn. 1952. *Culture: A Critical Review of Concepts and Definitions*. Cambridge, MA: Peabody Museum of American Archaeology and Ethnology, Harvard University.

Ladd, Everett C. 1993. "Thinking About America," *The Public Perspective* 4, 19–30.

Lazarsfeld, Paul F., and Herbert Menzel. 1961. "On the Relation Between Individual and Collective Properties," in Amitai Etzioni (ed.), *Complex Organizations: A Sociological Reader* (2nd Ed.). New York: Holt, Rinehart and Winston, pp. 499–516.

Lee, Chin-Chuan. 1979. *Media Imperialism Reconsidered: The Homogenizing of Television Culture*. Beverly Hills, CA: Sage.

Lerner, Daniel. 1958. *The Passing of Traditional Society: Modernizing the Middle East*. Glencoe, IL: Free Press.

Leung, Kwok, and Michael Harris Bond. 1989. "On the Empirical Identification of Dimensions for Cross-cultural Comparisons," *Journal of Cross-Cultural Psychology* 20, 133–151.

Li, Zehou. 1979. *On Historical Development of Modern Chinese Thinking* [Zhongguo jindai sixiang shilun]. Beijing: People's Press (in Chinese).

Liang, Su-ming. 1981. *On the Essence of Chinese Culture* [Zhongguo wenhua yaoyi]. Hong Kong: Joint Publishing Co., Ltd. (in Chinese).

Lichter, S. Robert, Linda S. Lichter, Stanley Rothman, and Daniel Amundson. 1988. "TV and the Family: The Parents Prevail," *Public Opinion* 10, pp. 19, 51–54.

Link, Perry. 1986. "Intellectuals and Cultural Policy after Mao," in A. Doak Barnett and Ralph N. Clough (eds.), *Modernizing China: Post-Mao Reform and Development*. Boulder, CO: Westview Press, pp. 81–102.

Liu, Alan P. L. 1981. "Mass Campaigns in the People's Republic of China," in Ronald E. Rice and William Paisley (eds.), *Public Information Campaigns*. Beverly Hills, CA: Sage, pp. 199–223.

Liu, Zhiqin. 1987. "Reflections on Li" ["Li" de fansi], in Fudan University History Department (ed.), *Reflections on the Traditional Chinese Culture*. Shanghai: Fudan University Press (in Chinese), pp. 121–137.

Machlup, Fritz. 1962. *The Production and Distribution of Knowledge in the United States*. Princeton, NJ: Princeton University Press.

Mao, Zedong. 1927. "A Report of the Investigation of the Hunan Peasant Movement," *Selected Works* (vol. 1). Beijing: People's Press, pp. 23–62.

McClosky, Herbert, and John Zaller. 1984. *The American Ethos: Public Attitudes Toward Capitalism and Democracy*. Cambridge, MA: Harvard University Press.

McGuire, William J. 1964. "Inducing Resistance to Persuasion: Some Contemporary Approaches," in Leonard Berkowitz (ed.), *Advances in Experimental Social Psychology*, vol. 1. New York: Academic Press, pp. 192–231.

————. 1986. "The Myth of Massive Media Impact: Savagings and Salvagings," in George Comstock (ed.), *Public Communication and Behavior*, vol. 1. New York: Academic Press, pp. 175–259.

McLeod, Jack M., Dianne M. Rucinski, Zhongdang Pan, and Gerald M. Kosicki. 1988. *Attention to Television News: Explicating its Meaning and Measurement*, paper delivered at the annual conference of the International Communication Association. New Orleans, Louisiana.

McNemar, Quinn. 1955. *Psychological Statistics* (2nd ed.). New York: Wiley.

Meyrowitz, Joshua. 1985. *No Sense of Place: The Impact of Electronic Media on Social Behavior*. New York: Oxford University Press.

Nass, Clifford I. 1986. *Society as Computer: The Structure and Skill of Information Work in the United States, 1900–1980*. Unpublished Ph.D. dissertation, Department of Sociology, Princeton University.

Nathan, Andrew J., and Shi Tianjian. 1993. "Cultural Requisites for Democracy in China: Findings from a Survey," *Daedalus* 122, 95–124.

Nelan, Bruce W. 1991. "Getting China Wrong," *Time Magazine* 137, no. 23 (June 10). pp. 35–36.

Nowak, Stefan. 1962. "Correlational Approach to the Control of Meaning of Attitudinal Variables in Cross-cultural Surveys," *Polish Sociological Bulletin* 5–6, 15–27.

————. 1977. "The Strategy of Cross-national Survey Research for the Development of Social Theory," in Alexander Szalai and Riccardo Petrella (eds.), *Cross-
national Comparative Survey Research: Theory and Practice*. Oxford: The European
Co-ordination Centre for Research and Documentation in Social Services, pp. 3–
48.

Osgood, Charles E., George J. Suci, and Percy H. Tannenbaum. 1957. *The Measurement of Meaning*. Urbana: University of Illinois Press.

Pang, Pu. 1988. *Liangxiuji: Collection of Papers on Chinese Culture and Philosophy*.
Shanghai: Shanghai People's Press (in Chinese).

Parish, William L., Jr. 1984. "The Family and Economic Change," in Norton Gins-
burg and Bernard A. Lalor (eds.), *China: The 80s Era*. Boulder, CO: Westview
Press, pp. 222–244.

Platte, Erika. 1988. "Divorce Trends and Patterns in China: Past and Present," *Pacific Affairs* 61, 428–445.

Porat, Marc U. 1977. *The Information Economy: Definition and Measurement*. Washington, DC: U.S. Department of Commerce Office of Telecommunications.

Przeworski, Adam, and Henry Teune. 1970. *The Logic of Comparative Social Inquiry*.
New York: Wiley and Sons.

———— and Henry Teune. 1969. "Equivalence in Cross-national Research," *Public
Opinion Quarterly* 30, 551–568.

Ray, Michael L. 1973. "Marketing Communication and the Hierarchy-of-Effects,"
in Peter Clarke (ed.), *New Models for Communication Research*. Beverly Hills, CA:
Sage, pp. 147–176.

Rogers, Everett M. 1983. *Diffusion of Innovations* (3rd Ed.). New York: Free Press.

Rokeach, Milton. 1973. *The Nature of Human Values*. New York: Free Press.

————. 1979. *Understanding Human Values: Individual and Society*. New York: Free
Press.

Rosen, Stanley, and David Chu. 1987. *Survey Research in the People's Republic of China*. Washington, DC: United States Information Agency.

Rosenberg, Morris. 1968. *The Logic of Survey Analysis*. New York: Basic Books.

Salinas, Raquel, and Leana Paldan. 1979. "Culture in the Process of Dependent De-
velopment: Theoretical Perspectives," in Kaarle Nordenstreng and Herbert I.
Schiller (eds.), *National Sovereignty and International Communication*. Norwood,
NJ: Ablex, pp. 82–98.

Scheuch, Erwin K. 1968. "The Cross-Cultural Use of Sample Surveys: Problems of
Comparability," in Stein Rokkan (ed.), *Comparative Research Across Cultures and
Nations*. Paris: Mouton, pp. 176–209.

Schiller, Herbert. 1976. *Communication and Cultural Domination*. White Plains, NY:
International Arts and Sciences.

Schramm, Wilbur. 1964. *Mass Media and National Development: The Role of Information in the Developing Nations*. Stanford: Stanford University Press.

———— and W. Lee Ruggels. 1967. "How Mass Media Systems Grow," in Daniel
Lerner and Wilbur Schramm (eds.), *Communication and Change in the Developing
Countries*. Honolulu: East-West Center Press, pp. 57–75.

Schuman, Howard, and Stanley Presser. 1981. *Questions and Answers in Attitude
Surveys: Experiments on Question Form, Wording, and Context*. New York: Academic Press.

Schwartz, Shalom H. 1992. "Universals in the Content and Structure of Values: Theoretical Advances and Empirical Test in 20 Countries," in Mark P. Zanna (ed.), *Advances in Experimental Social Psychology*, vol. 25. New York: Academic Press, pp. 1–65.

Siegel, Sidney. 1956. *Nonparametric Statistics for the Behavioral Sciences*. New York: McGraw-Hill.

Spence, Jonathan D. 1993. "Confucius," *World Quarterly*, Autumn, 30–38.

Spindler, Louise S. 1977. *Cultural Change and Modernization: Mini-models and Case Studies*. Prospect Heights, IL: Waveland Press.

Su, Xiaokang, and Wang Luxiang. 1988. *River Elegy* [Heshang]. Hong Kong: China Books Press (in Chinese).

Sudman, Seymour. 1983. "Applied Sampling," in Peter H. Rossi, James D. Wright, and Andy B. Anderson (eds.), *Handbook of Survey Research*. New York: Academic Press, pp. 145–194.

Sweet, James A., and Larry Bumpass. 1987. *American Families and Households*. New York: Russell Sage Foundation.

Szalai, Alexander. 1977. "The Organization and Execution of Cross-national Survey Research," in Alexander Szalai and Riccardo Petrella (eds.), *Cross-national Comparative Survey Research: Theory and Practice*. Oxford: The European Co-ordination Centre for Research and Documentation in Social Services, pp. 49–94.

Szalai, Alexander, and Riccardo Petrella (eds.). 1977. *Cross-national Comparative Survey Research: Theory and Practice*. Oxford: The European Co-ordination Centre for Research and Documentation in Social Services.

Taylor, Ella. 1989. *Prime-time Families: Television Culture in Postwar America*. Berkeley: University of California Press.

Tu, Wei-ming. 1991. "Cultural China: The Periphery as the Center," *Daedalus* 120, 1–32.

———. 1987. "Iconoclasm, Holistic Vision, and Patient Watchfulness: A Personal Reflection on the Modern Chinese Intellectual Quest," *Daedalus* 116, 75–94.

———. 1985. "Selfhood and Otherness in Confucian Thought," in Anthony J. Marsella, George DeVos, and Francis L. K. Hsu (eds.), *Culture and Self: Asian and Western Perspectives*. New York: Tavistock Publications, pp. 231–251.

Turner, Jonathan H., and David Musick. 1985. *American Dilemmas: A Sociological Interpretation of Enduring Social Issues*. New York: Columbia University Press.

Verba, Sidney. 1969. "The Uses of Survey Research in the Study of Comparative Politics: Issues and Strategies," in Stein Rokkan, Sidney Verba, Jean Viet, and Elina Almasy (eds.), *Comparative Survey Analysis*. Paris: Mouton, pp. 56–106.

———. 1977. "The Cross-national Program in Social and Political Change: A History and Some Comments," in Alexander Szalai and Riccardo Petrella (eds.), *Cross-national Comparative Survey Research: Theory and Practice*. Oxford: The European Co-ordination Centre for Research and Documentation in Social Services, pp. 169–200.

Wang, Georgette, Wei-wen Chung, and Godwin C. Chu. 1991. "Cultural Value Survey in Taiwan," *Journal of Communication Arts* (Special Issue on Cultural Change in Asia and the United States) 12, 71–80.

White, Leslie A. 1959. "The Concept of Culture." *American Anthropologist* 61. Reprinted in Frederick C. Gamst and Edward Norbeck (eds.), *Ideas of Culture:*

Sources and Uses. New York: Holt, Rinehart and Winston, 1976, pp. 55–71.

Whyte, Martin K. 1989. "Evolutionary Changes in Chinese Culture," in Charles E. Morrison and Robert F. Dernberger (eds.), *Asia-Pacific Report 1989: Focus: China in the Reform Era*. Honolulu: East-West Center, pp. 93–101.

Williams, Robin M., Jr. 1970. *American Society: A Sociological Interpretation* (3rd Ed.). New York: Alfred A. Knopf.

Wills, Garry. 1992. *Lincoln at Gettysburg: The Words That Remade America*. New York: Simon and Schuster.

Yang, Haiou. 1990. *Cultural Fever: A Cultural Discourse in China's New Age*, paper presented to the Workshop on Cultural Construction and National Identity, Institute of Communication and Culture, Honolulu: East-West Center.

Yu, Ying-shih. 1993. "The Radicalization of China in the Twentieth Century," *Daedalus* 122, 125–150.

Zhang, Xin-xin. 1989. "How Come You Aren't Divorced Yet?" in Perry Link, Richard Madsen, and Paul G. Pickowicz (eds.), *Unofficial China: Popular Culture and Thought in the People's Republic*. Boulder, CO: Westview Press, pp. 57–71.

Zhao, Xiaoyan. 1989. "Effects of Foreign Media Use, Government and Traditional Influences on Chinese Women's Values," *Revue europeene de sciences sociales* 84, 239–251.

Index

About the Book and Authors

This fascinating study is the first to compare the dynamic and ever-changing cultural values of contemporary China and the contemporary United States. Surveying 2,000 Shanghai-area residents and villagers as well as 2,500 U.S. citizens from all points of the compass, the authors examine the extent to which traditional Confucian values have persisted in China despite massive governmental attempts to obliterate them and, similarly, the extent to which there has been a loss of "traditional" values in the United States. The result is a sophisticated yet readable account of the value systems of two complex and powerful national cultures.

The book looks at value systems in both cultures associated with family and kinship ties, male-female relationships, and general interpersonal relationships—the fundamental social relationships comprising the social fabric of a society. The authors conclude that although both societies have experienced changes in this century, they have followed quite different paths. In exploring how this process has differed, the authors address the following questions: What traditional Confucian values persist in China after forty years of communist indoctrination and the recent "invasion" of Western culture? How are fundamental human relationships viewed in the United States? How do these two societies differ today, both in adherence to traditional values and in the dynamics of value change? These and many more issues are explored in this unusual study.

STEVEN H. CHAFFEE is Janet M. Peck Professor of International Communication at Stanford University. He is a past president and a fellow of the International Communication Association. His research has included such topics as family interaction, political communication, adolescent socialization, interpersonal coorientation, health and prevention campaigns, and survey research methods. His publications include *Political Communication, Television and Human Behavior* (with George Comstock and others), *Handbook of Communication Science* (with Charles Berger), and *Communication Concepts 1: Explication.*

GODWIN C. CHU is a senior fellow in the Program for Cultural Studies, East-West Center. His publications include *Radical Change Through Communication in Mao's China, Moving a Mountain: Cultural Change in China* (with Francis Hsu), *Cultural Change in Rural Taiwan* (with Ginyao Chi), *Social Impact of Satellite Television in Rural Indonesia* (with Alfian and Wilbur Schramm), *The Great Wall in Ruins: Communication and Cultural Change in China* (with Yanan Ju), and *Modernization vs. Revolution: Cultural Change in Korea and China* (with Jae-won Lee, Won-yong Kim, and Yanan Ju). His current research focuses on social/cultural change in Asia, including China, Japan, Korea, Taiwan, Thailand, and Indonesia.

YANAN JU, formerly deputy director of the Center for Communication and Cultural Studies, Fudan University, China, and associate professor of communication at the University of North Carolina, is currently professor of communication at Central Connecticut State University. He is co-author of *The Great Wall in Ruins: Communication and Cultural Change in China* and *Modernization vs. Revolution: Cultural Change in Korea and China*.

ZHONGDANG PAN, who received his Ph.D. in mass communication from the University of Wisconsin-Madison, is assistant professor at the Annenberg School for Communication, University of Pennsylvania. His current research interests include political communication, public opinion, and cross-cultural and cross-generational communication.